It Came from Hunger!

Frontispiece: Larry Buchanan, plotting (circa 1992)

British Library Cataloguing-in-Publication data are available

Library of Congress Cataloguing-in-Publication Data

Buchanan, Larry
    It came from hunger! Tales of a cinema schlockmeister / by Larry
Buchanan,
     p. cm.
       Filmography: p.
    Includes bibliographical references and index.
    ISBN 978-1540344625 (library binding: 50# and 70# alk. papers)
    1. Buchanan, Larry 2. Motion picture producers and directors—
United States — Biography. I. Title.
PN1998.3.B8A3 1996
791.43'023'092-dc20
  [B]   96-18684
                                    CIP

Manufactured in the United States of America

Cover Design by Jasser Membreno

IT CAME FROM HUNGER!

Tales of a Cinema Schlockmeister

LARRY ✦ BUCHANAN

To Jane
for, through it all,
her enigmatic smile

I have known Larry Buchanan and his work for over thirty years. He is one of the most inventive directors I have ever known. He is a maverick filmmaker who uses any guerrilla tactic in his arsenal to get his pictures to the screen. He is a quintessential survivor in independent cinema, while never compromising his reputation as a gentleman. In short, Larry cares for films, for his players, and for his craftspeople.

— Roger Corman

Larry Buchanan is truly an endangered species . . . among the last of those who made movies — good or bad — because making them was their life. He is a cinematic dinosaur, and deserves preservation!

— Paul N. Lazarus
Former Vice President, Columbia Pictures

I have known him for almost forty years as he wrote, produced, directed, and usually raised the money for his independent pictures. He always had to make good with a small budget, but no money was ever wasted. What Larry lacked in money, he made up for with imagination and originality.

— Samuel Z. Arkoff

Table of Contents

Foreword by Lynn Shubert

It was the late forties. There were 10,000 would-be actors, directors, producers, dancers, designers, singers and musicians all pounding the mean streets of midtown New York City. We each believed that we were the one in that 10,000 who would shoot to the top as a new celebrity; 9,999 of us were wrong. But Larry Buchanan was right. He was one of the chosen few to scale the slippery ramparts and become a legend in his own time.

I met him in 1947, at the stage door of the Alvin Theatre on West 52nd Street. He was going to audition for a part in *Mr. Roberts*. I had already been told the auditions had been moved to the Barrymore Theatre on West 48th Street. I volunteered the information to save him time. That short walk started our friendship which has spanned five decades. We have been best man at each other's weddings and have experienced many failures and many successes together. We know our friendship will last until we join the heavenly choir.

Larry, after a very humble beginning, was bitten early by the cinema bug. At nine years of age, while living at an orphanage in Dallas, Texas, he attached himself to an older kid who ran the movie projector for their weekly shows, cannily realizing that that kid was old enough that he would soon be leaving the institution. The projectionist's job would be up for grabs. Larry was determined to get that job to learn as much as could. Thus opened the door to his future success making 30 full-length features and many documentaries and commercials.

He volunteered his services as a gofer, and to his good fortune the older boy was lazy and let Larry run every sort of errand for him. The main chore was taking the heavy film cans back and forth on the bus to Dallas's "film row." The loaded cans were as heavy as he was, but he was happy to lug them. They were "movies," the "picture show." He was in the picture business to stay. He became a regular on the street of Dallas' professional movie center.

He made friends. The old-timers were only too happy to teach this eager kid what they knew about the cinema business. He learned distribution. He learned about "one sheets." He also saw firsthand some of the rotten sides of the business: the knocking down by the distributors of the producer's cut, the shamefully padded expense accounts, and the fraudulent charges levied against the picture. The flip side of the picture? He learned how to cut and edit a picture, how to salvage a film in trouble, and how a story can be trashed in the cutting room. On graduation, he said goodbye to his old Simplex projector and headed for Hollywood — "Baghdad on the Pacific."

1

Although he was prepared for Hollywood, Hollywood wasn't waiting with open arms. Just as in New York later, 10,000 hopefuls were already there. Larry knew he was that one in 10,000, but it appeared it would take him a while to prove it.

He managed to open a few doors. He worked as a bit player. He studied at the 20th Century–Fox acting school with the likes of Marilyn Monroe, William Eythe, and Jeanne Crain. He played leads at the Westwood Playhouse. To pay the bills, meanwhile, he worked at the Douglas Aircraft plant in Santa Monica.

It was tough. Hollywood was a closed door. The movie crowd was not as friendly and eager as that in Dallas to help a talented kid learn, and there was nothing like the university film schools that proliferate today. But learn he did — acting, directing, producing, and distribution.

He refused to throw in the towel as most do. He was determined. After six years of frustration, he concluded there must be a better way, and with his bag and jumbo guitar, he turned his gaze eastward to New York. New York didn't notice. But television was stretching out of its little box and threatening the movies. Here was a place where he could try his skills. Back at the orphanage, he had entertained the kids by plucking his battered Sears Roebuck guitar and singing Western ballads. Once again that skill worked for him. He set his table by singing and chording for the networks, commercials, and nightclubs.

One rule he learned early on. If they ask you if you can sing, the answer is yes. Can you dance? Yes. He was working as "atmosphere" on the *Lucky Strike Hit Parade* when the director, knowing he was from Texas, asked if he could spin a lariat. He could not, but he answered "Yes" and got the job. He had 24 hours to become a convincing rope twirler, and he did it. He threaded a bit of wire inside the rope to make it stand out. The studio, NBC, superimposed its logo inside the loop. The Lucky Strike Tobacco people followed suit, and Larry parlayed his cowpoke twirls into another week. Soon he was a regular on *The Hit Parade*.

While reading for a Broadway play, *Dear Judas*, he overheard producer Michael Myerberg say there would be a lot of fencing in the drama. Larry volunteered that he was in champion class with the foils and that he could teach the cast their swordplay. He had in fact been taught some fencing at the 20th Century–Fox lot, but that hardly qualified him as an instructor. He got the part based on his stated ability to teach the cast. That gave him one week to learn the discipline. He had noticed one of the dancers audition for the show with a mock swordfight and had been impressed, but the young, dark kid from Greenwich Village had no callback. Larry said he needed a foil and requested a callback of the dancer. (That kid from the Village was Tony Charmoli, who went on to big things as one of the best and most Emmy-honored choreographers in television and Broadway.) Together, they successfully choreographed the fencing scenes which were applauded on opening night at the Mansfield Theatre. Larry was, in a modest way, directing on Broadway!

Larry was up for a part in *My Three Angels* with Walter Slezack and Darin McGavin. They needed a harmonica player. Could he play the harmonica? Of course, he said yes, reasoning that a harmonica is just like a guitar except you blow into it instead of plucking the strings. He got the part. Now, he was "musical director" of a Broadway play.

Larry is a believer in the adage that "what goes around, comes around." He never hesitated to pass on a tip that would help a fellow thespian. I have seen him read for a Broadway show or incoming film shoot and lose out. Then he would call friends and coach them for the role, passing on tips that would help them get the job.

Larry's serious thoughts turned ever toward cinema. He worked in films at the Army Signal Corps Photographic Center, based in Astoria, Long Island. These huge studios were famous as the home of many silent films shot in the early days of film. The kid from Texas now felt he was in the picture business. Larry became a fixture at the SCPC facility. Cutting, acting, lighting, and scripting filled his days.

Finally, the need to produce his own pictures was overwhelming. He scratched for a few dollars and made a short subject in Texas and Manhattan's Central Park. He was so zealous in his determination that he was somehow given free wardrobe from Brooks Costumers and some citified horses which kept heading for the barn during the shoot.

Then we made a first feature, *Apache Gold* or *Grubstake*, depending on the version people saw. Backed by a modicum of New York money, we boasted, "An expedition that is well-planned usually has success." New York actors Neile Adams (who would later marry Steve McQueen), Jack Klugman and I headed for Big Bend National Park in West Texas, following Larry's crew. Larry and I had cowritten the script and were co-producing the film. Larry would direct.

In Big Bend there were no supplies. The nearest telephone was 120 miles distant. Mountains, snakes, lizards, the Rio Grande, and vistas with no horizons were all that surrounded us. We discovered we were woefully underbudgeted and understaffed. But we started learning. For six long weeks (or was it eight?) we sweated the Chisos Mountains, snatching images onto the film, until we finally had a wrap. We returned to New York over budget, dead broke, and a lot wiser than when we had left. Needless to say, the resulting film does not rank with *Stagecoach*, nor did it win an Oscar. But it launched careers and forged friendships.

Best wishes, Larry, both personally and in your continuing cinema (which for so long you called "picture shows"). You are fond of the expression "Trails cross." I am pleased to say, "Usted pasa por aquí."

Lynn Shubert

Foreword by Jeff Buchanan

Growing up the second son of Larry Buchanan has been, and continues to be, an experience to say the least. As is usually the case with sons and daughters, we find it difficult to speak of, or show our gratitude for, lessons learned and principles instilled. So when my sister Dee Myshrall (née Buchanan) asked me to recount any unusual events or incidents which readers might find entertaining or enlightening, I saw a chance to personally show gratitude to my parents and remind myself as well as my parents of a handful of funny, though somewhat pathetic, incidents.

I must start by outlining the eclectic household we were raised in. Imagine a small brick house in Dallas, Texas. In that house was a grand piano on which my mother Jane Buchanan, an Oberlin-schooled classical pianist, kept me quiet with renditions of Chopin as I played with my Matchbox cars underneath the piano during the hot afternoons when the others were away at school. In the evenings my father would pull out his Martin six-string guitar and sing folk songs and country tunes. It's difficult as a child to fully comprehend your parents' exploits when you grow up around them. I didn't realize my father was viewed as an enigma in the neighborhood — a "director," a "moviemaker." Dallas is a town not known for its liberal thinking or progressive nature, a place where most people were blue collar workers or housewives. In Dallas it had to be difficult for anyone to imagine a neighbor making a film entitled *The Naked Witch*!

I distinctly remember changing schools in the third grade (something we did quite often) and having to fill out a form with a question I couldn't answer, a little box which haunted me. It said, "Father's occupation? _____. I told my teacher, "My dad doesn't have a job, he makes movies." Looking back, I had no idea how profound this statement was. Years later, I cling to this notion: film is not a job, it's a passion. I feel very fortunate to have been raised with this principle. And now, almost three decades later, that third-grader is trying to follow in his father's footsteps, to not have a job. To make movies.

I started working in the cutting room with my father when I was 13. It was summer vacation and I spent the whole season in the blackness of the editing room. The film was *Strawberries Need Rain*. It is truly a wonderful film, made for nothing — and I'm not talking about contemporary Hollywood's idea of nothing being "just 10 or 11 million." I'm talking about nothing! So, as the sun came up each morning and set each evening outside 9255 Sunset Boulevard, I tight-wound miles and miles of outtakes at 50 cents an hour, as my father cut his "art picture." I loved the 14-hour days because that was seven bucks.

I'm not sure how he would recall this, but I believe what happened was that I became impatient just winding up the "outs" and started voicing my opinions about cuts. He pacified me for several days with the promise that if I could make a clean splice on the block, I could start making cuts. So I went at it, splicing endless pieces of workprint and three-stripe sound together until I made them clean, with no air bubbles. (Editors familiar with Moviolas and the old cutting blocks will know what I'm talking about here.) Finally, he started to let me actually have a say in dramatic decisions and questions of tempo. We built all the sound effects and foley in the garage with a cassette recorder. Until I went out on my own years later, I thought this was the way everyone did it.

At the finish of the cut we had an interlock screening with workprint and magnetic sound. This means that the print is dirty and scratched, with pieces missing and certain effects not laid in yet. My father got up and addressed the small audience in attendance, reminding them that they would be seeing a "rough cut" and that this was a work in progress. He was quickly silenced by several people proclaiming that they were "experienced producers" and reassuring him that they knew how to look at a rough cut. The lights were dimmed and the film was started.

We got perhaps four minutes into it when a grease pencil mark (representing a fade-out for the lab) ran through the gate. Two or three voices called out frantically from the dark, "Larry! Larry! There was something on the film! Stop the projector!" We phoned the booth to stop the film. Lights came up. My father got up once again and in his genteel Texas manner, patiently explained that this was truly a rough cut and by no means represented the way the general public would view the film. Several people in the theater, probably the ones so startled by the grease pencil mark, condescendingly reminded my father that they were "experienced producers" and asked him please to continue.

The film started again. A door closed on screen and the sound effect was not there because it was in the editing room on one of the FX tracks. Nervous voices called out again in the darkness: "Larry, shouldn't there be a door sound there? Did you hear? There wasn't a door sound there!" Again the film was stopped and the lights were brought up. My father, in that famous Buchanan mannerism, pressed his hands together and, staying composed, patiently explained again that this was just a preliminary cut, that there would be things missing, marks on the film, pieces of leader to replace missing frames, and so forth. "Of course, Larry, we know this, we're experienced producers." As you can imagine, the screening of an 80-minute film took three and a half hours. We stopped at every grease pencil mark, every rough splice, every missing effect for the next 8,000 feet. Such was my first exposure to "experienced producers" in Hollywood.

In years to come, I would work with my father in a variety of capacities. On one film, on which I was a member of the crew, I remember a particularly poignant statement my father made after dealing with one of a long series of opinionated actors. We were on a hillside, just the immediate camera crew: DP, first AD, gaffer, myself and Dad. After this actor delivered his less than compelling argument about his character, he went off to change wardrobe. As the actor descended the hill, my father turned to us and said, "On the stage you act; on film you behave." I've since used this piece of brilliance numerous times in dealing with actors with inflated egos.

Another time, an actor who was feeling ambitious rewrote a scene and offered it up on set during rehearsal. My father feigned his admiration and said, "Let's do it!" Afterward, I asked my father and the DP (out of earshot of the others) why we wasted time and film on that fruitless exercise. They both turned to me to explain that they had done a dry run. They hadn't rolled film! The slate, the crane move, and everything else had been faked. I asked my father why he had done that, and he replied simply, "Because for the rest of the shoot, he's in my palm." And it was true; that actor was so grateful to my father, he did all he was told for the next three weeks because he had gotten his scene.

The next recollection, which offers precious little humor, must come under the heading of "pathetic actions in the desperate city." Looking for music for a film about rock 'n' roll, we were invited to a songwriters' showcase on Hollywood Boulevard. As the evening wore on, we were subjected to prime examples of why so many don't make it in the arts. We were accosted by a dishelved older gentleman with a satchel overflowing with handwritten pages of poetry. He leaned over our chair backs and began telling us that his poetry would make our film come alive. He was ushered away by our host but waited for us at the bottom of the stairs. It was late, perhaps midnight, as we emerged onto Hollywood Boulevard, which was barren now, and started for our car which was parked two blocks away. The man stepped in behind us and began telling us intimate details about his unhappy life — a wife that recently passed away, being disowned by his children, and so forth. It was truly sad. We politely explained that we didn't need poetry in our film and headed for our car, which now seemed a desert away as this poor soul began reading his poetry out loud, increasing in volume as he fell farther and farther behind.

I'll never forget his voice resounding off the dirty brick walls of those austere buildings on Hollywood Boulevard at midnight as we jaywalked through scattered newspapers and trash-filled gutters. I kept thinking to myself, "This is Hollywood." I remember, after we got to the car, I could still see the old man, standing in the middle of the boulevard, which was deserted now by all but prostitutes and cruising johns, reading aloud from his poetry. My father and I both wondered where he lived and what he was going to go home to. Truly a sad thing to experience, but just one of thousands of stories that young filmmakers will encounter in their pursuits.

An experience that every filmmaker knows is the agony of cutting a film. There is nothing quite like it — especially when you must lose 40 minutes from the fine cut, as my father and I once had to. The result of extensive cutting is that whole characters and scenes are lost "on the floor." After being in the cutting room for three or four months, removed from production, you're less involved with the actors as people since they have become images on celluloid. It is very easy to assess pragmatically what has to be dropped once you're removed from these hopefuls as flesh and blood, so you cut them out because a distributor demands it.

Unfortunately it may happen that the secretary who creates the invitation list to the cast and crew screening just sends out the invitations according to the cast list, not knowing who no longer is in the film, so everyone is invited. Imagine standing in the lobby of the elegant Director's Guild theater on the night of the cast and crew screening as a stream of actors come through and say hello. They are jubilant, enthusiastic, expectant. You smile, nervously, instantly reminded of those long-lost characters and trying desperately to remember what reel they were in. As the film unspools, actors storm out of the darkness of the theater in humiliation, realizing that they have been cut from the film — or worse, that their part has been cut from three pages to two lines. Their dreams are shattered for the moment. It is not funny.

My father is a compassionate man, and he instilled that quality in his children. Such are the trials and tribulations of the filmmaker. These are the things which will never be taught or learned in film school.

Jeff Buchanan

1. Beginnings

"There are places in this world where fable, myth, preconception, love, longing or prejudice step in and so distort a cool, clear appraisal that a kind of high-colored magical confusion takes permanent hold . . . surely Texas is such a place."
— John Steinbeck

And Lost Prairie was just such a place. A "Depression" town. A wide place in the long two-lane blacktop between Dallas and Houston. I say "was" because it is no more. In the 1930s, the Southwest was stricken by its worst thirst in its history. Stubborn winds lifted parched yellow dust from the Great Plains, carried it hundreds of miles and spilled it onto the black loam of East Texas. Lost Prairie, population 316, died.

But before the Dust Bowl swallowed up this little hamlet, a minor event took place at the farm of Marcus Larry Seale, part-time peace officer, and Maude Dove Seale. It was January 31, 1923. I was born, the last of six children. I had one brother and four sisters.

I was born Marcus Larry Seale, Jr., and would keep that name for exactly twenty years until January 31, 1943, when I became "Larry Buchanan." I was about to sign as a contract player with 20th Century-Fox in Hollywood. Head of casting William Mayberry didn't like the name Seale. "Sounds like a circus act," he said bluntly. "What are your grandmothers' names?" I managed to remember that they were Dove and Buchanan.

Without skipping a beat, he blurted, "Dove is too passive, we go with Buchanan!"

Although painfully aware of the unsigned document on the desk, I challenged the big man. "Why the Buchanan?"

He countered, "The only Dove that ever made it in this business was an incredibly sexy female, and even she had a man's first name — Billie, Billie Dove."

Shyness gone, I suddenly realized this man was serious. "Okay, but who's ever heard of a Buchanan in show business?" I thought I had him.

"Well, for one there's Jack Buchanan, one of the biggest names in the U.K." Then he got the look I had been warned about by the day players I knew on the Fox lot. "That's it kid!" he shouted, tearing up my painfully honest biography he was holding. "We start a whisper campaign that you're the bastard son of Jack Buchanan!"

I tried to stop him. You would have to have known Bill Mayberry to appreciate how futile that effort was. The only person he ever yielded to was his boss at Fox, Darryl F. Zanuck.

Hollywood! Marcus Larry Seale, Jr., becomes Larry Buchanan, courtesy 20th Century-Fox Pictures. The studio photographer shot every contract player the same way in the same light. I was uneasy, but it worked.

He rushed on. "We'll have to lose that corny Texas accent. Six weeks with Josephine Dillion and you'll sound like you were to the manor born!"

Every actor in Hollywood of the forties, whether working or "between engagements," knew who Josephine Dillion was. She was the divorced first wife of Clark Gable. Fallen from the grace of Gable, she had turned to dramatic coaching and was highly praised by her pupils. More important, they loved her. A caustic and unkind rumor cast her as the opening curtain in Gable's calculated rise to King of the Silver Screen: Act One was Josephine Dillion to polish his hick image; Act Two was rich Ria Langham Gable to buy the tweeds, turtleneck sweaters, and touring cars, and fix the bad teeth; then Act Three was Carole Lombard as the one and only committed love. The final union with Kay Spreckels which produced his only heir was touching and wholesome but, to my mind, out of character for the King.

Bill Mayberry didn't have to sell me on Josephine Dillion. Eyeing the unsigned contract on the desk, I gambled. "Who pays Josephine for the lessons?"

His face flushing, Bill punched the intercom button and picked up his pen. The seductively sweet voice of the receptionist carried a British accent, a mid-forties chic. "Yes, Mr. Mayberry?"

"Make out a voucher for six weeks' coaching with Jo Dillion for"—he looked up at me with a scowl—"Larry Buchanan."

"Yes, sir, Larry Buchanan it is." I will never forget her voice—night-blooming jasmine. (An old phrase I still love, evocative of everything good and decent; at once clean, unfettered, stimulating, creative, sexy, remembered with a sigh.)

The scratch of Bill Mayberry's pen on the contract was the sweetest sound I had ever heard. How could I tell him I had been studying with Jo Dillion for three months and was about to quit for lack of funds?

Now for the punchline. After Josephine tirelessly and lovingly whacked away at my Texas brogue and polished my new "Continental expression," I got a call from Fox Casting. I reported. The role was a wet-behind-the-ears Texas fighter pilot in a World War II quickie called *Coming in on a Wing and a Prayer* with William Eythe and Don Ameche. It was to be played with full Texas brogue!

I might have learned a new way of speaking, but by no means had I forgotten anything of my Texas roots or my childhood in the Great Depression. The most accurate portrait of the Depression was captured by John Ford in his film of John Steinbeck's *The Grapes of*

My father, Mark Seale. Having lost his wife, the mother of six, he held three jobs to set his table: constable, partner in a livery stable, and proprietor of his own barbecue pit. But the Great Depression and the ravages of a Dust Bowl economy won out in the end.

Wrath. It starred Henry Fonda as Tom Joad and John Carradine as Casey. Years later I would work near both of these giants, but I only worked *with* Carradine. Fonda was unknowable for contract players or day players. He shed his coldness only long enough to conjure up the warmth of *Abe Lincoln in Illinois* or the sensitivity of Frank James in Fox's story of the outlaws Jesse and Frank James, co-starring Tyrone Power. Carradine, on the other hand, was out-going and helpful to neophytes. I will say more about these two and others later.

My family's lives were not spared the trauma of the Great Depression. When I was only nine months old, Mother died. Years later they told me it was pneumonia. Truth to tell, bearing and rearing children under primitive conditions, the barren frontier fare and humorless neighbors had all surely taken their toll. Her only solace was her children and church work wherein she played an ancient, wheezing organ. She sang standard Baptist-approved hymns such as "Satan's Jeweled Crown" and "Just as I Am." Rural mothers such as mine found their lives bearable only with the promise of "When the Great Day Breaks."

Papa tried. He was a peace officer, a constable. (The word "sheriff" was frowned on in that part of Texas.) As a body, peace officers, both rural and urban, were called "the Laws," so we used to hear expressions like "The Laws have been chasing him since Cain killed Abel" and "The Laws over't Fort Worth's got that mother's boy in their sights."

Saturday nights, Mother would practice for Sunday's service while Papa would take off with his battered guitar for the nearest dance. His repertory included "Corena, Corena," dirt farm blues, and songs made famous by the Blue Yodeler himself, Jimmie Rodgers, the *original*

"Jimmie the Kid." Serious scholars of American folk music now consider Rodgers the father of country and western music.

The good people of Buffalo, Texas, called. They wanted my father to be their constable. As in every other town in the Lone Star State, the farmers and ranchers of Buffalo were just scratching a living out of the dirt. They couldn't pay anything to speak of. The hours would be around the clock without a deputy. Worst of all, he and the family would be in real personal danger, for this was 1926 and hard times had spawned a terrifying change in the lives of country folks.

There had been an alarming and sudden increase in small town bank robberies. Otherwise decent, "Christian" boys, enraged at their impoverished lot, were prowling the Trinity River bottoms of East Texas in old Model A Fords and heavy secondhand Buicks. Their prey was not the well-guarded banks of Texarkana, Dallas, or Fort Worth, but rather the pitifully vulnerable, small family banks which rarely had an armed guard. Their heist was a miserly few dollars, sometimes taken at the life of some brave citizen trying to stop the robbery. Constables and other peace officers were fair game, and being a member of "the Laws" was dangerous to one's health. Papa was a target more than once. The most serious encounter was with Floyd Hamilton. Using a sawed-off .310 shot-gun, Hamilton pumped buckshot into Papa's chest. This was at long range and was not serious, but it was sobering.

Floyd and his brother Roy ran with Clyde Barrow and Bonnie Parker as their wheel men, both being expert auto drivers. One of my early reality-based documentaries was *The Other Side of Bonnie and Clyde* with folk-singing Burl Ives. Floyd Hamilton, then an elderly night watchman for a used car dealer in Dallas, was featured in the film. My partner and coproducer, Harold Hoffman, gave him a polygraph test on camera. I later took Hamilton on the road with the picture along with the actual guns used by Bonnie and Clyde in their savage waltz across Texas. These were loaned to us by the widow of Frank Hamer, the Texas Ranger who stalked Bonnie Parker and Clyde Barrow for years. He was very poorly depicted in the script for Arthur Penn's *Bonnie and Clyde*, but actor Denver Pyle made the most of the scenarist's material.

Papa made a gut-wrenching decision. He placed us in an orphanage near Dallas called Buckner Orphans Home. The largest institution of its kind in the world, it had been founded by young Baptist minister Robert Cooke Buckner after the catastrophic Galveston flood of 1900 orphaned thousands of children. Reading the somber telegrams and news accounts of the disaster, Buckner boarded a train for the Gulf Coast and rounded up as many orphaned children as he could. Having no funds of his own, he solicited help from strangers and the Texas and Pacific Railroad Co. and took the children home to the large frame house near Dallas that he and his new bride owned. We six entered Buckner Orphans Home on the condition that no single one of us could be adopted. It was all or none.

I was not aware of this condition and certainly would not have understood it if it had been explained to me. What I do recall is the pain of rejection when there were offers to adopt me, followed by silence and the dismissal that another had been chosen. My bewilderment changed to resentment. It wasn't that I hated my father; in my innocence, I was ashamed of him. I made a pledge in a bitter prayer that I would never desert any children I might have. It was years before I realized that, although nothing material was forthcoming from him and I was embarrassed by the rarity of his trips to see us at the home, he had given me the priceless love of my brother and sisters and the fellowship of an extended family of over 400.

At first, my new home followed the orphanage cliché—long on discipline, short on liberties. Buckner Orphans Home had its own school system plus a dairy and a farm. There was

Summer 1936. I was rewarded for my solicitation of "love gifts" from church groups throughout Texas for the benefit of Buckner Orphans Home. The bike came from the Southern Baptist Conference. The ten gallon Stetson sombrero was a gift from my seldom-seen father.

cotton to be chopped, hay to be baled, and cows to be milked. I remember the early years there as repressive.

I lived for Friday nights. That was when the big Chevrolet flatbed truck would stop outside the boys' dorm and we would load up for the seven-mile trip into Dallas and "the picture show." The chic word "cinema" and the hip expression "flicks" were unknown to this Depression-reared towhead.

The movie that changed my life forever was *History Is Made at Night*, directed by Frank Borzage. The year was 1937, and I was a bewildered youth of 14. Suddenly, this story of jealousy, divorce, and the discovery of true love grabbed me like a hay hook. The clichés of previous serious films were gone and forgotten. For ages, friends thought it a peculiar choice as a favored title for a filmmaker. Then, many years later, I was redeemed when esteemed film critic Andrew Sarris called this shipboard drama "not only the most romantic title in the history of the cinema but a profound expression of Borzage's commitment to love over probability." The film resonates to this day.

I knew what I wanted to do with my life. I sold packets of flower seeds and raised "squabs" (young pigeons) to gather enough money to buy a subscription to *Photoplay* magazine, the old oversized version loaded with sepia and green-toned portraits of my favorite stars. I devoured every page, every morsel and posed in front of my mirror as I imitated Colman, Cooper, Cagney and Errol Flynn. I sang along with Spencer Tracy when he won his Oscar for *Captains Courageous*. But when I wrote the studio, I asked for anything they could send me on director Victor Fleming, just as I had written about Frank Borzage when I was so moved by *History Is Made at Night*.

Any amateur analyst would have no difficulty diagnosing the emotional churning going on here and why it would be the obsessive behavior of my life. The only real existence I acknowledged was what I experienced in the supercharged darkness of a movie theater. As the beaded screen reflected belly laughs (Buster Keaton in *The General*), heartbreak (Lillian Gish in *The Wind*), epic sweeps of the camera (Errol Flynn in *Robin Hood*) and towering star power (Ronald Colman in *A Tale of Two Cities*), that other life of the orphan shifted into soft focus. I don't mean it became pleasant, it just became tolerable.

Early on, the matrons at the orphanage were monstrous. Low-paid and ignorant, they were suspicious of my curiosity and questions. A particularly sensitive area was the subject of the Nazarene. I had become interested in the historical Jesus, and they simply were not equipped to deal with my inquiries. Punishment was swift and terrifying, so much so that my big brother Earl worried for my sanity. If I wet the bed, I knew it meant I would be locked the whole day into the "wet closet," which was piled high with soiled bedclothes and rubber sheets. There would be no supper ("dinner" was the noon meal) and at lights-out I would be force-fed Epsom salts and cod liver oil as further punishment.

But I would relive last Saturday's *Jungle Princess* with Dorothy Lamour. The dark of the wet closet would become the balcony of the Capitol Theater on Elm Street in Dallas. The stench of urine would change to the seductive aromas of buttered popcorn and Mexican pralines in the lobby of the Capitol. And suddenly, there was Dorothy singing "Lovelight in the Starlight" to Ray Milland. Or was it "Moonlight and Shadows"?

Then the chorus of crickets outside the dorm would segue to the opulent Majestic Theater in Dallas, the flagship of the Interstate theater chain. We were on our feet, hoarse and happy, as stuntman Yakima Canutt worked his way from the shotgun seat of a stage coach to the lead pair of horses and dropped to the alkali desert floor between flying hooves and wheels, making himself a place in history with the greatest stunt ever in movies. I saw John Ford's *Stage Coach* 23 times.

I must have fallen in "movie-love" just as many times, but first and longest with Shirley Temple. The picture was *Bright Eyes*, the director David Butler. Was I empathetically ensnared because she played an orphan? I think not. It had to be her singing of "On the Good Ship Lollipop."

Years later, I would direct her first husband John Agar in three good-bad films: the infamous *Zontar, the Thing from Venus*; *Hell Raiders*, a World War II flick with one Sherman tank; and *Curse of the Swamp Creature*, a textbook horror title. We were both Aquarians, born on the same day and hour, so it was no surprise to me that we got on famously. Despite the privations of budget, wardrobe, and accommodations, we charged into the Caddo swamps as if we had money. When we finished *Curse of the Swamp Creature*, I boasted to John, "We just made a horror in nine days!" John cut me down pronto. "John Ford finished *She Wore a Yellow Ribbon* in 28!" Enough said. We talked often of director Ford and of Agar's parts in *Yellow Ribbon* and other Ford epics. Agar's friendship, his humor, patience, and his talent, are warm memories from my life in film. Neither of us ever mentioned Shirley Temple.

For most of us, our movie loves cannot be rated like thoroughbreds in terms of first, place and show. Rather, I think each should be saluted for some special sensual aura at a special place in our private time. Way back, there was Anita Louise — cool Dresden china, the Grace Kelly of her day. For her husky-voiced come-on in DeMille's *The Plainsman* and her tearful consent in *History Is Made at Night*, there was winsome Jean Arthur. Years later our family would live, as she did, in Carmel, California. I would nod to her as we passed on our morning walks around the famous beach of Monterey Bay.

When Greer Garson welcomed Ronald Colman back to the cottage at the end of *Random Harvest*, I was crushed. My only redhead. How can I forget Greer's music-box perfection? And that half-laugh, stopped midway, which said, "I love you." Her *Blossoms in the Dust* is one of the all-time most underrated films. *Mrs. Miniver* still brings tears.

Interviewing her for NBC in Dallas some 15 years after *Blossoms in the Dust* was a high point in my life.

Alice Faye was the embodiment of that old phrase "all woman." She was the darling of 20th Century-Fox and the distaff side of a winning cast combination that included Tyrone Power, Don Ameche, and a truly great guy, Cesar Romero. I can say I worked with these beautiful people but must confess it was at shouting distance of 50 feet away as a walk-on bit player. Fifty years later I would work with Alice on fundraisers toward the cure of diabetes. For me, Alice had lost none of the stable, quiet sex appeal she exhibited in *Alexander's Ragtime Band*, *In Old Chicago*, and my favorite, *Hollywood Cavalcade*. Alice and Shirley Temple made many films together at Fox. And that is fitting. To me, Alice Faye was a kind of grown-up Shirley, with Shirley's dimples and giggle replaced by Alice's sensual warmth and maturity.

And there was my only brunette, Ava Gardner, the only leading lady who ever snatched a picture away from Bogart. When Ava strolled through *The Barefoot Contessa*, she effortlessly enunciated what screen acting (or non-acting) is all about. At the end of her career, she was permitted only cameos by heavyweights such as Gable (*The Hucksters*), Heston (*Earthquake*), and Peck (*On the Beach*). Given anything more than ten lines, she would devour her costar. Witness *The Night of the Iguana*. On location in Puerto Vallarta, she was Earth Mother to an entire company of players in heat. While they bitched and suffered, she drew upon her legendary ability to adapt to outrageous circumstances: lovers' quarrels, free-flowing booze, inclement weather, exhaustion, and tropical lust.

My own love affair with the magic of movies continued. And so did the oppressive cycle of chores before and after school and the force-fed regimen of Christian fundamentalism taught by tight-lipped, anal-retentive matrons. The less strident of these were the pretty young schoolteachers just graduated from Baylor University and other ecclesiastically oriented halls of learning. Since movies, spicy Western and detective magazines, and other forms of erotic stimuli — even the Sears and Roebuck catalog, whose bra ads may have been deemed too explicit — were censored or banned, these young women from all over Texas literally became our sex education. Then, there was another one of those crazy turns in the road which would flip my life upside down. It began with a campus scandal and a "Tom Swift" (our nickname for the eager young studs at the orphanage who not only were peeping toms but were swift when the matrons came running). A handsome outwardly pious boys' basketball coach arrived to take charge of our basketball team, the Hornets. Within weeks the grapevine knew he was sleeping with a goodly number of girls at Teacher's Hall. Exposure brought a fallout heard in every Baptist church in the Lone Star State. It was time for reform.

At the time of the clean-up at Buckner, the U.S. government was preparing the nation for the possibility of entering World War II. Jobs became plentiful. Any male high school graduate could name the branch of the service he wanted to join. War-related manufacturing plants popped up everywhere in Dallas County.

Buckner Orphans home found itself the owner of thousands of acres of prime real estate in east Dallas, the direction of growth. With our new found wealth, our hand-me-down reputation became embarrassing. We no longer needed the threadbare donated clothing that had been sent in by the boxcar load in the early years. Now that Buckner's fortunes had improved, those of us who worked in the commissary were ordered to haul huge loads of the surplus gifts in the middle of a cane field and burn them. I vividly remember seeing the black smoke rise and wondering what those donors from small churches across the South, poor themselves, would think if they could see the flames lick at their sacrifice.

Change was everywhere. A professional and progressive new management team took

The look of earnest innocence that made me a success in soliciting funds for Buckner Academy.

charge. Gleaming new buildings rose across the undulating hills; a gym, stadium, Olympic swimming pool. These and a highly degreed staff defined the altered image of the largest institution of its kind in the world. Even the name was changed to Buckner Academy.

In my last year there I took advantage of the new opportunities. My brother had gone into the Navy. My sisters had graduated and found successful new lives in Dallas. As a senior, I began to discover the benefits of clout. I was editor of the school paper and president of the senior class. These pursuits were not prompted by any altruism on my part; the perquisites were many. I became a traveling ambassador for the Academy, speaking at churches all over the South and Southwest. I rarely saw a classroom that last year. A pair of tutors accompanied me as I made my pitch "Bucks for Buckner." Holding up a silver dollar, I would intone, "Render unto Caesar that which is Caesar's and unto God that which is God's." The bucks poured in.

I was a post-pubescent Elmer Gantry. I might speak to a congregation of only 15 people in the little town of Sweetwater, Texas, then go the following Sunday to the First Baptist Church in Dallas, boasting the largest membership of any single church in the world — nearly 10,000. There were up to five services a day to accommodate the faithful.

On the road, for the most part I mixed with the stalwart Soldiers of the Cross and listened to their narrow patter. The women, their perms hugging their heads like stockings, reeked of lavender. The deacons gave out their business cards to each worshiper as they showed them to their seats. The exceptions were alternately humorous and pathetic.

I remember coming to the town of Muleshoe (really) on a Sunday evening in 1938. By the time our big Buick rolled into the main street, the Christmas sky had already darkened the town except for a few neons. The holiday decorations were up across the street, tattered from too many packings and unpackings. Christmas was always a cinch for collections and a huge feast for supper. All over town 78s scratched out "Oh Come All Ye Faithful" and "Deck the Halls."

The Bijou lights of the only picture show in town blinked out the seductive words *Beloved Enemy* with Brian Aherne and Merle Oberon. The show would start in about an hour. I said nothing and waited until we reached the boarding house where we would be billeted before I made my move. I told my two chaperons that I wanted to go over to the church after supper and before the congregation started coming in, "just to get the feel of the place." They bought it.

After deep-fried chicken, dumplings, and candied yams, I headed out for the church. A dry run on the place was necessary in case I was late from the movie for my pitch. I slipped in the door and found a ghost-like silence. I was alone, or so I thought. The carpet runners muffled my footsteps as I went to the podium. I wanted to check to see if there was a microphone — a rarity, but I had to know. Without a mike, I "worked the room" with my silver dollar solicitation, but if there was a public address system, I knew I would be glued to the podium. That meant I would have to ensure there was a one-step riser to bring me up to height, for although I was shooting up like new corn, I still couldn't stand as high as these country clerics. I was almost to the podium when I heard them.

A male and female voice mingled in playful courtship in what I thought was the choir section. Then I heard the sound of splashing. Above the choir stalls there was a large opening in the wall, much like a bay window. A beautiful trompe-l'oeil painting of the River Jordan at Hijlah Ford flowing into the Dead Sea hung presenting a faux view out the seeming window. The scene was of the very spot where the Nazarene walked out of the desert and said to the tattered man in animal skins, "Now, cousin John, the waters." The palm trees, cane rushes and vegetation on the river banks glowed with a soft blue light.

Summer 1942. High school graduation day.

With a whoosh of delight, a pretty girl in a clinging wet dress shot up out of the real water of the baptismal font followed by an equally water-soaked boy who could not have been more than three years my senior. The illusion was breathtaking. He pushed her up against the waters of the Jordan and allowed himself to be locked in long legs that flailed as their bodies came together. After a flurry of grunts, he let out a yell, "Halleluya!"

Coming down from the passion, they were soon quiet, gasping for breath. I could not see the real waters of ablution, but as he helped her to the shore of this trompe-l'oeil masterpiece, he reached up and steadied himself with his hand on the aqua blue oil of the painting. That struck me as funny and is my single sharpest recollection of the visit to Muleshoe.

I slipped out of the church and soon was settled into a broken, trashed seat at the Chaparral Theater. The price of admission was two bits, so there was nothing left for a Mexican praline.

The silver nitrate glowed from the screen. Brian Aherne waited as his lover Merle Oberon slipped through the Black Irish guards and into a cellar, and fell into his arms. Nothing at the church later or before could top that.

I was awarded a ministerial scholarship to Baylor University at Waco, Texas, with one proviso: I would become a Baptist preacher after getting my doctorate of divinity.

But I would not be deterred from my chosen altar. I tried to enlist in the Air Force but

An essential prop in the studio, a man's pipe. Even if you smoked Lucky Strikes.

was rejected because of a perforated eardrum. (A Buckner bully had held me under water too long at Bull Pond, a swimming hole one mile from the Home, infested with venomous water moccasins. We called them cottonmouths.)

I hitchhiked to Los Angeles. For a Depression-reared Texan, Hollywood in the war years of 1942 to 1945 was a Fellini dreamscape. By day, thousands of workers poured into Los Angeles from all over America to snatch up the high-paying jobs in the war plants. The air was charged with the promise of sloe-gin fizzes and sex, sex, sex! On weekends, uniformed men and women out-numbered civilians ten to one on the streets of Hollywood. At nightclubs such as the Trocadero, Ciro's, Mocambo and the Cocoanut Grove, a guy and his date could mix it up with movie stars who relaxed their isolation for the war effort. Hollywood as Babylon lasted for a thousand and one nights.

And the movies? They were a strange pastiche of anti-Fascist fare such as *Thirty Seconds Over Tokyo* and *Mission to Moscow*, musicals as escapist fare typified by *Cover Girl* with Rita Hayworth and Gene Kelly, and occasional minor masterpieces like *Hitler's Children*, certainly an early "good-bad" film.

I figured that with many young Hollywood males called to battle, it would be a great time for a beginner. Right? Wrong. Truth to tell, although no one can ignore the great work done by the industry in selling war bonds and underwriting talent tours, or the great success of the Hollywood Canteen as a haven for lonely and hungry GIs, too much was made of the "sacrifice" made by such woefully unqualified figures as Ronald Reagan in suiting up to supervise military propaganda films. Too, there was a scandalous sub-culture of actors dodging the draft with a whole array of clever devices, including contrived disabilities ("faux 4-Fs"). No, the studios were not desperately looking for me or any other draft-dodger; that is, any guy in his twenties still wearing mufti.

But I had no real complaints. I worked enough to maintain my 1936 V-8 Ford and a hotplate apartment in Westood Village. I remember that interim in the Village with warmth. I spent thousands of hours in the UCLA library. I had a reasonably active social life dating extras, most of whom seemed to live at the Studio Club on Lodi Place in Hollywood, a famous sorority-type haven for innocent and sometimes not-so-innocent actresses with stars in their eyes. I swear to God, I never once waited in that lobby for my date to come down without seeing Mickey Rooney waiting for his. Night-blooming jasmine. That was the Studio Club.

Thirty years later my partner and cowriter Lynn Shubert and I created and shot scenes in the Studio Club for our *Goodbye, Norma Jean*, the first feature film on the life of Marilyn

Monroe. She, or rather Norma Jean Baker, lived there for a brief period, chronically late with the rent and depending on "Johnnies" for her one meal a day. She had not yet had her nose and jaw work done and she showed too much gum when she smiled. All of her plastic surgery would come after her introduction to ailing agent Johnny Hyde, who would claim her as protégée. She would have no truck with contract players like me or extras without money or contacts. Otherwise, consent was implied with the shaking of hands. Like all of us, Norma Jean was flawed.

As the war dragged on the cost of living in Hollywood (or, as in my case, Westwood Village) went through the roof, and wages for contract players and movie extras were stuck in 1939 figures. Meanwhile, the war plants were on a wage orgy. Hayseeds and unschooled farmers from the Midwest were suddenly making more in a month than they had realized in a year behind the plow. Lockheed Aircraft in Burbank and Douglas Aircraft at Santa Monica were the leaders of the

If a contract player could only afford one suit, it had to be a grey pinstripe. This was an edict from studio boss Darryl F. Zanuck.

payroll madness, for two reasons. First, they worked on government cost-plus contracts which allowed them to spend anything they wished for labor and materials and still guaranteed them a percentage profit. Second, they were being pressed by Uncle Sam to increase productivity, screw the cost. There were three shifts around the clock: day shift, swing shift, and the graveyard.

Like any patriotic American with overdue rent, I headed for Santa Monica, a suburb of Los Angeles, to work for Douglas. There was just one hitch. To keep my job with Fox and the small but welcome stipend it provided, I would have to work the swing shift. The problem was that all the single guys and gals wanted the swing shift. The money was premium. But the real perk was the nightlife.

The swing shift started at four in the afternoon and ended at midnight, which meant seven hours' work for eight hours' premium pay. When the chimes at midnight rang, several thousand swing shifters piled into their ancient vehicles (no new cars were being built) and headed for the Palladium in Hollywood and other enormous dance halls. There they would dance, woo and win until sun-up. A favorite was the Aragon Ballroom near the Pacific Ocean. The popular musical dance song was "Drinking Rum and Coca-Cola."

Visions of my dancing to that rhumba and holding some Kansas City doll in red shoes dissolved when the personnel officer said that the swing shift was full up. I was headed for the door when he noticed I had been flipping an ivory guitar pick in my fingers.

With my big brother Earl in 1943 at Earl Carrol's Dinner Theatre in Hollywood. Earl was shipping out the next day to the South Pacific to serve as gunner on an aircraft tender. I lied about how well I was doing, then showed him the town, not knowing if I would ever see him again. My 1936 Ford V-8 got him to boot camp in San Diego at 0600 hours, just in time for reveille.

"Whaddaya play?" His tone was not patronizing.

"Guitar." What harm could come of being courteous? Hell, I had already lost my day's pay at Fox.

"A good one?"

"Jumbo Martin Dreadnought." God, I was proud of that box. "And I sing. Leadbelly Blues, Woody Guthrie." There was no stopping me now. ". . .And Jimmie Rodgers, the Blue Yodeler."

He didn't miss a beat, a no-nonsense fellow traveler. "Ever hear of the Douglas Minstrels?"

I had. The Minstrels were made up of Douglas Aircraft employees who were for the most part musicians, actors, and olio acts. Weekends, they were bused all over Southern California to entertain GIs at boot camps and other bases. In addition to their hefty paycheck for working the line, they were given a bonus for the weekend. "I've heard about them, yes." I wondered where this was leading. He called in the director of the Minstrels. There were whispers. The director laid it all out as he walked back to his office.

"Be back here at three o'clock. Bring the Martin. I want to hear 'Bring a Lil' Water Silvy,' and if you can do a buck and wing, that will help." Pay dirt! I had chanced upon not one, but two people who actually knew who bluesman Huddie Leadbetter was. Suddenly, Deep Ellum in Dallas didn't seem so distant. And as for the buck and wing dance steps, I could always fake that.

It was a piece of cake. After all, I had heard the Master sing and play it a dozen times on his battered 12-string guitar. Once was on Deep Ellum (Dallas's Elm Street) before Leadbelly was sent to Huntsville Prison for stabbing a Browder Street pimp. (He composed a blues song about the prison and sang it to the warden who promptly pardoned him.) As for the dance steps, they never mentioned them, even though I had worked on them for three hours. No regrets. Those sleepless hours were absorbed by my philosophy, originally enunciated by Thomas Carlyle, that "Nothing is lost, all works for all."

The next 24 hours were as frantic as a greyhound race. A security clearance on me was teletyped from the FBI (sabotage was on everybody's mind throughout the conflict) and I took a physical exam and an IQ test. A photo was laminated onto a badge and by the start of the next day's four o'clock swing shift, I was given the pretentious title "Liaison Officer." Not once did I ever hear a correct French pronunciation over the loudspeakers. It was always "lieson offisuh Larry Bucknan re-poat to wang 'sembly Magnegick In-spection." Always with a Southern accent. In fact, the huge plant was a cacophony of accents from across America. I felt quite at home.

My office, high above the line of bombers being assembled, was to be shared with one other inspector. That first afternoon I was introduced to my office mate, the tallest man I had ever seen. He was Fritz Leiber, Jr., the son of Fritz Leiber, the actor who seemed to appear in every costumed picture ever made in Hollywood.

Me and my trusty Jumbo Martin Dreadnought guitar. That box was my salvation during the famine between casting calls.

Fritz Jr. was to become one of the most honored and prolific science fiction writers in the history of the genre. His Nebula and other awards and citations would fill a small museum. But the giant I met that afternoon was still searching for himself. Shy and unassuming, he was obviously overshadowed by his famous father. When he learned that I too was searching, bucking to be a filmmaker and having to do work as an extra in films to survive, a friendship was born. Truth to tell, we both had father problems, albeit with different spins. His was too much Pater; mine, too little Dad.

Fritz considered himself a failed actor and was experimenting with various literary forms, not the least of which was science fiction. His imagination was unbounded as he talked about "mousers" and "change wars." He never ran out of questions for me about anything on which I might have some expertise. He was especially inquisitive about the Texas mind set. I would like to believe that some of what I told him found its way into *A Spectre Is Haunting Texas* and my favorite of all of his sci-fi novels, *The Big Time*.

More than 20 years later, when I was working on the screenplay of *Mars Needs Women*,

I remembered those cerebral talks with Fritz. He was a talent light years ahead of his time, contriving plots that were galaxies distant from our predictable story structures.

Finally V-J Day came on August 15, 1945. President Harry Truman said it was all over with Japan and the Hollywood lights blazed again. GIs and civilians alike danced in the streets, paralyzing traffic for hours. The Hollywood Canteen was jammed with 3,000 servicemen in 48 hours. The hot war was over. My cold war was not far behind.

As the year came to a close, an ugly chapter in movie history opened. There was a troubling division in the industry over unionism and politics. There was a rush to collective bargaining with the major studios, orchestrated by the International Alliance of Theatrical Stage Employees, or the "IA" as it was called. Craftsmen wanted a bigger share of the incredible profits generated by movies. An emotional deep freeze set in between labor and management, and regardless of the lip service to the contrary, it has never really thawed. Arguably, the golden age of studios, nurturing actors and craftsman alike, ended with the horror of Hiroshima.

The big war over, I now divided my time between occasional day player gigs at the studios and the live playhouse known as the Westwood Village Theater. But the hunger persisted to make my own films. Therein lies a rub.

During the late forties in Hollywood, there was no such haven as university film schools such as one finds today at UCLA and USC and seemingly every other place of higher learning across the United States. As Jimmy Durante said, "Everybody wants to get into the act!"

Rather, it was seat of the pants, catch as catch can. A union card from the IA, the Directors Guild, the Writers Guild, or the Screen Actors Guild was prized and guarded jealously by the bearer. The independent filmmaker was yet to emerge as a creative force and no one dared incite the wrath of the majors. They owned the movie lots, and more important, they owned the theaters.

The brave independents who flew in the face of the powerful majors would open shop in the area of Sunset and Gower and make a pitiful effort to compete. They would then fold when the majors denied them playing time in their theaters. This phenomenon gave rise to the naming of the areas as "Poverty Row" and "Gower Gulch."

Show business abhors a vacuum. Soon the buzzword on the street was "go east, young man." Broadway. New York. Manhattan. Exciting things were stirring. Small independents, led by United Artists Pictures, were breaking all the rules. They were more concerned with content than megabucks. Others followed, and the Manhattan hustle was on. This migration was accelerated when federal law forced the major studios to divorce themselves from owning theaters.

I wanted to be a part of this movement. I would go to the Big Apple. Then the worst plague the show business gypsy faces raised its ugly head. Some call it the "it never rains but it pours" syndrome. A lot of insignificant calls for work made me postpone my trip to the big town on the Hudson.

Someday I would like to research this phenomenon. It goes like this. Just when you are exhausted from the Job-like slings and arrows of misfortune and are ready to cave in, the gods would like a laugh. So they give you a morsel to recharge your ambition and you come back for more punishment. The job goes nowhere and the cycle repeats itself. Such a lure presented itself.

Truth to tell, it was this final irony described below that stiffened my resolve to finally go to the East Coast.

At Fox Pictures, Darryl Zanuck had bought the movie rights to W. Somerset Maugham's best seller *The Razor's Edge*. It was meant for Tyrone Power, the king of the Fox lot, but he was still in Marine uniform in the South Pacific and no one knew when the war would end. So Zanuck, the little vermin, pulled off one of his most sinister and cruel stunts: He announced that the part of Larry in *The Razor's Edge* would be played by a newcomer! He would be surrounded by the best of the major stars on the Fox contract list including Anne Baxter, Gene Tierney, and the incredible Clifton Webb. Best of all, the young "stock" contract players on the lot would be given preference for the testing.

But, even if you were doing work as an extra and saw all of these people daily — Zanuck and Mayberry in casting, screenwriter Lamarr Trotti — protocol dictated that you did not approach them to solicit parts. Your agent did that.

Sure as hell, my agent Marie Crisp, estranged wife of the best character actor on the Fox lot, Donald Crisp, called.

"Have you gotten to page 17 of *The Razor's Edge*?"

"No," I confessed, "I don't have the book." She insisted I come right

New York City, 1948. I trade my ascot ties and tweeds for unfamiliar, drab overcoat and hat. The briefcase carries nothing but photo headshots and movie résumés; both prove useless in the Big Apple. I already miss the night-blooming jasmine of Westwood, California.

over to her house in Westwood. With no comment, she pushed the book into my lap and snapped it open at the bookmark. There it was. More correctly, there I was!

I was stunned. An actor without vanity is suspect to me, but I did not feel mine was of this magnitude. Maugham was describing me! And it was validated by Marie as she begin dialing the Fox lot. She asked for Bill Mayberry in casting. Marie could always get through to any executive at Fox with the possible exception of Zanuck. She was clever. She dispensed with the salutations and rolled right into reading page 17 from the popular novel. (The "I" in the excerpt is the character played by Clifton Webb.)

> Isabel's young man, Larry, said nothing. He looked very young. He was just over six feet, thin and loose-limbed. He was a pleasant-looking boy neither handsome nor plain, rather shy and in no way remarkable. He seemed perfectly at ease and appeared to take part in the conversation without opening his mouth. I noticed his hands. They were long, but not large for his size, beautifully shaped and at the same time strong. He was slightly built but not delicate in appearance; on the contrary I would have said he was wiry and resistant. His face, grave in repose, was tanned, but otherwise there was little color in it. He had rather high cheek bones and his temples were hollow. He had a natural grace that was attractive and I could see why Isabel had been taken by him. Their eyes met and there was in his a tenderness that was beautiful to see.

Mayberry allowed her to finish. Marie opened her pitch: "The young man just described by Maugham is seated in my living room." Marie was a helluva thespian.

Then, typically, he told her he had considered me but was worried about my Texas twang. This would not fit Larry, the World War I flyer seeking spiritual peace. She was right down his throat. "You've forgotten, Bill, he worked with Dillion; he's Continental" (the buzzword for a nonregional accent in mid-forties Hollywood).

Within five minutes, she had a promise of a test. Not the cornball "daughter of the theater owner from Kansas" variety, but a full sound test with Anne Baxter. The call was for Friday, early — two days away. And now, the clincher. Feeling invincible, I checked the change on my dresser at home in Westwood and found just enough for a couple of Old Fashioneds at Romanoff's bar in Beverly Hills. (God, I haven't heard a call for an Old Fashioned in 30 years!)

I had just asked for my booze when a familiar voice in the noisy room called to the bartender. "Make that two on my tab, José." It was William Eythe. We had only worked together one day on his starring vehicle *Coming In on a Wing and a Prayer*, along with the finest screen actor in cinema history, his costar Don Ameche.

We had hardly begun to sip the golden nectar when his guests arrived. It was John Hodiak pulling someone behind him through Hollywood's (or, more correctly, Beverly Hills') favorite watering hole. Serendipity. It was his wife, Anne Baxter! She of the great talent, good looks, and keen brain. Until now, we had had only courteous, nodding acquaintance confined to the Fox lot. Of course, it was too early for her to know that we would be working together on Friday. Thank heavens, I had by now curry-combed most of the gauche hayseeds from my manners, so I didn't mention the casting call. The bar time was quality with quality people. When the headwaiter announced that a table was ready, I discreetly begged off and headed for the foyer. Bill Eythe asked me to wait up and I stopped at the cloakroom.

"It's a scam, Larry."

"Pardon?"

"Yeah, another one of the lizard's devious machinations." I just listened. "You know Zanuck's an officer in the armed forces? He knows just when Ty Power is being mustered out. Ty telegraphed from the Aleutians or somewhere in the Pacific. He told DFZ that if he doesn't save *The Razor's Edge* for him, he's losing his favorite boy!"

I was numb. I knew of Zanuck's hatchet-man mentality. But why the treacherous plot, not to mention the expense?

"Simple. The studio is getting a lot of play from the scam. People who never heard of W. Somerset Maugham, *Rain*, *Of Human Bondage*, or even *The Razor's Edge* are talking about who's gonna play Larry. Sorry, pal."

I thanked him. Bill was a decent and talented man who never went into orbit as an actor but who went the distance. He is remembered as a nice guy who finished.

My disappointment was amplified when I got to my '36 V-8 Ford parked on Rodeo Drive and found an overtime ticket. Predictably, the Bentleys, the Rollses, and Joan Crawford's Cadillac V-12 were not tagged. I managed a wry smile. In the Hollywood of that point in time, valet parkers at the gin joints would resent it if you did not use their facility and tip like a sheik. Yet their overages on the lot would be placed on the street without fear of a tag from their buddy cops. Could the mean streets of New York be any less friendly? (They could.)

And *The Razor's Edge*? The next day the *Hollywood Citizen News* and the *Los Angeles Times* reported that Tyrone Power would play Larry. This was one of Zanuck's pet pictures, and nothing was spared to make it work. Although Ty Power, complete with corset, stumbled through the role never fully realizing its dimensions, the rest of the cast was a dream team. Gene Tierney had her usual edge of dementia. Clifton Webb in the role of Maugham

Broadway actress Marilyn Sable and I make *Life* magazine as models for Pepsi Cola. The money is good on these shoots, but a still photo is an unfinished movie to the movie-struck.

himself had just the right effete distance. And Anne Baxter walked away with the film. Without her all too early and tragic death, we would have had the special Eleonora Duse of the screen. Larry Buchanan, "special business extra," can be seen watching from a table in a Paris café, adoring this great talent.

Hocking everything except my Jumbo Martin Dreadnought guitar, I took the *Santa Fe Chief* to New York, unprepared for what I would find. I arrived in a winter rainstorm. A cab was out of the question. The downpour and indiscreet pigeons ruined my new English Burberry overcoat. I paid a fortune for a lice-infested hotel room until I could find a furnished flat. My enchantment with the Big Apple was fading fast.

And so was my stash. But then came another one of those mini-miracles. After three days of eating at the Automat, I took my last ten-spot, feeling very brave, and headed for a recommended but pricy eatery. It was the dining room of the Hotel des Artistes in the west Sixties off Central Park. This place had, and I presume still has, the sexiest murals in Manhattan. The service there was heavy silver and the color of the linens was what back home we called "titty pink." I ordered an Old Fashioned, light on the bitters. When the waiter returned he did not lift my drink from the tray but simply said, "Compliments of the Thorntons." He indicated a table where I saw one of the most beautiful women of my experience nodding along with a properly attentive gentleman.

"The Thorntons?" I was baffled. The waiter was discreet.

"They have an apartment here." I still must have looked bewildered. "The Walter

Thornton Model Agency is the most important in the city. They would like you to enjoy your cocktail with them before dinner."

We got on, as the English say, swimmingly. They insisted on picking up my tab, and I was to report to the agency at ten o'clock the next morning to sign with the firm. Life was suddenly very sweet. I was also about to receive a lesson in psychology. One could act for nothing Off-Broadway in turgid, downbeat Chekhov and Ibsen plays for months and never get a nibble from the producers uptown. But one good shot of the actor as model in *Cosmopolitan* or any of the slicks and the phone would ring off the hook for auditions. Suddenly, you had value commercially around Sardi's restaurant and socially with the ladies. Dastardly unfair, but there you have it.

One example will suffice. One of the prettiest young actresses in the mainstream theater world was Marilyn Sable. When she appeared in a hit comedy at the Mansfield theater on 47th Street, I wangled an orchestra seat from an usher friend and watched her with fascination. But at final curtain, I couldn't get past the stage door Johnnies that flocked to the dressing room with dinner invitations. I tried to introduce myself in the Automat, at museums, and in Central Park, but I was always dismissed because I was just a face in the crowd. An actor! An *out-of-work actor*! Reluctantly, I gave up.

Then, the Thornton Agency called. I was wanted for a *Life* magazine ad for a prestige client, Pepsi Cola. The publication was primo at the time. Even the location was platinum — the famous Versailles nightclub, the smartest night spot in New York. Actors and filmmakers avoided it because of the dinner tabs of $100. And that was in the late forties! I reported for the job, but the girl for the shoot was late. Just when the photographer and I both thought it wise to scrap the session, in walked Marilyn Sable. I had tried on at least five occasions to make an impression on Marilyn to no avail; I was not in her set. Now I played it cool when we were introduced. She betrayed not a flicker of recognition. Yet here, with my Thornton Agency credentials (they handled very few clients), my Italian shoes and tailored suit, I was accepted as an equal.

I finally came clean with her, and we both had a big but bittersweet laugh. But she was unyielding. Unblinking, she made her behavior perfectly logical. She wanted the big time and that meant choices she found hard but necessary. She confessed that she remembered each and every time I had tried to hit on her. She gave day and date and even politely told me that many times she had had second thoughts about the snubs.

Why this trivia? Because I have made a hobby of studying the winners, also-rans, and losers I have known in show business. And Marilyn Sable was a textbook case of the prime element of success in the world of entertainment. Before talent, before good looks — yes, even before hard work — are focus and perseverance. There is a distant aura about winners that is often mistaken for rudeness. But rudeness suggests that they even know you exist, and they don't. They have fashioned an image of themselves already enjoying their success. Asking them to "get real" or to "get a life" invites at most a shrug of the shoulder, and that only if they are feeling expansive. Expect absolute unawareness of your presence if they are recharging themselves with their tenacity and ambition.

This is not to say they are not good company. Take Ms. Sable. Marilyn had it all — good looks, talent, and focus. Wherever she is today, I would bet heavily that she is doing exactly what she pleases, with whom she pleases.

The modeling fees, of course, were very welcome, but the high jolt resulting from that chance meeting with the Thorntons was to come a year later. Irving Penn, the internationally famous photographer, was seeking a subject for a *Vogue* special dealing with the American working man. They were having trouble finding the right man to pose as a cowboy. Agent Walter took me over in person, and I got the assignment. I treasure the portrait. Penn was the Rembrandt of emulsion. (Even in this story lies a movie connection. Irving Penn was the brother of Arthur Penn, director of *Bonnie and Clyde*. Years later, my Dallas "stock company" and I would help Arthur Penn and Warren Beatty find Depression-era Texas locations for their watershed film.)

After the postwar artistic famine I had endured in Hollywood, I now began to enjoy what we used to call in Texas "a bird's nest on the ground." A trained actor could do Broadway or Off Broadway theater by night and films by day, much like the system in London. With the onset of summer, one could do summer theater throughout the Eastern Seaboard. It was great fun, although our supporting cast from the locals wasn't always that supportive. This gave rise to the expression "Summer theater, some'er not."

The Irving Penn photograph of me that made *Vogue* magazine's special on the working man.

I had been around movies, legit theater and cabarets for ten years, but I would designate 1951 as the beginning of my life in film. Again, my trusty Martin guitar would be my passport.

The old Biograph Studios in Astoria, Long Island, just a short train ride from Times Square, were famous for filmmaking since the days of silent cinema. The Army Signal Corps had taken the facility over as a photographic center and was using it to make "training films" to show to troops at military bases around the globe. The films covered such as "How to Dig and Use a Latrine." Although military brass managed and called the shots at the Signal Corps Photographic Center, the professional crews and cast were "civilian contractors" by law. Most important to me, it was a place where young, ambitious filmmakers could wedge a foot in the door.

Enter my Jumbo Martin guitar. I was a regular on a live weekly NBC telecast known as *The Gabby Hayes Show*. The budgets were small, so I doubled as actor in the frontier dramas hosted by George "Gabby" Hayes, comedy sidekick in hundreds of Western shoot-em-ups. I also performed the theme and background music, live. Each week, director Vincent

Yours truly as writer, musical director and performer on NBC's *Gabby Hayes Show*, telecast live weekly. No retakes.

Donahue would hire one promising actor as the lead. Lee Marvin. Robert Webber, Charles Bronson, Cliff Robertson — the list was endless as we churned out these weekly vignettes of the Old West. During rehearsals, I made many friends such as character actor Royal Dano, as well as walk-on acquaintances such as Steve McQueen. I don't believe Steve had any friends. His choice. Since both Steve and I were called "inmate" in our formative years, we traded many stories of the merits and demerits of the institutional life.

But the lucky star for me was Rod Steiger, who, like Steve, was beginning to be noticed by Hollywood. We had traded beers at the Theater Bar in the west Forties, but I really didn't know him until we brought him aboard for a role on *The Gabby Hayes Show*. He was to play Jim Bridger, great frontier scout in the American West. Rod was a stickler for script integrity and a lover of folk music. Knowing I was a Western buff, he would defer to me on points of authenticity.

My end-of-show guitar theme for that week was "Sweet Betsy from Pike." We had just faded into black when Rod snapped his finger at me. "Ever done any training films at SCPC?" I had to say no. He continued, "They're looking for an authentic hillbilly who can play guitar and act. Get out there."

The following morning, I was being fitted for a private's uniform as the lead in *Homer Goes Hygienic*. This was to be a musical and the most expensive SCPC training film to date.

One film followed the other. I was in hog heaven. Imagine, after all the guarded nonsense of the unions in Hollywood, to be encouraged to write, shoot, edit, act in, and score film after film, and be paid for it !

One of the many friends I met at SCPC was a movie nut like myself who was still in Uncle Sam's regulation uniform, Alexander Singer. Alex would go on to direct features such as *Psyche 59* with Patricia Neal and dozens of Movies of the Week, garnering his share of Emmys and other awards for television dramas which included *Glass House*.

I remember him most for two introductions. One was my initiation into the wacky, all-night movie world of the Screen Building at 1600 Broadway in Manhattan. The second was meeting his friend, would-be filmmaker Stanley Kubrick. The Screen Building was an ancient ten-story office structure devoted entirely to the post-production of film. There were cutting and screening rooms as well as equipment rental floors, and the rooms were always jumping. Insiders referred to the place simply as "1600." It was a great place to network. And one could take a cutting room and work all night for half price.

As the lights of the Great White Way would zap on to greet playgoers to *Mr. Roberts*, *South Pacific*, or *A Streetcar Named Desire*, 1600 would hum with Moviolas in that magical dream factory. At midnight, everybody split for the Jewish deli across Broadway for hot

My Jumbo Martin guitar is my open sesame to the lead in the Army's biggest film to date.

pastrami on rye and potato salad. I sometimes would muse to myself "I hope to God kosher pickles have some nutritional value." They were a staple of my diet. Even there, the buzz was film, film, film. I knew this was where I would edit my short subject *The Cowboy* if I could ever get the cash to shoot it.

As for Alex's friend Kubrick, he had already shot his short subject, a one-reeler about professional boxing called *Day of the Fight*. Encouraged by this effort, his dad, a dentist, helped him put together $80,000 to make his first feature, *Fear and Desire*.

In the wee hours of a Broadway dawn, Stanley was showing Alex and me his rough cut of *Fear*. There was a scene wherein a plate of beans was hurled to the floor and a soldier walks into the frame — from the wrong side of the camera. Stanley, a sternly focused loner, was beside himself; the scene was not working. Patiently, Alex explained that in the camera setup, Stanley had crossed the director's line (an imaginary line between the noses of the two actors nearest the camera; see glossary for further details). This elementary mistake destroyed the continuity of the scene. The only solution would be to flip the negative in printing, but that would leave the low-key scene "soft." Fiscally, reshooting was out of the question. Stanley, without a word, slipped into the dark hall of the sixth floor of "1600." Alex and I followed. We found this tough Jewish kid from the Bronx trying to hide the tears smarting in his dark, penetrating eyes. Stanley Kubrick does not now acknowledge *Fear and Desire*.

I loved *Day of the Fight* but found *Fear and Desire* pretentious. Less than seven years later, Stanley directed *Paths of Glory* starring Kirk Douglas. A great film. What do I know?

Thus when I hear a Kubrick detractor declare that Stanley's rise to eminence was without a payment of dues, I can only invoke the words of a great old vaudeville routine and say "Vas you dere, Charlie?" (Charlie and Moe were a comedy team whose most famous sketch had the ever-enthusiastic Moe telling skeptic Charlie some fantastic tale of his latest adventure. As the story became increasingly grandiose and implausible, Charlie would become red

faced with fury and finally explode into accusing Moe of lying. Moe would listen patiently through his diatribe, then, in his Yiddish accent, respond simply "Vas you dere, Charlie?" The punchline was that the audience knew Moe was always telling the truth about his escapades.)

The greatest gift New Yorkers gave to embryonic cinéastes was the Motion Picture Library at the Museum of Modern Art on 53rd Street. In Texas we would call it "in high cotton." A tyro actor-musician-filmmaker could take a date to see *Battleship Potemkin* or *Open City* then walk up to 57th Street to the Russian Tea Room for dinner. There we would argue the merits or demerits of the feature until the place closed. The Tea Room was affordable then and we never were thrown out for hogging a table. It is very chic now, inaccessible to neophyte filmmakers.

There was never a contest amongst our crowd as to the greatest film ever made: *Les Enfants du Paradis* (*Children of Paradise*). Privately, after more than 40 years, I see no reason to alter that opinion. Having made my declaratory judgment, however, I hasten to add that I am in awe of the films of the late David Lean, the greatest filmmaker in the history of the art.

I linger on Marcel Carné's masterpiece, *Les Enfants du Paradis*, for two reasons. First, it was one of the early examples, and still the finest, of guerrilla cinema. Made under the heel of the Nazis and subject to hellish privations and compromise, it is a triumph of dedication over adversity. Second, it was a shock treatment for me. Although I knew I could never even touch the garment of director Carné, I could perhaps learn from the master and begin.

The night I saw *Enfants*, I pulled one of my cowboy boots from the closet. I dumped all of that day's remaining one dollar bills and change I had into the boot. This became a daily ritual.

Somehow, I was going to Texas to make my one-reeler.

Opposite: The U.S. Army Signal Corps Photographic Center at Astoria, Long Island. The old Biograph studios had become a cinema center for training films, and the best film school in the world. One day I was directing, the next day I was a make-believe prisoner of war. I'm the dark-shirted speck facing left immediately below the central doorway.

2. The Cowboy

Consciously or unconsciously, I chose the right subject, something in which I was well-versed. In the live television shows I had done in which the West was portrayed, I was frustrated by the ignorance of television writers from the Bronx and their perception of Western folklore and mores. I tired of explaining to the scenarist that "you-all" was a Southern expression, born of the ante-bellum days, and that west of Fort Worth the only correct idiom was "y'all." Also, the mesquite tree was not "*mess*-keet" but "m'skeet." And so on.

My worst peeve was writers' references to use of Western regalia and working clothes. Their expression for this wardrobe was "colorful." I don't believe they ever discovered that every garment the cowboy wore had a practical function. The large bandanna was in reserve for a dust storm that might suddenly spring from the desert floor. The wide brim of the sombrero was for the unforgiving sun. The vest was for pockets to hold his makings for a cigarette, usually with Bull Durham tobacco. The leather chaps protected his legs from the chaparral shrub, a bothersome growth in the West. His high heels were to dig into the dirt when he was bull-dogging a calf for branding and for locking his boots into his stirrups. Even the long duster coats, favored by Italian director Sergio Leone, functioned as an all-weather standby.

At 1600 Broadway, I picked up a 100-foot-load Eyemo Camera and 30 rolls of 35 mm black and white negative. The Bell and Howell Eyemo is an indestructible combat camera of World War II vintage. This dependable, and expensive, jewel is still used by the major studios when they do a crash and they want a subjective shot of the action. They just tie it down in the car, train, or elevator and "let 'er rip!" The Eyemo should be placed in the Cinema Hall of Fame.

I closed my coldwater flat and, overloaded with gear, struggled to the Greyhound station. I took the express to Dallas. My brother Earl, alerted, waited with his 1947 Chevy. We headed west to San Angelo. The flat, characterless vistas of Central Texas turned to arid washes and beckoning mesas. We shot day and night, ignoring inclement weather. A pinto pony stepped on my light meter and I was reduced to guessing exposure. I was unstoppable, many times forgetting to eat or drink. After all, I was on location! I was making my first film! I was out of my friggin' mind.

And out of film. We returned to Dallas. I could not wait for the dailies to see if I had a picture, so we processed at the only laboratory in Texas: Jamieson Film. This decision would affect the rest of my professional life. Stay tuned.

Lo and behold, thank you Jesus, the great light of unspoiled Tejano panoramas splashed across the screen. It wasn't Ford's *Stage Coach* or Seastrom's *The Wind*. But it was in focus and we didn't lose a shot!

I headed back to New York and the catacombs of 1600 Broadway. By the time the one-reeler was cut, I was out of budget money for the narration, negative conforming and the mix, the final compositing of the elements. The reason for this state of affairs was a truism of show business: out of sight, out of mind. My absence from the city and my long hours in the cutting room had taken their toll. Larry who?

The first rule of the manual of guerrilla cinema is improvisation. One of the ambitious filmmakers at 1600 was a fellow Texan, William Free. He owed me. When he was casting for his first no-budget "street" picture, he couldn't find the right young leading man. I had remembered the work of a dark youth who came on like Gangbusters on film but who had never had a lead. I recommended Mark Rydell to Bill. It worked. This same Rydell went on to directing and is responsible for some of the screen's very best moments such as found in *On Golden Pond* starring Jane and Henry Fonda, and *The Rose* starring Bette Midler.

Bill Free, as it happened, was one of the best voices in town, and he was happy to oblige. But that left the mix, for which there was no money. The madness couldn't stop here, so we charged ahead. We did the unthinkable: a live mix.

Remember, if you will, this was before magnetic recording had been perfected, with its high tech capabilities. Rerecording was on 35mm optical film. A mistake meant starting over with the dollar clock churning above the screen. So, with me on the Jumbo Martin guitar winging Western standards and Bill Free laying in his sonorous, pear-shaped tones, we made it on the second take. Ecstatic, we picked up some cineastes from 1600 and retired to the Theater Bar on the West Side for beer and veal cutlet parmigiana. Sardi's, the "in" watering hole, was too pricey.

On reflection, I may have celebrated too soon. The bookers were less than enthusiastic. "So you have a short, kid. Shorts don't get rentals. They're just filler material. The shelves are loaded with 'em." To my chagrin, I learned they were right. Short subjects were and are a give-a-way. My mentor, Sam Arkoff, would later call them "artsy fartsy, self-indulgent showcases for questionable talents."

I was crushed. How could they talk about my masterpiece like that?

Then, wallowing in the quagmire of self-pity, I was reintroduced to an old fantasy acquaintance, Judge Roy Bean. Yes, the same historical character who illegally set himself up as the judge of the little West Texas town of Vinegaroon. In literature and the movies, he has ruled with his six-gun and sharp wit, becoming one of our culture's most enduring characters. He has been portrayed by such disparate types as Paul Newman in *Judge Roy Bean* and Walter Brennan in the *The Westerner*. Roy Bean's homilies and quotes are a kind of shorthand of raw philosophy and comments on the frailties of the human animal. Long before Lyndon Baines Johnson claimed authorship to the adage, Roy Bean had made his rulin', "If it ain't broke, don't fix it!"

Ever since the time I read about "his honor" in the fifth grade, whenever I have a personal crisis, Roy Bean suddenly appears in my own mind-flick about his exploits. Thus, when *The Cowboy* had been rejected by just about every booker in Manhattan and I was at a new low, broke and despondent, I should not have been surprised to hear the spurs jingle from Roy's boots as he stepped up to the bar (whiskey bar that is) and slammed his Colt 45 onto his Bible.

"What's the nuisance here, Junior? You look like a motherless calf!"

"Well, Your Honor, I made this little movie about the real cowboy and the gear he wears and all, but the people that run the picture shows are hardly bustin' gut to put it in theaters."

He bristled. "These picture show people — any of them been west of the Pecos?"

I had to tell Roy that I doubted any of them had been west of the Hudson River.

"Any of these tenderfoots have a streak of maverick in 'em?"

Then, I had to tell him that the only company in town with guts and the daring to step out from the herd was the new United Artists. They were making waves by taking chances and nurturing new filmmakers and offbeat material for their films. I also had to tell Judge Roy Bean that I had not tried to see United Artists.

"Then you ain't ploughin' as well as you know how!" Grabbing his pistol and Bible, he bellowed. ". . . And that's my rulin'." Then he was gone.

The crusty old bastard was right. The newly resurrected United Artists was the grand-child of the UA formed by Cinema pioneers Chaplin, Griffith, and Douglas Fairbanks when films were in their infancy.

Then it hit me like lead from Judge Bean's hog-leg revolver. I knew someone at UA! He was Francis Winnikus, a rising young executive and personal assistant to one of the head honchos, Max Youngstein.

Like a bat out of hell, I grabbed my reel and sprinted to midtown and the offices of United Artists. I had hardly said hello to Winnikus when his boss Max Youngstein stuck his head in inviting Francis to lunch. Francis looked at me with a straight face. "Well, Larry and I were just going to the Stage Deli after I look at his reel."

Youngstein uttered the magic words, "I've been thinking about a hot pastrami all morning. Mind if I tag along?"

In the screening room at 1600, the chords of "On Top of Old Smokey" faded into the end title of *The Cowboy*. Max Youngstein, in no hurry to leave, placed his feet on the seat-back in front of him. For the moment he had forgotten his hot pastrami. He mused, "Miller's *Salesman* preems next week at the Vic. The producer won't sit still for a Bugs Bunny or a Pathé. That leaves nothing for a chaser." (Translation: *Death of a Salesman*, the film version of playwright Arthur Miller's great play, was to open on Broadway at the Victoria Theater, a flagship movie palace. There would be no cartoon or newsreel. That means there was no "filler" to unreel as customers walked out after the screening.)

"*Salesman* is brilliant but it could be perceived as a downer, a kitchen picture." (Translation: A "kitchen picture" is a film of talking heads, wherein one player walks to the kitchen, pulls out a chair for a companion and utters the most damaging words in cinema, "Sit down, I want to talk to you.")

Max continued, "What they need is something with vistas, a filler that will distance the audience from those dark *Death of a Salesman*, studio interiors." (Translation: What they need is *The Cowboy*!)

The world premiere of *Death of a Salesman* with *The Cowboy* riding piggyback was in December 1951. I worked a bread and butter commercial that day, so I was late getting to the theater near Times Square. When I turned into Broadway from 47th Street, I was not prepared for what I saw.

Pickets? Yes! Organized, vocal, sign-carrying, meanspirited picketers making their turns outside the theater where *my* picture was playing. Not the most auspicious debut for a career in films.

The country was currently hostage to Red baiters, and zealous patriots were on a Communist witchhunt. Led by Senator Joe McCarthy, America-Firsters were on a feeding frenzy. They targeted anyone in the theater or in films who exhibited the most minimal concern for his fellow man. Lives were threatened and careers were ruined as McCarthy and his ilk rolled their ambitious juggernaut across the land of the free.

Their target that evening was not my modest little offering. Rather, their venom was divided between Arthur Miller as the creator of *Death of a Salesman* and the distinguished film actor playing the title role of Willy Loman, Fredric March. Both were listed, by the hatchet club known as the House Committee on Un-American Activities, as "sinister leftists."

Arthur Miller was able to vivisect the ills that gnawed at the best that was America, and so he did, with unmatched skills. And Fredric March, as Willy Loman and other characters, played Everyman better than any actor of his time, warts and all. To those who would say that they were out to destroy this country, I pose this query: "Vas you dere, Charlie?"

Death of a Salesman was liked by the critics and moviegoers. It played nine weeks at the Victoria, carrying

Jane McVayne in a photo from around the time I met her. George Cukor knew that, as his assistant, I was breaking his cardinal rule of not hiring the same extra twice. And he knew why.

The Cowboy along with it. I was paid $100 a week in "film rentals" for a total of $900! That was exactly what I had spent on the film in air fare, equipment, laboratory time, sound, and titles. Years later, I would be called again and again a minimalist. Could it be that *The Cowboy* presaged that moniker?

What is important here is that audiences liked *The Cowboy* too. Had they not, the short would not have gone the distance on the run. I was invited to put the reel up for competition for The Peabody Awards. I came in a close second to a short subject about a Bronx housing project. Imagine my chagrin not only to lose to a kitchen picture, but to lose to one with 200 kitchens!

Not to worry. I was now, in however modest a way, a player in the production of films. There was no turning back. Reeling in the intoxication of seeing my first effort on the big screen, I grew impatient. I was absolutely certain that I was ready to do a feature. If I could do one reel, I reasoned, I could do ten.

But my hiatus from commercials and making Army training films had left the exchequer flat. I had to hustle work, not only to set my table but also to sharpen my image if I were to raise even modest dollars for a feature. That meant lunches at Sardi's, a new blazer and Countess Mara ties, replacing my tattered briefcase with a Spanish import, and so forth.

Out of a crisp, fall Manhattan blue came a call from a fellow thespian with good news. Director George Cukor was coming to town to direct Judy Holiday in *The Marrying Kind*. He was looking for an assistant director (unofficial of course, considering union rules). The requirements were an ability to find and negotiate locations, acquaintance with a lot of hungry actors, and some experience in directing extras. I got the job.

September was host to the most exciting discovery in my young life — namely, that a woman could be more, much more, than a date, companion, bed partner, and a sincere, friendly, compadre with whom one could argue films at the Russian Tea Room. The right lady could be all of the above and more. Explanation is in order.

George Cukor was a rigid taskmaster. Rule number one was that no extra be hired for more than one location. The appearance in one of his films of a face getting off the bus at Rockefeller Center and then, in a totally unrelated scene, the same mug crosstown in a night-club, meant instant dismissal and blacklisting for the hiring assistant director on all future films out of Hollywood.

Cukor loathed crowd scenes in contemporary dress. He preferred his day players to be in a classic drama and with all concerned in period wardrobe. On frigid evenings on this shoot, George directed from the heated back seat of a limousine. He would quickly outline the scene to his assistants then raise the car glass to keep out the cold.

On one particular evening I left George to line up six couples on Fifth Avenue. They were to stroll to the canopy of a tall apartment building and enter, being careful not to bump into our principals, Judy Holliday and Aldo Ray.

Standing in the light of the streetlamp I noticed an odd extra — that is, one without a partner. Since we were ready for action, I began to walk in step with our odd one. I did not look at her or speak to her, being concerned with the scene's progress. It was only when we called for a second take and walked to the first positions that I focused on my partner. I was suddenly struck with an affliction alien to me: speechlessness. She had the most radiantly beautiful face I had ever seen. Adios, Ava. Goodbye, Greer. It was nice knowing you, Anita, Alice, Shirley.

When we wrapped shooting for the night, I learned that two other guys had asked her to supper. I wasn't going to let this one get away, so I joined them. We went to Macario's, an Italian bistro just off Central Park South, behind the St. Moritz Hotel. There began a verbal fencing for the shy smile of this lovely stranger. The chic cocktail of that time in Manhattan was the Old Fashioned. They flowed. Then, wary of an escalating dinner check, we ordered Veal Cutlet Parmigiana. And finally, that most obvious rip-off in America's social scene, the after dinner drink.

Long after the two Lotharios had given up and gone, I walked her home through Central Park up to 86th Street. That was when Central Park was for lovers. The thought of not seeing her again was troubling, so I hatched the most successful plot of my checkered career.

I explained to her director Cukor's firm rule of no call-backs for extras. But not to worry, "Do you have a blonde wig?" She did. That took care of the following day's work. In succession, she wore horn-rimmed glasses, sunglasses, exotic makeup, crazy hats — anything that would get her another day on the set, although she balked at cross-dressing. I was very pleased with myself. After all, in the eyes of Ms. Jane McVayne, lately of Erie, Pennsylvania, I was some sort of Houdini.

This little subterfuge went on right up the day the Hollywood Film Company was to return to the West Coast. When George Cukor said goodbye to his New York staff in the lobby of the Essex House, he didn't shake my hand. With that sly smile and his slight, effeminate lisp, he brushed by me and whispered, "Lawrence, dear boy, why don't you marry the girl?"

I did.

There is a peculiar postscript to this story. When *The Marrying Kind* opened in New York in spring 1952, the theater was (you've probably guessed it) the Victoria. As Jane and I turned into the limelight of Times Square, the familiar sight of pickets greeted us. This time the object of their displeasure was Judy Holiday, the star of the show. Again their charge was the unfocused accusation "Commie!"

I will never forget Judy's costar, film newcomer Aldo Ray. He prowled the lobby of the Victoria, standing eye to eye with a hundred pickets. He threw his dinner jacket to the lobby floor and in his gravel voice dared not one, but all, to slug it out with him, not necessarily under the Marquis of Queensberry Rules.

Inside the theater, Judy Holliday was giving the dramatic performance of her brief career.

3. *Apache Gold* (a.k.a. *Grubstake*), a Family, and a New Job

Girded by the emotional support of my new bride and the modest success of *The Cowboy*, I intensified my efforts to write, produce, and direct a first feature film. I wrote the screenplay of *Grubstake*, a Western, and designed it to be made for nothing. In short, it would come from hunger.

I pounded the pavements of Manhattan and boarded every elevator in town looking for the seed money that would make this drama a reality. Nobody challenged the authenticity of the dialogue or the feeling of place; these elements were my strong suit. But a recurring criticism was that the story lacked tension. I had always associated tension with whodunits, spy capers, and horror films, but I now learned a great lesson: tension is the absolute, indispensable ingredient in *every* film, be it a love story, adventure, comedy or pornography.

Enter Lynn Shubert. Lynn was a former P-38 pilot and an actor and playwright who had sold some live television dramas. We had met when we read against each other for roles in Thomas Heggan's *Mr. Roberts* which was later directed by Josh Logan and starred Henry Fonda. As competitors we lost in the auditions but became lifelong friends.

Lynn agreed to a joint rewrite for a deferred salary and a few points in "profits, if any." (These are two of the most potent weapons in the arsenal of the guerrilla filmmaker.) Living on hot tea and lemon and working on Lynn's kitchen table, we completed the rewrite in a nonstop 72 hours.

Within ten days after mimeographing our lean, mean oater, we had pledges for a measly $25,000. That, I was sure, would bring the film to an answer print. Intoxicated, we started to look for our cast leads.

The leading man was easy, and his wife (we'll call her "Edna") would go along as an unpaid makeup person and seamstress. Done deal. Edna was shy, quiet, and plain beside her Arrow shirt model husband. He never seemed to have a kind word, only petty criticisms. Edna was one of those who suffered in silence.

Our real challenges were our villain and the fiery, smoldering, sexy, Mescalero Apache trail guide. (They are always fiery, smoldering, and sexy.)

For the Heavy I remembered an intense, rumpled actor whom I had worked with just five weeks before in an Off Broadway play that flopped after a short run. The play was Irwin Shaw's *Bury the Dead*. Although the actor was street — smart and suspicious, he was also shy

Jack Klugman as the Heavy and Lynn Shubert as the Gunslinger drifter in *Apache Gold* (1952).

as we rehearsed the play, which was his first time on the boards. He was an amalgam of Jean Gabin, Fernandel, and Spencer Tracy. But he couldn't carry a tune in a bucket. In the play, strumming my trusty Martin Dreadnought, I sang and my protégé was to chime in on the refrain. Boy did he chime.

On opening night, Jack Klugman blew us all to hell and back.

> Oh bury me not on the Lone Prairie
> Those words came low and mournfully
> From the pallid lips of a youth who lay
> On his dying bed at the close of the day.

There wasn't a dry eye in the house.

Jack suffered from the oldest of maladies in show business: he couldn't get a good part because he did not have an agent and he couldn't get an agent because he did not have a good part.

The day after the play opened, Jack and I dropped into the William Morris Agency on Madison Avenue. Don't misunderstand me, I could never get the bastards to sign me on, but I could at least get past the girls with the English accents. All I did was make an introduction. The rest was Jack's magic. Pumped up from his personal success in the play, he devoured those ten-percenters and was on his way.

Now I had another reason to contact Jack. He returned my call from his home and asked simply, "When do we leave?" We had our heavy.

Now for our "fiery, smoldering" Mescalero Apache trail guide. A new musical had opened on Broadway, and my writing buddy, Lynn Shubert, had caught the opening and was sure that the girl we were looking for was in the show. At final curtain he had mixed with the cast and was captivated by this waif.

There were three ways you could see a Broadway show in those days. You could pay the monstrous ticket price. You could scrounge for "Annie Oakleys" (free promotional tickets, sometimes called "papering the house"). Or you could always count on one of the ushers being an actor friend "between engagements" who would sneak you in after the house lights dimmed. Via the latter route we found our leading lady, Neile Adams.

Careers in show business are subject to mercurial swings. Like a rocket, they can go ballistic or crash with the same intensity. A casual contact can be the magic moment that connects an artist with his or her destiny. Neile was certainly the classic Hollywood success story. That night in Manhattan she was dancing and singing her heart out in her first role. Within five years, she would win a scholarship with terpsichorean great Katherine Dunham, play a featured role in *Kismet*, star in a Broadway production of *Pajama Game*, and marry a young actor named Steve McQueen. She had been born in Manila to a British father and a Spanish mother. Her parents divorced when she was an infant. She never knew her father. When the Japanese invaded the Philippines, she was a runner for the guerrilla resistance. She smuggled information through the lines of the invaders. Caught, she spent time in a concentration camp. Once the war was over, she and her mother moved to New York.

She was everything my partner had promised and more. Her tough but waifish independence would make her ideal for the Apache guide. She could have stepped out of a Brady tintype print of Chief Geronimo and his Mescalero nomads.

The Big Bend National Park lies in extreme west Texas. It is formed where the Rio Grande dips into Mexico then heads north. This is the last frontier in the continental United States — rugged, awesome, scary, primeval. Igneous rock, square miles of every variety of cactus, ocotillo, Spanish Dagger, diamondback rattlers, gila monsters, and mountain lions. It is unspoiled and foreboding.

The little town of Marfa was the last we would see of telephones, iced drinks, and soft beds for the next several weeks. As the early morning lights of the town faded in the rearview mirrors, our small caravan looked more like a Gypsy troupe which has just been asked to vacate the premises by the sheriff.

Our destination was the Chisos Mountains ("Chisos" meaning "phantom"). We faced more than 80 miles of unfinished roads and creekbeds. Tires blew, radiator caps popped, and tempers strained. We averaged about ten miles per hour.

Then, just as neither man nor vehicle could muster any more energy, we entered the foothills of the Chisos. The sun, no longer curling our lips and draining all salt from our bodies, turned to a tolerable orange color. Then suddenly, there were the High Chisos, dominating the high basin. Specks of light from coal oil lamps beckoned from a small cluster of frame cabins and a lodge deep in the mountain valley. It was like a painting by Maxfield Parrish. We put the vehicles in low gear and let them roll the four miles to the hunter's lodge that made up the park headquarters.

To the small band of hunters and surveyors that greeted us, we must have seemed to have dropped from another galaxy. There was Neile Adams, in her Chino Poblano skirt, swirling away in practice on a Baile Tipica. Steve Wyman, our leading man, practicing the throw of a Bowie knife. Sol Fol, our Jewish assistant cameraman, painstakingly explaining

Apache Gold stars Neile Adams and Steve Wyman.

kosher cooking to the weathered old sod who would be responsible for feeding the company. He had never heard of bagels and lox. Kort Falkenburg, our sound man and a Mel Torme buff, playing "Blue Velvet" on a portable wire recorder. My friend and partner Lynn Shubert arguing with the wrangler who had promised us horses at five dollars a day, then mysteriously escalated the price to twenty bucks now that we were hostage to this primitive wilderness. Our cameraman Carl Sturgess (we did not call them cinematographers then) and me trying to repair a Mitchell noiseless camera that was chattering like a small cement mixer.

And Jane, my bride of six months, holding the script while our heavy, Jack Klugman, rehearsed his lines. But Jack was impatient. He had brought several double-breasted suits and some bright ties in his luggage in anticipation of some fun and games in some romantic border town. His fantasies of the West were, as for anyone from the inner city, a pastiche of MGM musicals. The villages of La Jitas, Vinegaroon, Terlingua, and Study Butte were composed of barren, crumbling adobe huts. Lonely old prospectors stumbled in and out of the abandoned silver mines wistfully holding on to the dream of the big strike. Mamacitas, their stomachs spilling over aprons, beat corn into tortillas. Chickens, which could not produce an ounce of fat if fried, pecked in the alkali and borax. This was the reality of the sunbaked border towns where we would shoot *Grubstake*.

I told Jack to put away his double-breasted suits. I promised he would like the town of Boquillas where we would shoot the first day. Boquillas, meaning "mouth," is at the mouth of a deep canyon on the Rio Grande. The canyon was sliced out of the rock by the river over

On location in the wilds of Texas and Mexico for *Apache Gold*. I'm at left talking to assistant cameraman Sol Fol. Seated are Neile Adams and Jack Klugman.

many thousands of years. When Jack Klugman saw the vultures circling the mud huts of Boquillas with nary a dark-eyed señorita with mantilla to be seen, he threatened to drown me in the Rio Grande. He was only half-kidding. Neile, like Jack and myself, had experienced a tough childhood. She asked us to take ten seconds and a good look at our behavior. And Jack, this rumpled soul, could not contain himself when he realized the humor of the situation. That face, which could be so tortured as when he dominated the play and the film of *Twelve Angry Men*, now spread into an elfin smile as wide as the Rio's Boquillas. Neile had broken through the tough street exterior and found the kid caught in the cookie jar.

The company had more than one daily crisis, but managed to get through the shoot without losing anybody. Shooting a movie in the boondocks produces a lot of perils physically, emotionally, and politically, any one of which could sink the project and leave a disastrous fallout.

One such crisis, a seemingly simple incident, I remember in particular. The Department of the Interior and the park rangers are very touchy about what has come to be called roadkill in recent years. It seems that in the barren wild of this treacherous park, roadkill is not always accidental. For impoverished families and desert rats (the human kind), the occasional roast venison or antelope steak can be a feast fit for a king. So to take out an animal at high speeds at night or even to leave the road and down the prey is no big deal, except to the authorities. It only leaves a dent in an already severely bashed pickup truck.

Such was not our scenario. On the second day of shooting, our little caravan was driving in the early dark trying to make the dining shack before our cook opened his bottle. Hypnotized by the high beams of the car, a doe, its eyes flaring like coals, raced towards us and slammed into the radiator. By the time we were able to stop safely, all of the cars were some distance from the deer. We all converged in the ditch to see the damage. The pitiful doe was losing blood through its nostrils and sucking for breath for its lungs. We all knew it was sure to die.

We stood transfixed. Our first thought was to end the suffering with a shot from one of our prop rifles, but the park officials had confiscated all of our live cartridges. All we had were cowboy blanks. Hollywood had met reality.

Please picture this. The unforgiving sun had given away to a cold evening wind. Several grown men, young and able, watched, hoping someone had some magic solution to either save the frightened animal or stop its pain. Then came the unexpected. Shy, quiet Edna, followed by my Jane, pulled off her corduroy jacket and ran to the animal. She directed Jane to tie the churning forefeet with her belt. Then she wrapped her corduroy around the nostrils. The deer's eyes were still wide, filled with terror. Edna looked directly into the brown pupils and held her gaze. In a few moments the wide eyes softened but the lids did not close. The struggle stopped. I stooped to see the last glow of life in the beautiful head. I have no way to describe the moment but I think there was communication between these two. I know there was acceptance in the brown pupils of the dying doe, a kind of recognition that she was joining a collective memory of her kind. And Edna? The next day she was back at her sewing. An actor's vest was split, needing mending. That was her concern now.

Out of money, we returned to New York. The picture, with some gaping holes in continuity, had a modest exposure in black and white on early television. By selling bits of it, some of which were stunning, as stock footage, we were able to return our backers their "nut" and a small profit. The negative lies smoldering in the recesses of some laboratory on the East Coast, and I pray no one tries to screen it. It is composed of nitrate stock. Nitrate film has the same ingredients as gunpowder.

Jack Klugman went on to carve a unique slot for himself in theater, films, and television as star of *Quincy* and *The Odd Couple*. Neile Adams continued her work in the New York theater and feature films until she met and married superstar Steve McQueen.

Jane and I returned from the wilds of the Big Bend Country to a rapidly changing New York. Many of the studios doing live television and commercials had moved their base of operations to Los Angeles. The theater was in a spiral of decline. Jane went to work at Manhattan's B. Altman's store, selling perfume. There were a few flop plays for me, *Dear Judas*, and *Texas 'Lil Darlin'* in the mainstream and a lot of Off Broadway.

But between the flops there were happy and productive detours. Memorable was getting to know Robert Flaherty, the father of the American documentary. He took his place in motion picture history with masterpieces such as *Moana of the South Seas*, *Nanook of the North*, and *Louisiana Story*. Our meeting was a happy fluke. The Arriflex Camera Company of Germany, later to become one of the giants of Cine Camera Equipment, had opened a modest office on 47th Street in Manhattan. Up a flight of rickety stairs, on the second floor, they had rented a small room to this independent filmmaker. The small directory on the wall read: "r. flaherty 2nd floor." I finished my business with Arriflex and climbed the stairs. The sepia-toned still photos on the wall were from *Moana*. They were sensual and warm. The Polynesian faces beamed back to the cameraman their trust of this unassuming man. He had gone to Tahiti with what he called his "thesis of non-preconception." He refused to read up on the island and its people and did not open his camera cases for months while he searched for the unvarnished essence and truth of these beautiful people and their culture.

Many years later, while I was actively producing and directing in Texas, we brought Robert's widow to Dallas where she lectured at the city's main branch library. We showed *Moana.* The innocent, childlike performances of the natives were mesmerizing. The black and white images were stunning. They had been developed on the islands in a "slop tank" for lack of laboratory facilities but they dazzled the eye. Ambitious neophyte filmmakers would do well to make studying Flaherty's films part of their homework. They are accessible on video.

And there was another happy excursion in 1953. I was hired by director José Ferrer to replace Eric Fleming in the Broadway comedy hit *My Three Angels* by Sam and Bella Spewack. Eric had signed to a Hollywood television series to be known as *Rawhide.* The producers got a bargain in me. I played the young French naval officer, understudied two other roles and played the harmonica in the wings for incidental music.

Our star was Walter Slezack, the warmest, funniest, and most generous actor I've had the pleasure to know and work with. It was sheer joy to report at curtain time to laugh with this mountain of a man with the impish wit. I simply could not believe that this prankster was the Nazi character in Hitchcock's *Lifeboat* and other World War II dramas.

Upon my solicitous inquiries on the nature of the great Hitchcock, Walter's eyes lost their laughter. "Monstrous . . . monstrous" (he would always repeat himself). "A sadist. He was bitter because he did not have one of his blonde, blue-eyed, thimblebreasted hostages in the boat. So he got his kinky sexual kicks in drowning us repeatedly with take after take when he knew damn well he already had the scene in the can. Everybody but Tallulah Bankhead got a cold; that's because she had the balls of a moose." Walter stole the show in spite of Hitchcock's shabby treatment.

As Christmas 1953 approached, the producers of the play decided they would go on the road with *Angels* the following January. At first I balked. After all, wasn't I a movie producer-director-writer now?

Then Jane came to the theater one evening to tell me that the "rabbit had died." She was pregnant with our first boy, who would be named Barry. So it was the road for me, and Jane went home to her mother in Erie, Pennsylvania, to wait for the baby. Predictably, with Walter's antics and great comic talent, the show was a smash on the road. We were out 22 weeks.

Probably the craziest unbroken four weeks of my life was when we played Chicago. Our theater had a common backstage with another where the comedy *Time Out for Ginger*, starring Melvyn Douglas, was playing. A young lead in the play was Steve McQueen. Both companies were billeted at an actor's hotel, with a long cab ride to the theater. In those days Equity actors had to pay for their own hotel bills, meals, and out-of-pocket expenses. I sure to hell couldn't take cabs as I was sending all I could home to Jane. So we all walked — that is, all except McQueen.

Steve was always in motion, but backstage and around the hotel, he was hyper. He had been waiting for the delivery of his first sports car. Payments had been made for the used vehicle, an MG-TC roadster. The Chicago run had provided the last dollars for the delivery of the car with its high fenders and glistening wire wheels. Years later this remarkable talent would have garages and warehouses bulging with the world's great racing vehicles, sports cars, motor bikes and even biplanes from World War I. But I can attest the whole bundle did not give him the thrill of the early runs in his MG in and around Chicago. Steve McQueen was born to roll.

He would tool around the gin joints of Chicago from final curtain till sunrise. He seemed mindless of the Chicago cold and refused to put up the top on the sportster. He was very careless with his stash and owed all of us for money to gas the MG. Perhaps it was our common orphan's experience, but he was at least civil to me and on rare occasions talked in confidence. He was perpetual motion, never stopping for anyone or anything beyond his very low boredom threshold. Because of our common but separate youth experiences, he was transparent to me, or was so until the end of our run in Chicago.

Shortly before curtain time, I was called to a Chicago police precinct. Steve had, in one evening, managed to be charged with speeding in his open-air MG, possession of hash, and statutory rape. Only the last of these offenses was hokum. A would-be actress had resented his "flip-off" after their diversion. I convinced the sergeant that she was a local Sadie Thompson, attached to touring musicals which came to town.

I would like to boast that my con talents got him off, but it was really that shit-kicking innocence he deployed so well that made the Sarge show us to the door. We just made the curtain for both of us. Later, he shifted from foot to foot, never looking directly at me. I was surprised when he spoke very low. "Tex . . . you keep asking me what's my hurry? Maybe it's because I've got such a fucking long way to go and I've already used up eight of my nine lives."

Bored with the road, broke, and anxious to get on with his career and his vehicle hobby, he was constantly asking for a raise from the producers of the play. The last time I saw Steve was at the moto-cross track at Indian Dunes north of Los Angeles in 1975. We both had sons riding the Dunes every Saturday without fail. Neither of us talked of films, or theater, or even of when we had met; it was only about the boys and their bikes. I really believe he was starting to get what it was all about. I was sure he had forgotten our times in Chicago and his little MG roadster, when, having finished loading his vehicle, he shifted to his low gear and leaned out the window. "You know that play in Chicago? Those bastards fired me from that show!" Then, ghost-like, he was gone.

In the summer of 1954 the road tour of *My Three Angels* finished. I returned to New York and we welcomed our first new member into the family, my son Barry. I was in a quandary. I didn't want to raise a kid in the mean streets of that city, and I didn't want to split for Hollywood and its nepotism, hothouse mentality, and anal-retentive cowardice. Truth to tell, Hollywood wasn't calling me anyhow.

I heard from a friend in Dallas that the only studio in town, Jamieson Film Co., was looking for a producer-director to head up its commercial and documentary departments. I procrastinated. I interpreted the idea as a setback.

Enter Judge Roy Bean, my alter ego, sitting on my shoulder. "What's riling you, waddie? You look like nine miles of bad road." I outlined my dilemma. He paused uncharacteristically long, then said, "I think it's time for you to bite the bullet. That little sashay into the Chisos Mountains should have taught you that you've got a lot to larn about making picture shows. What better place to get that larnin' than in yore own home town?"

I tried to interrupt, but he was having none of that.

"Hush up and listen! When you left Big D, you were on a high lonesome. Now there are three of you. Yore still wet behind the ears. I know yore sick with the maverick fever. But you've got time. And the kid — his birthright is to breathe at least a couple of years of that blessed Texas air. What in God's name have you got to lose?"

What indeed. Looking out our apartment window, I could see sleet and rain spoiling the already mean streets of Manhattan.

I filled my lungs with air, crossed my fingers, and called long distance to Dallas, I had met the Jamieson sons when they processed the film on *The Cowboy*, so I was able to ask for Hugh or Bruce by name. They both got on the line and, typical of their Scottish frugality and candor, told me not to waste money on the phone but get my butt down to Texas. They would love to have me aboard.

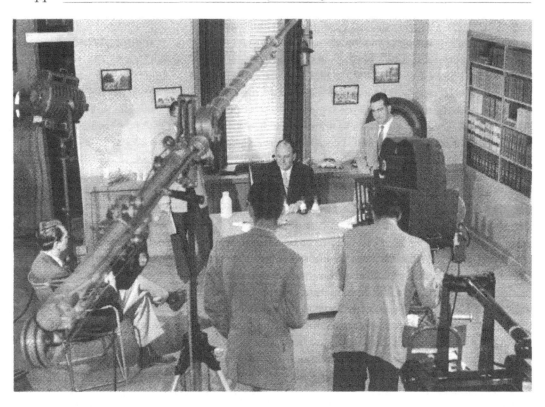

Top: Politicians, industrial giants and pitchmen all came to Jamieson Studios to tap into the burgeoning television markets. It was a gold rush for all concerned. That's me seated on the left.

Bottom: The tedium of television commercials was relieved by documentaries on location. Here, with cameraman Ted Liles, I interpret my script "San Antonio, City in the Sun."

With script in pocket and hand on the big sky-pan light, I discuss with the agency exec what will be an historic TV spot. The shoot is the first for a small Dallas company making something called Fritos. The gaffer standing on the ladder had walked into the studio that morning looking for work. Soon he would be the director of photography on several of my early stumbling efforts. Filmstruck Ralph Johnson was also to become a great friend.

I was in, but I had not articulated my one condition. I sweated. It could be a deal breaker, but I knew it had to be out front. They were suspicious.

"You're looking to sweeten the pot. What's it gonna cost us?" I shot back, "Nothing." But I explained that I had to have the freedom to continue my feature film efforts on my own time and without conflict with their commercials.

Then came the sweetest words I had heard since my first "action" cue at SCPC: "You're on. You can use our camera package on weekends and we'll do the lab work at cost."

Thus began four years of intensive production of commercials and documentaries. A third type of production was what we called "industrials," 16mm color films for corporations such as U.S. Steel and General Motors. Our output was awesome.

Jamieson Film Co. was no Mickey Mouse operation. The firm was the oldest continuous professional film lab and production house in the United States outside of the venerable Hollywood names such as Pathé and Peerless. It was founded by Hugh Jamieson Sr., who had been a contemporary and assistant to Billy Bitzer, who photographed *Birth of a Nation* for David Wark Griffith. Now, while the boys ran the lab, old Hugh Sr. would putter around in the machine shop, developing patent after patent for use in the rapidly evolving regional film processing business.

It was a very nurturing environment for me, and I treasure the professional friends I made there. Many of them would later constitute my crews when the production roller coaster took off on my "good-bad" films for American International Pictures.

4. *Venus in Furs*

Irony of ironies, I was still in the early stages of my first moonlighting flick when I had an interesting visitor. He was a young Dallas oil baron who was under pressure from his bimbo mistress for some material demonstration of his affection. The Rolls-Royce, the diamond bracelets, and a condo on Dallas' upscale Turtlecreek Boulevard were fine, thank you, but she wanted to "express herself."

Let's call him "Bubba"; it's not his real name, but it may protect the ever-changing innocents who hang on his arm these 40 years later. They prowl the pricey private clubs of Dallas as if money grew on trees. Of course, for Bubba it does. (Today's low-profile oil well pumps are called "Christmas Trees.")

Bubba wanted me to make a film starring his Caprice. More correctly, Caprice wanted to make a movie and he would rather lose the bucks than lose Caprice. He didn't care what I did as long as it was classy and sexy. He wanted no control over the money as long as he gave it to me in cash. His name was not to be on the credits. Most important, we were not to shoot anywhere in Highland Park where his wife presided over the biggest French Provincial manor in North Dallas.

So there it was. My first moonlight flick would be a scam. The man who bathed in the applause at the Victoria Theater when *The Cowboy* ended, doing an exploitation rip-off? How could I do it? Easy. We now had a new addition to our family, a brown-eyed girl named Deborah.

How could I do it indeed? It came from hunger.

Now the picture. I had remembered reading a short piece by the Marquis de Sade called "Venus in Furs." My weekend was approaching, so, working from memory, I feverishly wrote a script which follows. You read correctly. Not a "treatment." Not a "synopsis." Not an "outline." This is the actual script we shot.

VENUS IN FURS

We are in France at the time of Louis XV. An audacious young man from a distinguished family, the Marquis de Sade, is married off by his family against his will. He throws himself into a life of debauchery in his *petite maison* at the village of Arcueil. He invites prostitutes to his house where he brutally beats them. Satisfying the erotic whims and deviations of their customers is expected of the girls, but this is dementia. In two words: De Sade, "sadistic." They complain to the police, but before they can arrest him, he splits for Provence with an opera

46

singer. In the dark streets of his village he is stopped by a destitute young woman (Caprice) who begs for money. On the pretext of giving her work, he takes her to his villa. There he tortures her beyond anyone's sickest imagination. The poor girl is dragged to the attic where he makes his opera singer mistress undress her. He ties her hands behind her back and whips her until blood runs. Then, curiously, he takes a box of salve from his pocket and applies some of it to the wounds and bandages them up. The next day, he tears the wounds open with a penknife. Deranged, Caprice breaks free and throws herself out of the window. She survives long enough to give an account of the horrors and pain inflicted by de Sade. De Sade tells the police that all he wanted to do was test the properties of a new Salve!

With the blessing of my bosses, I moonlight a soft-porn feature, *Venus in Furs*.

This exercise in deviation was my first real experience in Guerrilla Cinema. The phrase suggests a film that is off the wall, made without resources and a filmmaker who is driven to covert machinations to make the film work at any costs in human effort, honestly trying to give the patron exactly what he has bargained for.

We delivered. Then there was a surreal conclusion to this wild, Kafkaesque nightmare. Because I literally had my own laboratory, I cut and scored the film in one week. There was a frantic call from Bubba. That midnight, he and I screened the print. It was eerie as there was no one else in the plant. As it ended I turned on the overhead lights.

"Well?" I felt that, for the money, we had done a good job. "*I love it!*" he gushed. I really didn't need stroking. A sincere "I like it" would have sufficed.

"Everybody paid off? You come off okay?" I assured him the books were clean and we were quite happy with the deal.

He then asked me to put the negative and print in the trunk of his Rolls-Royce Silver Cloud in the parking lot. We drove to his weekend house at Lake Dallas, 40 miles north of town. There, in his speedboat, we drove slowly to the middle of the lake. Ceremoniously, he dropped can after can of film into the deep, dark water. He fixed us bourbon and seven from his little bar. Finally he spoke.

"She left me. Fucking cunt left me for a disc jockey. They flew outta Love Field last night. My contact out there said they had tickets to Mazatlan."

He finished the bottle and I skippered the boat back to the pier.

After nearly 40 years, on the bottom of Lake Dallas, his Caprice and the Marquis de Sade sleep in each other's arms and gather barnacles.

5. The Naked Witch

Other than the very welcome fee, I profited from learning certain valuable lessons from *Venus in Furs*. One such lesson, never taught in film schools, is the gender of film. I am convinced that that gender is female. Consider that an actress, say Emma Thompson, with reasonably prepossessing looks and some talent can sit absolutely motionless on rolling film and the scene will hold. There need be no overt physical action. On the other hand, should Sly Stallone not move for the equal duration, the scene would be suspect and provoke derisive laughs. The difference is that we almost hear Emma thinking whereas Stallone has gone on cerebral hold. The camera is kind to the female form. This is remarkably verified in scenes of near nudity wherein something is withheld. Sophisticates who would be turned off by unvarnished pornography are pleasantly stimulated by tastefully directed erotica.

These were the thoughts on my mind as I listened to a caller on the phone in 1957. He was Claude Alexander, an independent road-show distributor of exploitation product. He was the last of a special breed of movie men that roamed the country in the fifties and sixties. They worked outside the system, had no studio ties and were fierce loners. Their product was a devil's stew of African rites ("Karomojo!"), birth reels ("See the birth of triplets! Nurse in attendance!") and young people and drugs ("The Marijuana Story!").

Most of these loners worked in drive-in theaters, their offices the trunks of their gargantuan Cadillac sedans. Their films were just a come-on. The real moola was made by the sale of French Tickler condoms and birth calculators ("Approved by the Catholic Church!"). We will never see their like again.

Claude was different. He wanted to make a real movie. More out of curiosity than need, I agreed to meet him at a favorite Dallas chili parlor. Knowing some of the local exploiters, I expected to see a sleazoid monster with yellow teeth and crunchingly bad grammar. Instead, I came to know a kind, intelligent, immaculately attired, courteous, and courtly gentleman. After nearly 40 years, he remains one of a very few close friends.

I might also add that Claude was one of the greatest salesmen it has been my pleasure to know. After mesmerizing me with his bizarre stories from his life on the road with his schlock films, he blurted out his reason for calling me: "I want to make a drive-in picture with lots of nudity and very little dialogue and all I can spend is $8,000!"

Red flags went up all over my left brain, prompted by the madness of the idea. But Claude was too smart to dwell on the impossibility of the proposal. He went for my Achilles heel by promising me total artistic freedom. "Make whatever you want. All I demand is color and eighty minutes running time." Making a movie by the minute? By the pound? Of course, with only eight grand, the idea was insane.

But I was intrigued. And Claude persisted. So I told him of one of my scripts in the trunk *The Naked Witch*. I was inspired to write the story when I first visited the hill country west of Austin, the capital of Texas. The little town of Luckenbach, among others, had been settled by Germans from the Old Country around 1836. Sparkling springs gushed from the limestone rocks. The flowers and climate reminded the settlers of their homeland, and they cluster there to this day. They are an industrious and clannish people who hold annual holidays called Saengerfests (singing festivals) and Shutzenfests (shooting festivals). Their homes are such as you might see along the Rhine, and their lifestyles are almost Amish in their simplicity.

The ready props, houses, backgrounds, and folklore begged for a screenplay, even if I had to write it on speculation. In the spotless little library in Luckenbach I had found a folktale of a witch who returns from the grave after 100 years to kill and maim the descendants of those who had put her to the stake. This story gave me the basis for a screenplay.

Claude was ecstatic. To sweeten the deal, he would have his lab in Colorado Springs do the processing. When could I start?

My bosses at Jamieson Studios

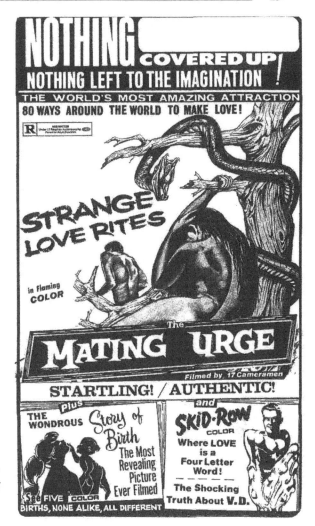

On pictures like these I was charged with sifting through miles of other people's footage in search of a coherent plot that could be spliced together. I came to be known as "Dr. Buchanan," but I must confess that not all of my patients emerged from surgery alive. I never took screen credit for my work on these films — not out of shame, but because a credit would cost the producer more money (and anyway, credits only bored the audiences, who were waiting for skin).

were reluctant but granted me ten days, no more, for principal photography. Our chances for success were those of a snowball in hell. The only hope was to shoot in 16 millimeter and optically blow up to 35 millimeter for the drive-ins. My characteristic optimism was being sorely strained.

Then I found my witch! In Dallas, no less, which was just fine for me. Earlier I mentioned that film is female in gender and kind to the right face. I had no need to screen test my find. She radiated Gothic mystery. My enthusiasm was boundless. Suddenly the shortages and lacks of the project dissolved. We headed for the German hill country and the old mill.

For the beginning filmmaker, unless his family is in the scrap metal business or his uncle is Steven Spielberg, the safest choice of subject matter is horror or science fiction. They are forgiving. Should the novice come up with something less than what he dreamed in his preparation, or if he just comes up with a tiresome dud, he can always lay the turkey off today onto video cassette release.

That's guerrilla cinema. Some wiseacre fanzine critic once described my *modus operandi*, with fair accuracy but little kindness, as follows:

Buchanan has truly big ideas. But for most of them there is a fate worse than death. Puny, shrunken life. One scene at a time, one extra at a time, one dollar at a time. His divine inspiration is dwindled down to size. Malibu State Park stands in for Kilimanjaro (*Mistress of the Apes*). The avalanche is a bucket of rocks (*It's Alive!*). Into the valley of death ride the . . . six (*Sam*).

The rest of the world sees the foul pop to left field. But Buchanan closes his eyes . . . he still sees the home run in his head.

Evolution of a minor success. My new friend, roadshow man Claude Alexander, wasted no words. "Give me a piece of key art and a good title and I don't care what you shoot with that camera. *They pay on the way in!* This sketch for *The Naked Witch* was an amalgam of all the narco-mystical brainwashing that I had endured in movie theatres. He loved it!

As part of the all-day Saturday guerrilla cinema seminars that I conduct now, I walk novice and stagnated filmmakers through the treacherous minefields of home video. This can be a safe harbor for their efforts. In 1957, there was no home video. Our safe harbor then was the drive-in theaters.

Thus it was with *The Naked Witch*. But even so, there were hard and fast rules and parameters that had to be met. Among these were minimal dialogue (no talking heads), relentless action scenes (even if unmotivated), murder (preferably more than one), and sex (in as many varieties as time would allow). Imagine our cast and crew slipping into the little village of Luckenbach, Texas, armed with these mandates from my new friend Claude Alexander. We were going to have a naked maiden prowling the hills at night. We would disrupt graves and churchyards. We would make the spring water that spilled over the Mill Race churn with make-believe blood. And all of this would have to be covertly executed in a community whose sexual mores and patterns of social behavior were stuck in the nineteenth century. This was not George Cukor shivering in the back seat of a limo, nor 50 union crew members tallying up their double time on Dixie cups, nor a prima donna needing reassurance from a dozen people before she could deliver five monosyllabic words. This was no man's land. This was war!

The first hit my little platoon took was when, after a 16-hour day on location, there was an urgent message from the color laboratory in Colorado Springs, Colorado. Since labs work around the clock, I was able to phone back at 3 A.M. I was not prepared for what followed.

Colorado Springs is one of the most unapologetically conservative cities in the country. Maybe it's the water. At any rate, when the technicians saw our naked witch emerge from the chemical bath water, they went ballistic. Fact was, our actress Libby Booth was wearing a skin-colored body stocking and was about as naked as one of today's TV soap opera queens dressing for dinner.

But the lab technicians were unbending in their fundamentalist zeal. The film was to be confiscated as obscene and turned over to the authorities! I was zombie-tired and, obviously, scared. I was so exhausted I actually fell asleep pleading on the phone for my case.

In the nightmares I then slipped into, I encountered my old phantom friend, Judge Roy Bean, the hanging judge of Vinegaroon. When I told him my woeful tale, he roared with laughter. I said I saw no humor in my predicament and would he please stop his imitation of Walter Huston in *Treasure of the Sierra Madre*. Then he laid it on me. "You just struck the mother lode and you're too blind to see the yaller gold! Dare those mother lovers to hold on to that fillum — then call the newspapers and give 'em the story. Junior, you were just dealt a flush hand. Play it!"

I came up in the bed in a cold sweat. The old bastard was right. Unlettered, caustic, and smelling of rotgut whiskey, he had gifted me with another life lesson that has stayed with me through the perilous nights of my career. Call it, if you will, the "Vinegaroon Varsuviana." Roughly translated, the lesson was that what at first appear to be slings and arrows of outrageous fortune can often be turned around to save the day.

At first light, I called the Luckenbach weekly newspaper. The pretty editor, about whom there will be more later, joined me for breakfast. She loved the idea, and a special edition of the sheet was prepared with a lurid headline and story of the fussy film lab that "called an old German folk tale obscene!" My new editor friend sent a mockup of the bogus paper to Colorado with an inquiry as to when the lab thought would be an appropriate time to run the story. We received our developed negative by return express mail, and I called my old standby Jamieson Labs in Dallas to tell them to expect the rest of my dailies. We kept rolling.

We pulled it off, and *The Naked Witch* was, within the realm of exploitation pictures, a smash. Roadshow man Claude Alexander had multiple booked us into six drive-ins in the greater Dallas-Fort Worth Metroplex. They were good houses, which was a relief. Most of the other "ozoners" were known as passion pits, with patched and torn screens, speakers missing, snack bars reeking of hog fat. Used condoms and "French ticklers" littered their ramps. I blessed Claude for his choices.

I smiled when he reeled off the theater names: The Chisholm Trail, Bruton Rd., Lone Star, South Loop, Kaufman Pike, and, most interestingly to me, the Buckner Blvd. Yes, there it was, the Buckner Blvd. drive-in. Dallas had spread its limits to enclose Buckner Academy, and in the place where once I had run rabbits, chopped cotton, and had my ass switched for wetting the bed, there was now a marquee emblazoned with THE NAKED WITCH in big letters.

We killed 'em! I wasn't sure when I saw the ads in the newspapers. But, God bless him, Claude knew his audiences and what turned them on. As we drove in his big black Caddy from drive-in to drive-in, we were locked in long lines of pick-ups and family sedans as their occupants shelled out those magic bucks to see our picture. I was reminded of Joel McCrea in *Sullivan's Travels*. A Hollywood producer, he goes on the road disguised as a bum to "get to the real people" and find out what they want in their entertainment. He could have asked Claude Alexander and saved the trip.

THE STRANGEST STORY EVER TOLD!
She had the body of a goddess,
but the soul of a witch.

THE Naked
WITCH

What would YOU say
to a naked witch?

Our second trial campaign; the first flopped, so we switched the top and bottom copy for this result. Still no business. Claude stared at the artwork with renewed intensity. "Bingo! I've got it! It's not just the copy — look at that face. It's a friggin' teenager. And those eyes — scared shitless. Defensive. That's the way the *victims* should look! We need more mystery. Show her from the back — threatening. And lose that corny line 'What would you say to a naked witch?' It's not what you would say to her, it's what that mean mother is going to *do* to you!"

This pattern repeated itself the following weeks in San Antonio, Austin, Houston, and New Orleans.

By the end of summer, Claude's second string reps had more screening prints of *The Naked Witch* and were spreading out onto America's drive-in circuit. It was the golden age of the drive-ins. The drive-in replaced Lover's Lane in America's social fabric and became a babysitter as young marrieds could opt for "one buck for a carload" nights. And frugal seniors had found an entertainment bargain for severely strained Social Security budgets. At this writing, sadly, drive-ins appear to have become a dying breed. Their foremost defender is film critic Joe Bob Briggs — a fellow Texan, I'm proud to note. It is hoped that he will also be their Boswell. For although he was in diapers when the behemoth passion pits and ozoners were packing 'em in, he has his own real passion for these symbols of an incredibly important chapter in a uniquely American sociology and guerrilla cinema.

The drive-in fare of those years might be called a barometer of the uptight, straitlaced sexual mores of the time and the beginning of their loosening. I looked at the screen as our witch (Libby Booth) ran naked through the village of Luckenbach bathed in moonlight and breathed a sigh of relief, remembering the crazy and surreal close calls we had while on location.

The first such incident was personal and comes under the heading of "God, the things I do for my picture!" The editor of the Luckenbach weekly newspaper was an attractive woman in her thirties. Let's call her Miriam. In the early stages of our work, when we were scouting for locations and feeling out the mindset of the locals, she had been invaluable. In fact, she had been and was (as we started shooting) critical to the success of our little effort. Unfortunately, for reasons that escaped me at the time, she had an instant crush on yours truly, and Miriam was persistent.

I told her the truth from the first: I was a happily married husband and father. She dismissed this stance as corny and said she was surprised that a sophisticate with years in Hollywood and New York would use that as a defense. I was walking on eggshells. Miriam was our linchpin in getting around the daily obstacles of shooting in such a conservative community with such a delicate subject. She had gotten us huge discounts at the motel and with the caterer, and when we needed props, she secured them from some friend's attic. Valuable? Miriam *was* our picture!

One night she went the distance for me. (Note that I say *for* me, not *with* me.) On the outskirts of town in a grove of mesquite trees was an ancient graveyard. Baroque, filigreed, and crumbling gravestones marked the graves of the dead, some gone since the founding of the village in the 1800s. The best art director in Hollywood could not have designed a better setting for our film. In the moonlight, created by our blue gels and our one big light and generator, ghosts of the early community seemed to swirl about the stones. It reminded me of Walt Disney's *Haunted Mansion*.

I was nervous as we started putting shots in the can. This was a pivotal scene in the script. Things were going smoothly. Libby as the witch moved from filigreed headstone to polished marble, noting the names of the dead. Without a word of dialogue, she conveyed the tenor of the scene. Some of the dead were her own kin and she

Eureka! The old pro was right. Once this ad hit, the local gendarmes could not contain the traffic leading out to the drive-in theatres. A great showman had found his hook.

would be misty-eyed. Others were the very ones who had run a stake through her heart when she was discovered coupling with her lover a hundred years before.

I became so intrigued with her performance, I did not at first notice the approach of an automobile on the back road, its lights on dim. God, I thought, this could be disaster. Here, without permission from the elders of Luckenbach, I had a lovely woman running naked over their forebears, gesturing with a bloody stake, her satin skin sparkling in the movie-made moonlight.

Miriam took charge. She told my gaffer to douse the moonlight and kill the generator. We waited. She had hoped the car would move on down the road, but the dim fog lights told us everything. At about one hundred yards from our shivering company, the shrouded, slow-moving car was recognized by Miriam. Squinting in the darkness, she gasped, "I know him. It's Joe Kramer. His poppa owns this whole south forty — and this graveyard."

Then she turned to me. With an enigmatic smile and a husky voice she whispered "You owe me one." In her cowboy boots and gingham dress she was quite a sight. She jumped over gravesites and dead bouquets of roses, running to meet the vehicle and Joe. She did not go to the driver's side but slipped into the back seat of the big sedan. There was a pause, during which we will never know for sure what was being said, then the car slowly backed away into a clump of big oaks were we lost sight of the big old Buick. At first we stood stunned. Then there were snickers. After about 15 minutes, the car emerged from the oaks and took off toward town, now with full headlights on.

Miriam, her cowboy boots kicking up holy ground, ran back to the set. By now, she knew the movie lingo. "Let's roll 'em. I can't count on everybody that shows up being an old high school sweetheart!" We got our scenes.

After that, my tap dancing around Miriam's advances became more difficult, to put it mildly. I used every weapon in the arsenal of the pursued. My excuses were hardly original: "There's a production meeting;" "I've got to call the lab;" "We've got an early call — 4 A.M."

My final excuse was not contrived. The weather changed and we were behind on the schedule and there was no reserve for contingencies. Our shooting day went from 10 hours to 18 hours before we could sleep. Since Miriam was our liaison and fairy godmother, she witnessed the exhausting days and nights. She even began to feel sorry for me as I called the lab every midnight, hoping for a good report on the negative. We were blessed. Our cameraman, Ralph Johnson, is owed a million dollars from my bank of appreciation.

On the last day of the shoot, we broke at 2 A.M. Since some of the crew wanted to head out to Dallas without sleeping, we had our wrap party at the old mill. We had used the mill race in which to dump the dead bodies killed by the naked witch. The water was clear and sparkling now, cleansed of the fake movie blood made of Karo syrup and food coloring.

The night was magical, mainly because we were "in the can." When the booze was almost gone, Miriam approached me for a dance. The country and western band was winding down with "Candy Kisses," a plaintive old Eddy Arnold tear-jerker. But when the old guy on fiddle saw Miriam pull me to the dance floor, he signaled to his boys. The strains of a waltz filled the garden with magic perfume. When the music stopped, she asked if we could walk along the mill race for just a moment.

I wasn't worried. She had been very decent about the libido thing since she had learned we were dead serious in what we were doing and could be seriously dead if we didn't deliver. Then she made a confession. I knew she was a very good writer, though I had thought that was confined to the little local weekly. Now she told me that she was writing screenplays and had determined upon our meeting that she would use me to get to agents with her bucolic gems. She could not let me leave without knowing the truth. I understand this hunger and gave her the best advice I could, knowing the pathetic odds she had of ever getting a screenplay by the agents, suits, and second-handers of our business. She listened. She awkwardly started to kiss me on the cheek but hesitated and squeezed my arm instead. Then, without a word, she turned and walked toward her beat-up Volkswagen.

Movie directors are strange observers. The most memorable image of that shoot for me was not the bloodletting or the nudity nor watching over our shoulder for the sheriff. It was Miriam when she got to her VW. She had carried her cowboy boots all evening and danced barefooted. Now, she kicked up fine sand as she reached the car and without a look back slipped into the boots and disappeared.

Why can't we directors shoot more scenes like that? Or find writers that can capture that kind of scene?

The hack writer would have me, after some years, see her credit on a feature film in some multiplex theater or applaud her as she went to the podium at Dorothy Chandler Pavilion to get her Oscar. But life writes dirty scripts. I never saw her again.

6. *A Stripper Is Born* (a.k.a. *Naughty Dallas*)

I was learning fast. Film is visceral, tactile, voyeurism legitimized. A quick buck could be made with satin skin and even thinner storylines. With the success of *The Naked Witch*, the night people of Dallas emerged from under the rocks. Some were decent, some sleaze, some sinners, some smart, some all of the above. For the most part, their source of money remains a mystery to me to this day. The word was out that Dallas had a professional filmmaker who had turned an $8,000 investment to $80,000 in less than a month in the marketplace. That, to slouch into lazy cliché, was the bottom line.

There were plenty of offers. The well-heeled oil tycoon caving in to his mistress who wanted a shot at the big time, the lavender-haired, oil-rich widow willing to spend an inheritance for a film about her late wildcatter husband, and a vast array of rich, bored wastrels who just wanted to get into the movies for the kicks. And there were the kinkos.

Nothing of merit was on the horizon. But I wanted to keep my crew together, knowing that they would fragment if there was not continuity. I had promised them I was going for broke to develop a real Dallas film community, and I couldn't let them down. In Hollywood, if a craftsman is not available, you just thumb the list until you find the person you want. We did not have that luxury. Instinctively, I knew I must build a film family. I looked to them for loyalty, and they looked to me for jobs. In short, my decision to make my next film again came from hunger.

A Stripper Is Born is worthy of discussion — not because of its production challenges or the fact that it made money, but rather because of the perverse relationship it had to night-club owner Jack Ruby and his place in the tragic fall of Camelot, and because of Candy Barr (nee Juanita Slusher).

I wanted to use Candy as a lead in *A Stripper Is Born* (a.k.a. *Naughty Dallas*). With her baby face and incredible physique, we would have a classic. And Candy was ready, willing, and able. But certain mysterious forces were having none of it, as I confronted a series of dark threats. The persons making them ranged from city fathers who used go-betweens to contact me, on down to small-time Dallas hoods and even a spokesman for Hollywood mobster Mickey Cohen.

Reluctantly, Candy and I decided the better part of valor was to scratch the idea. But I decided to follow the career of this remarkable woman nonetheless. How do I count her ways and sketch her portrait in a minimum of words? Enter Johnny Hicks, who knew Candy better than most.

Hicks was one of the most dependable members of my cinema stock company. He played leads in *Free, White and 21*; *Under Age*; and *The Trial of Lee Harvey Oswald.* Johnny was not just an accomplished actor and friend but also a successful and prolific songwriter. His hit single "The Ballad of Candy Barr" was inspired by her incredible story.

Candy was the most famous and infamous exotic dancer of her time or any time, and her rise and fall is like a Greek drama, a chronicle of the hypocrisy, perversity, and political chicanery that plagued not only Dallas, but the whole nation. It is a ballad of lust, child abuse, pornography, Hollywood gangsters, drugs, husband shooting, FBI harassment, dirty politics, prison time and third-rate religion. Her life could be called a preview of America in the nineties. *Oui* magazine (June 1976) called her "Burlesque queen, ex-con, Jack Ruby's pal, porno's first (reluctant) star and a real lady."

Candy left an impoverished family and repeated child sexual abuse in Oklahoma and headed for Texas while still in her early teens. Although she had a baby-doll face, her body had blossomed svelte and full. She began working nightclubs, not as a dancer but as a waitress. She passed for 18 until the prim members of the Dallas Alcoholic Beverage Commission discovered her. As she put it, "It was as if they had radar on my ass. No matter where I worked, they'd find me." Also, the "harness bulls" (young cops in uniform) would threaten her with vagrancy if she didn't put out. There were times when in desperation she would backseat it with the boys in blue.

In 1951, when she was only 16, she made the notorious, classic stag film *Smart Aleck.* It seemed to play every smokefilled bachelor party in the Lone Star State, where viewing it was a mandatory ritual for any bridegroom. Later, through piracy and tawdry, grainy duplication, it went national and international.

The Candy Barr roller-coaster went ballistic. She married a "box man" (a safe cracker) without knowing of his work. When he was sent to the penitentiary, she divorced him. He was later shot to death. Candy went to work as a stripper (she preferred to be called an "exotic").

There were three important strip clubs in Dallas at the time. The Carousel Club was owned and run by Jack Ruby, who would in time kill Lee Harvey Oswald. The other night spots were Barney Weinstein's Theater Lounge and the Colony Club, run by Barney's brother Abe. With her outlaw .45s blazing with blanks and her 38s flipping with tassels, Candy packed the house. Large corporations would schedule their conventions in Dallas so the suits could catch Candy's show at the Colony Club. The little girl from Texas wowed 'em with her pony tail and tits. The legend grew.

Her boss, Abe, sent her to headline in Los Angeles. This led to Las Vegas and standing room only at the Silver Slipper. The sharks began to circle and she made some dubious friends in high places. She returned to Dallas to fulfill her contract with the Colony Club.

She married a second time, but the union was cut short with divorce and separation. Fearing for her life, she bought a rifle. Her ex-husband, jealous of Candy's male attractions, followed her home in the wee hours of the morning and kicked in the door of her apartment. He assaulted her and forced her against the wall. They fought down the hall to the bathroom where she pushed him into the tub. She ran to get the rifle. He came at her not believing she would pull the trigger, and she pumped a .22 bullet into his belly. The wound was not fatal. He never pressed charges. Abe had to add a third show to accommodate the crowds at the Colony.

The city fathers were incensed. Somehow they had to derail the saga of Candy Barr. One of her showgirl friends was living with a narc. Remember, if you will, this was a time when the "M" word was taboo and the drug squad spelled terror to anyone who dared puff on the euphoric weed. The narcotics officer was ordered to use his girlfriend to plant hash in Candy's apartment, even though anyone who knew her could swear that the stripper was not a user. The narc moved into the apartment across from Candy, and a tap was put on her phone. One night Candy, tired from a grind at the club, had hardly latched her door when there was a knock. Pretending to be from Western Union, the narcs and cops pushed their way in and "found" marijuana and extensive paraphernalia for fixing. Candy was thrown into the slammer. Once out on bail, Candy appealed all the way to the Supreme Court but failed in her attempts to expose the phony bust. One night, after a show, she got a note in a champagne glass from mobster Micky Cohen. It read "Don't be afraid, little girl. You still have friends." A torrid affair with him followed. This did not sit well with the Cohen organization. The threats that followed pressured Candy to walk out on gangster Mickey.

Returning to Vegas, she had hardly begun her first bumps and grinds when she was informed that her bond had been forfeited and that she was a fugitive from justice. The FBI put her under arrest after checking her car to make sure it was not rigged with explosives, courtesy of the mob. Candy Barr, exotic extraordinaire, was given 15 years.

Something unexpected happened to Candy in the penitentiary. She got religion. She sang in the choir and performed in the prison rodeo, and was paroled three years into her sentence on April Fool's Day 1963.

Ugly elements, both personal acquaintances and agents of the Dallas "good ol' boys club," harassed her. On many occasions they tried to manufacture evidence of parole violations. As she put it, "There were a helluva lot of people who wanted me back in the joint."

Her parole terms were so strict that she moved to the little Texas town of Edna to get away from the temptations of Big D. This brings us back to Jack Ruby and the strange cast of characters you have met and will meet in the drama of November 22, 1963.

Candy had known Jack Rubenstein since she was 14. Although they had become good friends and confidants, she had never worked in his club. Seven days before Kennedy was murdered, Ruby visited Candy in Edna. Twenty-four hours after the shooting of the president and Governor John Connelly, the authorities were in Edna, Texas, in a surprise visit to Candy Barr. The visit was cut short by a mysterious telephone call. Candy Barr, along with many other expected candidates I knew, was never called by the Warren Commission. Shortly thereafter, Candy (née Juanita Slusher) was pardoned by Governor John Connelly. The mind boggles.

To return to *Naughty Dallas*, a.k.a. *A Stripper Is Born*, I had originally planned to shoot the film in Jack's strip joint, the Carousel Club. I had looked at every stripper in town with the exception of those working at Jack's club. The reason, bluntly, was that Jack Rubenstein was not well liked. In fact, he was detested. He was cheap and a cheat, inarticulate, antisocial, a bully, a trouble-maker, profane, and a pathological liar. He was a bisexual who loved to fist-fight, constantly trying to validate his manhood.

The Carousel Club was reached by two flights of stairs up from the street in downtown Dallas. I once saw him taunt two young plowboys from east Texas. Their age for entrance into the club was in question. He threw the first punch. For a full three minutes, he battered them down the steps to the street. He returned, smiling, stuffing his shirt back into his pants and wiping blood from his knuckles with a cocktail napkin. He was in hog heaven.

The reader may question the logic of any association with Ruby, given his obnoxious character. The reason is simple. Jack Ruby was the first of the strip club owners to introduce an Amateur Strip Night. Innocent young country girls would come into Dallas from small, dying, and impoverished towns across Texas, Oklahoma, Arkansas, and Louisiana, hoping for a piece of the good life. Sadly, most failed and returned to Miseryville to marry mechanics and farmboys. A precious few, with minimal talent and blessed bodies, could earn handsome weekly bucks. If the talent and body were accompanied by brains, real stars would emerge. Examples of the latter were headliners like the favorites of Dallas, Candy Barr, and Niki Joye.

Sociologists would do well to study Ruby's Amateur Strip Night. In ill-fitting costumes, fashioned by some grandmother or bucolic seamstress, and shaking off-balance on unaccustomed high heels, the girls would glide nervously across the floor, out of rhythm with the drums.

But the boys loved them. Here was woman at her most irritating yet most mysterious — on the one hand, offering sweet nectar through gestures beckoning to a world of sensual fantasy; on the other, so awkward and unpracticed that the gawkers' gentlest instincts stirred. They wanted to protect these little girls from the terrors of the cold city.

So although we had stars such as Candy and Niki, it was the amateurs that intrigued me as a story.

There was a problem in that Jack Ruby's club had a very low ceiling above the runway. There was no place for hanging movie lights. So, in the true spirit of guerrilla cinema, I plotted a coup de grâce. We would take Ruby's girls to the Theater Lounge, the most elegant strip joint in town, for the shooting. Abe Weinstein's Theater Lounge was large with a balcony and boxes for visiting celebrities and butter-and-egg men, and screened cubicles for the city fathers.

To stroke Ruby's overgrown ego, we would shoot a night or two in his place and give him a small role. Then, in the emerging tradition of guerrilla cinema, we would deep-six the footage with the explanation that we had lost the film in the processing laboratory.

We played out our little deceit. On color film, Jack Rubenstein introduces two of his girls, flashes his vulgar finger rings, pushes the drummer aside and stubbornly pounds the skins, and finally works the room. Then, totally unrehearsed, he takes on three gate crashers who refuse to pay the cover charge of the club.

It was this last move about the room that later came into question during the Warren Commission's investigation of the murder of John Kennedy. Lab personnel testified that they had seen Ruby with loner Oswald at a back table in our footage. What was not mentioned was that plenty of rookie police officers working the late shifts would frequent the Carousel to hit on the naïve strippers from Amarillo, Odessa, and Tyler, Texas, and any number of the young men in blue could have confirmed that Lee Harvey Oswald was in fact a regular at the Carousel. And many of the night people, who were sleepwalking through the underbelly and after hours life of Big D, were prepared to shed light on the Oswald connections. But the Warren (or more correctly the LBJ) Commission was having none of it. These revelations would not have fit the Johnson plan for cover-up.

But all of this would have been later. Oswald was not in the city when we shot our ridiculous scenes with Ruby. Nor would this be the last encounter I would have with the misfits Ruby and Oswald. We would meet again artistically, four years later, when we made *The Trial of Lee Harvey Oswald*. The original; there have been two imitations to date.

Somewhere, on a dusty shelf in the dark recesses of a Dallas film laboratory, lies a can containing 400 feet of 16mm Eastman Color original ER (for "extended range") film. It is marked "N.D." for *Naughty Dallas*. It is a portrait of a coarse and pitiful man in action in his snake-pit of an environment, a man who changed history. If that film can had not been discarded and lost, it could have secured my lady and me a house in Provence or on the island of Majorca. That's show business.

7. *Common Law Wife* (a.k.a. *Swamp Rose*)

My next film really came from hunger. After all, with the birth of sons Jeff and Randy, there were now four children in the Buchanan domicile.

What I thought I had made was *Swamp Rose*, a low-country sex drama, in color, influenced by the writings of my role models Erskine Caldwell, Tennessee Williams, and William Faulkner.

What wound up on the drive-in screens of the southern United States was *Common Law Wife*, a grainy potpourri of out takes that I had rejected in my cut. To save money, the owner-distributor had printed his release prints on black and white stock. Drive-in audiences loved it. The critics and the filmmaker were bewildered.

I linger on this potboiler for two reasons. One, for my lead I found the most remarkable redheaded sexpot I have ever directed. We're talking risk here — she had never acted, modeled, or even been a stripper. But when cast and crew gathered at my house, ready to leave for location, Lacy Kelly arrived and paralyzed the neighborhood. When she waltzed up to me, I noticed she had prematurely put on the tight green dress in which she would seduce the heavy in the script. Our nearest neighbor stopped mowing the lawn. A delivery man, mouth open, could not start his vehicle. A number of men in the neighborhood were late for the office that morning. The magic of Lacy Kelley was, as with Marilyn, her affinity to camera. Neither that movie company nor I will ever forget her.

Nor will I ever forget the first steamy Saturday night into the shoot. We were on schedule and we accepted the "mule" from some locals. This is illegal home brew, sometimes called White Lightning.

By 2 A.M., everybody but me was sleeping off the strong stuff. Two strapping hulks appeared at the door of my motel room with ax handles under their armpits. They mumbled something to the effect that they wanted to show me some "local color" since I had the next day off. Nobody had ever informed these hayseeds that Sunday is a director's toughest day. I really thought it unwise to argue with these bigfoots.

The ride in the pickup truck nearly suffocated me, thanks to the overpowering odor from their lack of personal hygiene. Five miles out of town, we stopped at a wharf shack surrounded by giant cypress and drooping Spanish moss. Ten or fifteen more brutes, much like my honor guard, snickered as the leader of the motley group read me the riot act.

59

From left to right, the remarkable Lacy Kelly, producer John Rickert, and in the Butch Cassidy hat, actor Pat Cranshaw. The picture was *Swamp Rose,* later known as *Common Law Wife.* Conservative Dallas suddenly became nervous.

"Listen here, Mr. Hollywood pervert, the boys and me —"

I tried to interrupt. "I'm not from Hollywood, I'm from Dallas and —" Whack! His ax handle bent the fender of his pickup.

"Shut yo mouth! The only gum-beatin' here tonight is gone be by me. So hush up or I'll push this ax handle down yore queer throat!" I listened. "You people think you kin come over here with yore makeup and yore money, carrying on with yore screw parties, buying up all the mule likker in the county so's they's nothing left for the price we can pay. Now, we're good Christian people in this low country and we're goddammed pissed off the way that actress shakes her ass all over town. That pussy should be whipped like the wild filly she is. And there's a lot of the boys here that have the switch to do the job!" Big laugh.

Nothing more was said. Someone started the engine of the pickup. The door was opened by hulk number one. He didn't get in but slammed the door after me with a laugh through missing teeth. Only when the vehicle had turned and started back to the motel did I notice the driver was not one of the original monsters. He was a kid, maybe 17. He didn't smell of mule, or sweat; he was clean cut and respectful. He offered his hand and his name, "Matthew, from the Bible."

When we hit the two-lane blacktop, he started talking. He was sorry he had to be there tonight. He had been to a western dance party with his girl and was ordered by the others to join the gathering. He hoped she wouldn't be mad.

He wanted to talk. He talked about being stuck in this swamp town with no way out, about having to leave high school, about his girl planning to go away to college in Fayetteville, Arkansas. I had no words of wisdom for Matthew. When the pickup pulled away from the front of the motel, I felt I had somehow let him down.

My second reason for detailing *Common Law Wife,* notwithstanding wonderful Lacy, was that this was when I realized that somehow I had to break out of "regional" cinema. My dilemma was nothing unique; I suppose it is experienced by any artist. My sweating over the cutting bench, making silk purses out of sows' ears, was taking its toll. My funder-distributors were provincial in their thinking, happy to play off the films in a few states while giving them precious little foreign exposure. I knew I could be a real player in film poker, but I also knew it was risky. It was time for some soul searching.

Until this time, I had done it all: scripting, casting, fundraising, producing, directing, cutting, advertising, and sales. Yet I knew instinctively and by experience that filmmaking at its best relies on collaboration, and if I was to take on Hollywood, I needed help. My first thought was my good friend Lynn Shubert, but Lynn was by now an executive with the TeleprompTer Company and raising a family in Los Angeles. Enter Harold Hoffman, advertising whiz, painter, photographer. Harold was everything I was not. Most important, he had a good business background, knew how to keep books, and was a keen negotiator. This latter capability would be vital as I had for too long given away the store just to get the films before the camera. We decided that Harold would be executive producer and that I would continue with a free hand as director.

Our first decision was that our introductory venture had to be a powerhouse film. We had to be noticed.

Boy, did we get noticed!

8. *Free, White and 21*

Someday, sociologists and students of racial relations will turn to Dallas, Texas, of the early sixties and discover a noble experiment that worked: "the bloodless revolution."

All across the rest of the South, African-Americans (known then by Southern whites as coloreds or niggers, depending upon one's level of decency or sophistication) were confronting the horrors that accompanied attempts at segregation. It is not my intent to recount the well-documented pain and abuse heaped upon people of color during that nightmare. Other scribes more gifted than I have done that exceedingly well.

But I can attest to what happened in Dallas, how and why it happened and its pertinence to my first breakthrough (read "hit") picture, *Free, White and 21*.

Dallas was and is run, not by vox populi or propositions, but by committee — to be exact, the Citizens Committee, an elite group of power players made up of the local captains of industry. The elected officials are a rubber stamp. This is not a criticism; the Committee rules very well. Their motto is "The business of Dallas is business." Recognizing that any social unrest is bad for business, the Dallas creed makes no distinction between commerce and cries for equality.

So as heads were bashed, storefronts were smashed, jobs evaporated, and racial violence escalated in Arkansas, Mississippi, and Georgia, Dallas watched. The Committee called for urgent meetings with the black leaders of the Dallas–Fort Worth Metroplex. Newsreels were unspooled showing the carnage and its effect on payrolls, Mom-and-Pop stores, and schools. The message was loud and clear: This madness was bad for business. That, reasoned the Committee, made it bad for blacks. The meetings became marathons, lasting into the wee hours. Propositions were argued, amendments were proffered, commas were replaced, ifs and buts were dropped and added.

Then came a strange development. A short, distinguished gentleman, respected by all present, asked for the floor. Quietly, he traced his family's move to Dallas decades before. He brushed aside his father's struggles as a Jewish merchant in a harsh and alien land bristling with a frontier ethic. Rather, he recounted how his family had succeeded by appealing to the women of Texas. He pledged to them uncompromising service to their needs and fantasies. His emporium would be their oasis and home when they left the lonely and bleak outbacks and visited the overgrown cattletowns of Dallas and Fort Worth. Would they come? They came. And Neiman-Marcus became a global contender.

"What is important here," the soft-spoken Stanley Marcus continued, "my father did not run from an ethnic contest, he simply changed the playing field and did what was best for his adopted city." Then Marcus's delicate voice stiffened in timbre and reached everyone in the hall. "Why can't we discard the paperwork — subsection this, paragraph that — and shake hands on one guiding principle: No more agitation . . ." The merchant hesitated for emphasis. The blacks sat up erect. Had they been "woofed" again? The short man continued, ". . . and no more segregation!"

The hall was hushed. The utter simplicity of it was stunning. Everyone present knew integration was the law of the land and inevitable. More important, they knew the short sting of embracing the statutes would be minor compared to the fallout of futile attempts to disobey them. In short, it would be bad for business. The committee closed its notebooks and put away its charts and graphs. Without major incident, the black and white communities of Dallas came together in a cooperative spirit that became a model for other cities across the commonwealth.

What did this transition have to do with guerrilla cinema in general and *Free, White and 21* in particular? Plenty.

There were those who believed the "quiet revolution" was a sell-out for the blacks, but on the whole they were soon convinced and joined the sweep towards harmony. Yet there were outsiders who saw the climate as rich with opportunity for someone with a personal agenda and ambition.

Such a player was Greta Mae Hansen.

A stunning blonde from Sweden, Greta had organized an integrated bus tour in Mississippi and was following a carefully calculated route through the South and Southwest. Her final destination with her "brothers and sisters," black and white, was Hollywood. There she would cash in her publicity chips for a career in flicks.

Today, our video channels bulge with the sensational exploits of ambitious men and women snatching at their Andy Warhol–allotted fame of 15 minutes. Nothing, not even murder, is off limits as they plot their notorious or merely lurid acts that promise endorsements, book deals, and pay offs. Greta Mae had the gift. As her bus lurched from town to town, she would inflame her audiences with a recitative of their plight and the "enemy." But on the long nights on the road, while the others slept, Greta Mae would stare out of the window. She didn't see the towns or the railroad crossing lights. She saw herself on every drive-in screen that flickered along the two-lane blacktops in Biloxi, Fayetteville, New Orleans, Texarkana, then Dallas.

Dallas . . . and Tony Davis.

You just had to know Tony. My partner Harold and I did. Tony was a part-time disk jockey on a South Dallas radio station. He was also part owner of a run-down motel, an announcer, actor, radio time salesman, and part-time model. In fact, he was just about part-time everything. We knew him as a lovable, jovial con man who was fair in his dealings, a somewhat overweight bon vivant, a gatherer of bar tabs, a hustler with a heart, a man in love with life.

He was no rapist.

Harold and I were shocked when, at our respective breakfast tables, we opened *The Dallas Morning News* to find a headline shouting, "Swedish Freedom Rider Cries Rape." Then, in only slightly smaller type, "Disc Jockey Held," and finally, "Well-known figure in the Negro community, Tony Davis, says it was a question of consent." *A Question of Consent.* Hmm.

Harold and I spent the next ten minutes trying to phone each other. Finally, I told the operator to cut in since it was indeed an emergency, "a matter of rape." She put me through to Harold pronto.

There were no "hellos" or "good mornings." We both spoke simultaneously: "What a title!" We had found our movie subject.

Harold, ever the conservative, lowered the excitement in his voice. "Did he do it?" My adrenaline escalated. "Tony Davis doesn't have to resort to rape or prostitutes for country pleasures." Harold agreed, but wanted me to face the sobering reality of filming such an inflammatory happening in the city limits of Dallas. He had always concerned himself with the political and social currents of our home town. The gentlemen's agreement that had saved Dallas from becoming a Dante's Inferno was just beginning to bear fruit.

We agreed to meet at a favorite coffee house, out of hearing of our long-suffering wives.

"It will be a struggle," Harold pointed out. Finding the money, however minimal, might be iffy. We could be sued by one or both of the parties."

Harold knew our city, but entertainment law was my department — not by any formal curriculum but through knowledge gleaned from my sojourn in New York. I quoted verbatim, "Once a person throws his affairs upon the mercy of a court, his right of privacy is compromised." (The "right of publicity" is the new scam being used by entertainment lawyers as an extortion device to pillage for bucks in events involving public figures.)

Harold, realizing I had a vast reservoir of self-serving precedents, insisted I listen very carefully.

"We both have families and kids. You could wake up at night and find a burning cross on your front lawn. Worse, we could be in physical danger. Remember, if we take on this challenge, we have to ride it out. Given the race mind of the city, the verdict could go either way. If Tony is guilty, Dallas could be a reprise of Selma. If he's judged innocent, the rednecks will torch South Dallas. Either way, for us, there is no turning back."

There was a full three minutes of silence. Harold stared out the window, watching a light Dallas rain pelt the panes. (Crises like these are always accompanied by rain. It's part of the script.) I was absentmindedly writing on a yellow legal pad.

Harold knew this was my response to being faced with a vital decision. "Read it," he ordered. My attempt at nonchalance was transparent. But I began.

"*A Question of Consent* could be destructive to the fragile truce that restrains the hotheads of Big D. It could put an end to our careers in Dallas. It very well could put our families in harm's way." I stopped for emphasis. "But it also could be our open sesame to Hollywood — it might even make us rich!"

Zap! Fate had set a course for both Harold and me in our mother's wombs. He had struggled up from the bleak landscapes of Oklahoma to a university degree with honors. I had taken much too long to scrub the sandy loam of Texas cotton fields from under my fingernails. And though we both had been reared in hardshell Baptism, we were tired of turning the other cheek. The idea of taking on Hollywood *and* making some real money was seductive and sweet.

In a small office above a bowling alley, we began. We worked from the court transcript of the trial, which was fed to us by a friendly court reporter at a dollar a page. Needless to say, we did not discuss the undertaking at home. Since we both were excellent typists, we worked in turns, one pacing while the other pounded the keys on the typewriter.

The schedule was grueling. It was oppressive because we had no clue we could ever excite conservative Dallas businessmen to invest in our daring adventure. By day, we typed and checked facts from the transcript. Evenings were for pitches to anyone with a fat wallet who would listen to our projections. It was a drag-ass routine even for zealots.

Then, abruptly, Tony Davis was acquitted of rape and was a free man! Within 48 hours, we had our pledges for the budget, minimal as it was. We were embarking on a feature shoot with only $40,000, a sum that would not buy the lunches for a modest Hollywood horror film. Shaking off that spectre, we picked ourselves up and whispered a little prayer of thanks.

I knew all along whom I wanted for Tony Davis role. We had to establish integrity in this casting. The actor had to possess impeccable credentials. He had to be attracted to the substance of the piece rather than the paltry monies we could afford. Truth to tell, I had to have his trust in this delicate venture.

I wanted Frederick O'Neal.

Our friendship had begun in Hollywood when he was brought west to play a lovable con man in 20th Century–Fox's *Pinky*. I was an extra on that one, which starred the lovely and considerate Jeanne Crain. Fred missed his New York friends and the theater. We hit it off. I introduced him to eateries such as Barney's Beanery and (when we were flush) the Copper Room in Beverly Hills for dinner. He turned me on to what he called the "legit" theater and a different world of literati than I had known, featuring works by stalwarts Maxwell Anderson, Somerset Maugham, Arthur Hopkins, and George Abbott. Fred would go on to win an Academy Award nomination for his role in *Pinky*. Later, when I split for New York, we renewed the friendship and worked together in Off Broadway plays.

Crossing our fingers, we called Fred long distance in New York. We awkwardly tried to summarize the story only to stumble miserably. Here we were, a racist-reared Texan and a second generation Okie, conversing with one of the most esteemed black actors in the Broadway theater. Even as we spoke, he was serving as president of the prestigious Actors Equity Association, the union serving professionals everywhere. Charitably, Fred interrupted us. "Send me the script."

Four days later, he called. His first words were, "I just finished reading *A Question of Consent*. I'm your Tony Davis."

A Question of Consent went before the camera. I use the singular "camera" because that's exactly what our pitiful budget allowed. We had only two weeks to shoot a feature film, and although much of the drama was in a courtroom, there were other locations throughout the city. Imagine, if you will, a stunning Swedish Greta Mae in a form-fitting, luminous cocktail dress, and high heels, walking under the street lamps of the underbelly of South Dallas; toward a "twist" nightclub.

Our script followed the court transcript with meticulous fervor. At the club, our Greta Mae (played by Annalena Lund) meets Tony Davis and discovers he is part owner of the motel where she is billeted. They return to the motel and play out the drama which is the crux of the photoplay.

Although shooting was like walking on hand grenades, we came in on time and on the spartan budget. There were no crosses on the lawn, and family and friends were very supportive.

We were hardly through with the editing in our office above the bowling alley when we received a conference call from Samuel Z. Arkoff and his partner James H. Nicholson, executive producers and owners of American International Pictures. Notwithstanding the anecdotes I recounted earlier about Sam and Nick, this was our first contact with these fabulous characters and American International Pictures.

Would we give them "first refusal"? (I have always detested that phrase because it suggests an inevitable turndown.) At first we played coy. Then Sam, as subtly as he could, which was not very, reminded us that they virtually owned the laboratory where our picture was being processed, namely Movielab in Hollywood. He then recited the outstanding negative arrears we had there. Not to worry, they "might be able to help." They call it leverage. We were naked before the enemy.

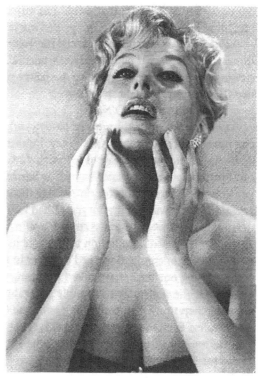

Frederick O'Neal. We had worked together in New York Theatre. I sent him the script with fear and trembling. He called. "I'm your man." Bread on the waters.

Annalena Lund. The real life plaintiff was from England but when we saw Annalena, we took some artistic license and made the part Swedish.

I wish the movie game were a huge poker arena, so at least one could call his play, be it five-card stud or whores, fours and one-eyed jacks. Then with a little bit of luck and some skill, the odds would scramble and one would have a prayer of winning. But making movies is a gamble only to those creative masochists in the trenches: the writers, directors, and independent producers. The second handers deal only on a sure thing.

The real clout is with those at the roulette wheel: the agents, the bankers, the lawyers, the nepotists — second handers all. These cold-blooded, devious players take no prisoners. And they have an incredibly effective communication network. If an independent producer runs into trouble and is short of cash, the second hander will know overnight what he owes the lab, equipment houses, and actors. He monitors the progress of the film. If the dailies are looking good, his laboratory shill will inform him of that. He will make his move early and buy into the promising film on his usurious terms. If the early footage is less than expert and looking iffy for distribution, the second hander will bide his time until the producer is destitute. He then makes his move, a strategy that virtually gives him the bulk of ownership. The creators find themselves in servitude and their precious effort on the block for a quick sale. Very little if any of the conversion finds its way into their pockets.

The above-cited example is just one of many ploys at the second hander's command. The question, then, is why deal with these unsavory people? Why not find another responsible distributor? The questions ring hollow because the above scenario is not an exceptional case. It is the norm, whether employed by a major or by the fast-buck go-between on Poverty Row. It is the only game in town.

Back to *A Question of Consent*. We had a distributor — or, more correctly, a distributor had us.

The first use of their clout was good for all concerned, although at the time, we were shocked. "We've got the release title. Are you both ready for this?" We were not, but they rattled on: "*Free, White and 21*." They were throwing out the title! "*A Question of Consent* sounds like a courtroom picture," they pointed out.

But, we argued, "It *is* a courtroom drama!"

"Yes," they continued, "but we don't want them to *know* it's a courtroom drama. We could never exploit that!"

That was final. We had struggled hard to make an "art house," interracial statement. Now, we realized, it very well might become a naked, intense, exploitation pander. The juggernaut began to roll. We were learning from the masters.

Free, White and 21 opened at the Fox Theater in Detroit for a test engagement. The Fox is a famous movie palace of humongous seating capacity and vaulted ceilings. At that time, as the civil rights movement was seething and about to explode, the Fox was the premiere "colored" house on the American scene.

By the end of the first two days, the Detroit AIP film exchange knew something important was going on at the

YOU
ARE THE JURY!
YOU MUST SEE THIS MOVIE
FROM THE BEGINNING
TO CAST YOUR VOTE.

AMERICAN INTERNATIONAL
PRESENTS
THE CONTROVERSIAL BOX OFFICE HIT....

"**FREE,**
WHITE
and 21"

......**A QUESTION OF CONSENT**
A FALCON INTERNATIONAL PRODUCTION

A print ad for my breakthrough picture. At least our original title made it into the ad copy.

Fox. Sam and Nick, back in Hollywood, couldn't believe their ears and asked their people to recheck the numbers that were coming in.

At the end of the week, *Free, White and 21*, had grossed $42,000 and had broken the house record! Movielab was ordered to work overtime to produce more release prints, and the film was booked throughout the domestic and foreign markets. In the spring of 1963, *Free, White and 21*, produced for under $40,000, was one of the ten top grossing pictures in the United States!

In all the hullabaloo that followed, no interviewer for radio, print, or television ever picked up on the pertinence of the fact that the film was made by two Baptist WASPs reared in the racist South.

We had tapped into the market that wasn't there. To the industry of that time, blacks did not exist outside of a few valiant efforts such as Mark Robson's *Home of the Brave* and 20th Century–Fox's *Pinky*, which introduced our Frederick O'Neal. The blaxploitation floodgates now opened. *Shaft, Superfly, Sweet-Sweetback's-Baadasssss Song, Dolemite*, and dozens of lesser titles inundated the theaters, and cash registers sang.

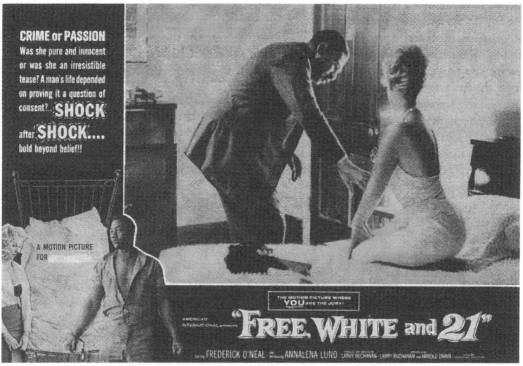

Top: This lobby card was stripped from its case by religious stalwarts in Mobile, Alabama.

Bottom: This lobby card was allowed only when experts in Memphis gave warrant that Frederick O'Neal was not actually touching Annalena Lund.

The *New York Times* reviewed the film on June 20, 1963, in less than glowing fashion. Eugene Archer wrote,

> No attempt is made to take sides in the case, with the result that both protagonists emerge as unpleasant and unsympathetic characters. Possibly some socially conscious spectators will find the subject matter significant enough to overlook the film's unconvincing dialogue, awkward acting and total absence of cinematic technique.

Mr. Archer was subsequently apprised of the fact that every single word of dialogue was taken verbatim from the transcript of the trial.

For me there was no turning back. No matter how many worthy and sensitive concepts and scripts I offered to the "money," I was branded like a motherless calf. Even now, thirty years later, no matter how passionately I present the material, their eyes glaze over until I reach into my bag of tricks and reveal some exploitation adventure.

Thus, when staging one of my guerrilla cinema boot camps, I close by paraphrasing Francine du Plessix Gray: "So goodbye, dear class, and Godspeed. Never worry about what category or genre your films might fall into. The world, alas, will pigeonhole you before you know it, griping and caviling when you stray from the niche into which they've glued you. For the time being each of you is free to gambol, as lambs gambol, and frolic in the delectable, Lord-given vineyards of cinema. How I envy you."

With my new minor celebrity came choices — some delicious, some anguished. American International Pictures (read Arkoff and Nicholson) had an option for a second picture. I could do commercials and consulting but no features until they found the right script. The commercials I did were the first, national television spots for Frito Potato Chips (later Frito-Lay), Dr. Pepper, and Blue Cross of America, all of which were home-grown Dallas businesses that opted to go global. I mention this because there is a lesson to be learned here for the filmmaker. I realized the marketplace demanded a quantum leap if I as an artist was to survive. The commercials with their obscene fees enabled my family of six to move into a new home in North Dallas.

The consulting also paid well, but it presented another seduction. I would like to recite just one early example, which I call the LBJ Caper.

A certain U.S. senator from Texas died in office. Lyndon Baines Johnson, the powerful and power-mad Democratic Texas Senator, used his chokehold on just about everybody concerned and had a wealthy friend of his appointed to fill out the term. The buddy was William Blakely, who was the largest stockholder in Braniff Airways and one of the largest land owners and oil barons in the state. He was also shy, of high principle, old-fashioned, and incorruptible — a truly decent man.

But once he had tasted the intoxication of political Washington, he wanted to return as a duly elected choice of the people. Problem: As a campaigner, he was about as exciting as a game of dominoes, and his opponent, Ralph Yarborough, was an old pro who was making his bid to get back into the game he loved so well.

Blakely turned to LBJ, who had one of his aides, Wick Fowler, call me. My job was to coach Blakely on television deportment and delivery. I was also to have my crew film every speech of Bill's in every hamlet across the state. Cost was no object. Wick Fowler was a kind of covert stand-in for LBJ, who could not be shown to be running the show. This kind of ploy was Lyndon at his best — manipulation without obvious involvement.

Wick will be remembered not as a great newspaperman (which he was), nor as a crafty political pro (which he was), but as the concocter of Wick Fowler's Chili Powder, sold commercially everywhere. I speak as one conversant with good Tex-Mex when I say nobody did it better.

The speechwriter for the campaign was a young, bespectacled beginner just out of Baylor University, with an ecclesiastical background. This fellow Baptist, Bill Moyers, and I got on well. We talked of religion in America, of Schweitzer, Bonhoeffer, Muggeridge, Graham, and other spiritual giants.

The third member of the Blakely brain trust was Jim Blundell, who wrote the checks and was the conduit to Johnson.

The campaign was heated and grueling. It seemed we made a speech in every backwater town in Texas. My crew would capture every word and gesture as our man Bill strained in his uncomfortable pursuit. The film would be rushed to the Jamieson labs for processing, then put on a plane to LBJ in Austin, or Washington or his ranch on the Pedernales River.

Then the fur would fly. If Lyndon found fault with any nuance of the speech or the lighting or soundtrack, all four of us would hear him bellow his rage on a telephone, night and day. This chameleon Johnson used sweet talk and praise as control techniques when he was on the record, but privately he was a mealy-mouthed, profane 18-wheeled truck. He crushed his way to the presidency.

This book is not the forum for an honest look at the man Lyndon Baines Johnson. In time, gifted scholars will piece it all together: the truth behind box 13 in Duval County, which gave rise to the expression "Landslide Lyndon"; the suspicious death of his private pilots in a storm near Austin; his relationship with Billy Sol Estes; his part in the suppression of the book *A Texan Looks at Lyndon* and the mysterious death of its author; and finally, his jealous, neurotic hatred for John F. Kennedy.

Back on the Bill Blakely campaign trail, we planned the most expensive, colorful, and electric finale for our candidate in the town of Longview, in East Texas. It was to be televised across Texas at exorbitant time charges. We had a hundred square dancers, country and western stars from Nashville, a circus elephant, the state's most winning high school football team for the year, and even the tasseled Rangerettes, arguably the sexiest cheerleaders that ever took to a high school stadium on a Friday night.

In Dallas, at the KRLD television station, sat Ralph Yarborough alone, waiting for his cue to deliver his own solo message to the people of Texas, a people he knew well.

Our expensive and bloated show went off like wet firecrackers. Our man Bill was . . . well, sincere. He finished just in time for us to rush to the black and white monitors which would carry the Yarborough speech. The KRLD announcer was brief. "Ladies and gentlemen, the candidate for the U.S. Senate, Ralph Yarborough."

The little sound room at the Dallas station was deathly quiet. Yarborough waited through a pregnant pause, then reached to a table and lifted a large Bible into frame. Not a crisp new Bible with a hard cover, but an old, worn one that sagged in his grasp. The gilt had flaked from the edges. He placed his right hand on the open scriptures and spoke, almost in a whisper.

"My fellow Texans . . . friends . . . especially those of you who have sent in your quarters and dimes so that I can talk to you tonight, as God is my witness, I swear on this good old Book that I have only rehearsed what I will say to you one time, and that was on my knees, alone to the Almighty. I asked him to be with me tonight." Suddenly, I was back on the solicitation circuit for Buckner Orphans Home begging for "Bucks for Buckner." Jesus, he was good!

The red hotline from Lyndon Johnson lit up in the remote sound truck near the stage in Longview. Neither Jim Blundell nor Bill Moyers was present, and the technician could not find Wick Fowler. He pushed me into the trailer. I picked up the receiver to tell the big man that the others were not present, but he didn't let me get out one word. He was already shouting.

"Y'all see Yarborough?" Without waiting for my answer, LBJ rolled on. "When he put his cotton-picking right hand on the good Book, all your fancy dog and pony shows and all your cheerleaders with their tail-snapping pussy just went into the toilet. This dog won't hunt." He slammed the phone down.

We lost heavily in the election. Johnson, meanwhile, continued his devious rise on the political scene. I had already encountered him another time, at least in an indirect way, through a story I did about a famous Texas attraction.

The Chicken Ranch of Southeast Texas is not mythology or mere Lone Star braggadocio. This infamous brothel was opened at the turn of the century and operated until it was closed for good (or bad) 70 years later. It spawned a thousand jokes, uncountable published articles and even a successful Broadway musical called *The Best Little Whorehouse in Texas* which in turn begat a dull, tiresome movie with Burt Reynolds and Dolly Parton.

The joy palace called the Chicken Ranch was not in any town. Its cluster of tacky frame shacks was situated about an hour's drive southeast of Austin, a hundred yards off the main highway, on a dirt road. It was cold in winter when the "northers" whipped out of the Panhandle of North Texas, yet in summer it simmered with sticky humidity and 100-degree temperatures.

The ranch was a long haul from the town of Bryan, the home of Texas Agricultural and Mechanical College, the students of which were the butt of decades of unsavory jokes. I would hope these dissolved with the closing of the doors of the Chicken Ranch, but in the late fifties, students from A&M made up the bulk of the tricks that barreled down the blacktop to the Chicken Ranch eager for poontang, spicy Tex-Mex grub and cold Lone Star beer. This rite of passage continued for more than six decades.

The pulpiteers and pamphleteers were indignant and puzzled as to why they could not shut down the pleasure shacks. Of course, they were ignorant of the fact that some of their own church members had prompted the name "chicken ranch." During the great Depression, farmboys and errant husbands often didn't have the four bucks which would be their open sesame to the country pleasures of the ranch, so chickens and eggs became the toll. Another accepted form of tender was Texas pecans in season, the best in the world.

During my tenure as director-writer at the Jamieson film Studio in Dallas, our cash crop was a weekly television show, called *Texas in Review*, which aired over 45 stations throughout the South and Southwest. It was an omnibus magazine show of offbeat subjects and personalities. When I heard about the Chicken Ranch, I convinced my bosses that there was a story here of historical import. Much of what my two-man crew and I found behind those shutters could not be aired in the Texas of the late fifties. Talks with the Madam turned up political shenanigans going back to the twenties.

Many of the girls were University of Texas students working to pay their tuition. To hide their extracurricular activities, they assumed the names of movie stars and dressed and made up like their namesakes. Back in the thirties one could enjoy the company of "Pola Negri" or "Paulette Goddard." During World War Two, "Betty Grable" and "Hedy Lamarr" were favorites. At the time of my Chicken Ranch escapade, the Aggies and farmboys could ask for "Ava," "Marilyn," and so on.

But the most captivating story I uncovered was that of Senator Johnson's bordello playpen. On his infrequent visits to the best little whorehouse in Texas, LBJ didn't come for the girls. The Chicken Ranch was an escape valve for Lyndon. It was also where he conducted serious, arm-twisting political business, scaring the hell out of dissidents and juggling more than one clandestine business enterprise. The Chicken Ranch kitchen, which was separate from the "cribs" and the girls, served as his nerve center. The three telephones were a constant annoyance for the black cook fixing blackeyed peas and collard greens for nine girls and the Madam.

It took me weeks to convince the chesty lady with the titian hair to let us do a movie story for *Texas in Review*. Finally, we agreed that only a cameraman and I would be allowed into these storied rooms. We got on well and we checked in to do the story. There was, curiously, one rule: we could not use or even enter the large kitchen. I thought nothing of this, and we got a fairly passable story, considering we had to be sensitive to our viewers on Monday night. When the piece aired, I was pleased with this bit of real Texana and promptly turned my attention to other things.

Then Millie called me from the Chicken Ranch. She was furious—but not with me; she loved the story. She rushed and tumbled over her words as she talked of how that "mealy-mouth sidewinder" had given her the worst screwing of her life, "and without laying a hand on me!" She finally wound down and whispered, "So if you want a real tacky story, come on down and we'll chew the fat."

Without alerting my associates or even calling Jane, I grabbed a CineSpecial camera, jumped into my big Chevy station wagon and headed south on the Austin highway. A few hours later, before the sun left the sky, I walked into the Chicken Ranch. The place was alive but not with the action you might expect. "Ava Gardner," in a loose-fitting calico, was hanging up her personal laundry on a clothesline which ran from one shack to the next. I was taken with the seeming innocence of the scene. "Joan Crawford" snapped green beans. "Linda Darnell" was on the porch writing a letter to her boyfriend in Texarkana. There was something surreal about all this. I had seen them all dolled up while we were shooting the story, with their rouge and eyeliner and net stockings, and they were far from a turn-on— perhaps because we were so dammed rushed for our story. But now, as they hung their laundry, wearing old robes and chemises and cleansed of all the veneer, I was moved. The light evening wind blew their thin cotton robes, showing peeks of flesh. They actually blushed and tucked the open robes together. They were suddenly innocent, suddenly real.

The redheaded Millie led me to—wonder of wonders—the inner sanctum, the kitchen. There were three dial telephones, one of which was the red "incoming" line. She closed the door after me but did not dismiss the cook. Millie wasted no time with niceties. Her expletives were torrid, even for the madam of a brothel.

Johnson, who by now was the most powerful and feared senator in Washington, was putting the screws on a small-time madam of a country whorehouse. It seems that Millie was being "advised" to give up her shares in a very lucrative cash crop, namely the combine that controlled the border greyhound race tracks along the Rio Grande. The four major betting tracks were Juárez across the Rio Grande from El Paso, Villa Acuña opposite Del Rio, Nuevo Laredo facing its sister city Laredo and the inland Mexico city of Monterrey. Except for Millie's interest, the ownership by LBJ cronies was all centered in Austin, the state capital.

One of these cronies was facing mayoral re-election, and the challenger was making threatening noises. His ace in the hole was that his opponent was not only participating in the take of the border race bets, but was doing so in partnership with a brothel keeper. Thus Millie had become a potential liability, and LBJ was called in. It is a fascinating commentary on the Texas mindset that the incumbent could withstand the leak that he was being enriched by the gaming tracks—Hell, mister, that's just the frontier ethic!—but that the rumor of a whoremonger as a partner had to be squashed. Millie jumped, startled, when the red phone interrupted her with a shrilling insistence. The senator was on his way to the Chicken Ranch and could be there any time. I wasted no time in packing my camera case.

Johnson's legend included some distressing whims when operating a vehicle in Austin and the hill country surrounding the capital. Although as senator he had an official driver, he would always take the wheel himself and barrel down the backroads at 90 miles per hour. He would chugalug bottles of beer and hang his left arm out of the window even at those speeds. I was only about ten miles out on the black top when our vehicles passed, and sure enough, the first time I laid eyes on the senator, he was upturning a Lone Star beer and hitting at least 80 with one hand on the wheel. It would not be my last sight of LBJ.

I have often pondered what international intrigue festered, what promising careers were ruined, what lobbyist-bought legislation affecting us all was passed in the kitchen of the best little whorehouse in Texas.

9. Under Age

What Arkoff and Nicholson wanted from me was more sexploitation. They had capitalized on a market segment that the majors had allowed to slip through the cracks — namely, America's post-pubescent youth. While the big studios slumbered, AIP pounced. They combined the horny, eager drives of teenagers with the seductive pleasures of California dreaming. The results were *Beach Blanket Bingo, Beach Party, Ski Party*, and any other excuse for getting guys and gals down to their bikinis and trunks. The surf was up and the drive-ins sold oceans of Orange Crush and countless underdone hot dogs. Frankie Avalon, Annette Funicello, Fabian Forte, John Ashley, Jody McCrea, Tommy Kirk, Deborah Walley, Yvonne Craig and others all became teenage idols, and in time I would direct five of these eight AIP Stars in feature films. (In the case of Tommy Kirk, there would be two starring roles: *Mars Needs Women*, and *It's Alive!*) But for the present, AIP would not give me any "above the line" money for stars, gifted or otherwise.

The success of *Free, White and 21*, was beyond their greatest expectations. We had proven that the courtroom drama, with minimal exterior relief, was a viable genre of film for a neat profit on a shoestring budget. Sam Arkoff never minced words on long distance. "When can we have another one?" he wanted to know.

So for my partner Harold and me, it was back to the courthouse. Our mandate was to find another closed court case with the same electricity of *Free, White and 21*. And since AIP knew where their popcorn was buttered, the leading parts had to be teenagers.

Our search ended when we found the case of *The People v. Wanda Duckworth*. In a small town in Dallas County, a pretty blonde cheerleader fell in love with a Hispanic boy. He was 17, the son of a prominent and wealthy Mexican merchant. She was 15, a WASP, and living with her working class mother who was divorced from her father.

Wanda, the mother, saw a path out of her drudgery and despair and encouraged her daughter to "go all the way" with the young man. She tutored her daughter in birth control methods and even arranged to be away from the house shopping so they could have a bedroom after school.

Wanda Duckworth was unschooled and ignorant of the law, and this would be her undoing. Just a few years before, Texas had passed its "Parental Rape" law. In essence, it declared that should either parent encourage a child under the age of 16 to have intercourse with another child or an adult, or engage in a homosexual relationship, the parent would be charged with rape.

Wanda was indicted, charged, and found guilty of rape. She served a term in prison. Her daughter changed her name and moved away to another state where she sought psychiatric counsel, married and started her own family. Sins of the mother? Sounds familiar today, doesn't it? It took the networks 30 years to scramble this same theme into countless "crime or disease of the week" movies.

Our title for the new work was *Under Age.* Partner Harold, a gifted musician, wrote a title song which gave a velvet layer to the child coupling that was the centerpiece of this outing. When the picture opened across middle America, business at the hard top theaters was disappointing. The next platform of release was the border states from California to Texas. The returns there were so encouraging, AIP went wide to cities with large Hispanic numbers and then into the Caribbean where the managers added extra shows to accommodate the crowds. After that, Mexico and South America were a shoo-in. (We never did any business in Europe on any of our courtroom dramas, though; the Europeans called them "tribunals" and regarded them as

Explosive in 1964. Today it would make a mild movie of the week on TV.

featuring too much talk and not enough action.) We were getting good at this courtroom format, but we swore *Under Age* would be our last. We already had our Rule One of guerrilla cinema — "Don't shoot kitchen pictures." Now we added Rule Two: "Never shoot in a courtroom." Shortly, I would learn the third lesson: "Never say never."

The large playoff of *Under Age,* other than the Hispanic markets, was not due to any inherent qualities of the film. It was played internationally double-billed with *The Wild Angels* starring Peter Fonda and Nancy Sinatra.

Partner Harold and I decided we would mellow out of the gritty material by working on a science fiction idea we were developing. We began pacing and pecking on the keys at Tanglewood Lodge, an upscale resort at Lake Texhoma on the border of Texas and Oklahoma. We thought that was a good touch for two guys from those storied landscapes. The work was progressing well, and, feeling expansive, we called our wives and told them to drive on up the 80 miles for a great seafood dinner.

As we walked across the lobby to the bar, there was what we thought was a disturbance.

We heard voices at high pitch, unintelligible exclamations, shouts of "No, No!" A guest, scotch and branchwater in hand, rushed past us. He was muttering, "Kennedy's been shot! They got the sonofabitch."

I was able to catch Jane before she left to pick up Harold's wife. We would return to Dallas pronto.

10. The Trial of Lee Harvey Oswald

On November 22, 1963, shots were fired in my home town Dallas. The echoes were heard around the globe. They still reverberate. A charismatic president, terribly flawed and tragically ill, slumped from a frontal bullet to the head. The patsy, Lee Harvey Oswald, was arrested for firing diversionary shots from an ancient building along the fatal route.

It was late in the day by the time I had dropped Harold off at his place and reached my house in Lake Highlands. We had listened to two hours of car radio on the run south. The conflicting reports on just what had taken place were cruel and repetitious. We found it hard to work on anything as remote as science fiction.

That was the case until Jack Ruby murdered Lee Harvey Oswald in the basement of the Dallas courthouse. When Harold and I heard the news, we mused. "Now, we'll never know the truth," Harold opined. "A trial would have silenced all the conspiratorial scenarios. Now, the poor bastard will go down as the worst heavy in history."

I tried to make a joke. "Maybe we should give him his day in court."

But Harold wasn't laughing. He stared ahead as if he could see the judge's bench. "Exactly, we give him the trial he was denied by Ruby's bullet!" Then we said it together: "*The Trial of Lee Harvey Oswald.*"

We had proved that we could deal with matters of law. But *Free, White and 21* had come from the transcript of a real trial, whereas this venture would be pure fabrication. We wavered. But only for a moment; then Harold said the magic words: "Charlie Tessemer!"

In our courthouse rounds, we had met and become friendly with the most famous and highest paid attorney in the Lone Star State. Colorful and histrionic, he was a bon vivant who loved show business. And we were the talk of Young Street, Dallas's film community. Charlie loved the idea and took us on contingency. He would build a legal defense for Oswald and a prosecutor's case against.

This was high concept. Raising the money was a breeze. American International wanted to give us an ordinarily coveted negative pickup (an advance of costs to date at completion), but we balked. We wanted creative immunity on this one. No producer in Hollywood threatened to steal the concept because by now, they all knew nobody in the business could beat us to a finish and a release date.

The Trial of Lee Harvey Oswald was a peculiar failure.

Not for lack of paying audiences. The premiere opening at the Warner Theater in Milwaukee and the subsequent engagements were characterized as good business. Nor did any

An ad for the ill-fated *Trial of Lee Harvey Oswald*.

critic find the dialogue awkward. Nor was there a lack of interest by the media; in fact we were bombarded with requests for interviews from both the domestic and foreign press.

The film was politically sensitive. It remains so today. Every attempt to re-release it fails.

I can understand the reader's sigh and mutter—"Oh God, not another conspiratorial fairy tale!" In fair defense I would point out that, after years researching the death of Marilyn Monroe, I was the first to go public on the manner in which she died. Her death was not murder, it was not suicide, and it was not an accident. It was an act of mercy. In the second of my projected trilogy of films on the superstar, *Goodnight, Sweet Marilyn*, a longtime male friend of hers administers a lethal, strychnine-loaded suppository, anally. He was making good on a standing pledge between the two as he had promised to do if Marilyn ever started seeing her mother in her mirror, bound by a straitjacket. Marilyn's friend was nicknamed Mesquite. Later, when we explore *Goodnight, Sweet Marilyn*, I want to say more about this remarkable man.

An interesting footnote to *Oswald* is indicative of how the political climate can change with new blood in Washington. Less than ten years after our picture premiered and was summarily shut down, a producer named Chuck Fries made a color film for television not surprisingly entitled *The Trial of Lee Harvey Oswald*. What was surprising was that he shot the film in Dallas using some of the same actors we had used in the original. His star was Lorne Greene of *Bonanza* fame. Another film, which was nothing more than a collection of clips made into a faux documentary, came and went much as ours did. There was even an Off Broadway play with the same title and theme which enjoyed a modest run.

After *The Trial of Lee Harvey Oswald*, I began the strangest odyssey of my life in film. The contract I signed with American International Pictures was for an initial three titles with an option for more. These were so successful for AIP that they picked up their option again and again. In the next five years from 1965 to 1970, I wrote, produced, directed, edited and planned the ad campaigns for nine feature films. It was C.O.D., and all had deadlines to meet. It truly was fast and furious, to borrow the title of a history of the studio. I preserved my sanity with one non-negotiable clause in the contracts that stipulated that I could do other outside pictures if AIP dragged their feet in approving one of my scripts for them. So, including five films outside the AIP package, I made a total of fourteen features in a little under five years. This does not include my documentaries and commercials.

I press this trivia because the reader must understand that at that juncture in the saga of Hollywood, even the most expedient and schlocky offering in the most remote drive-in "passion pit" credited several contributors. To wit: *Born Losers* was produced by Donald Henderson and directed by Tom Laughlin (under the pseudonym T.C. Frank), from a screenplay by E. James Lloyd. *I Was a Teenage Frankenstein* was produced by Herman Cohen, directed by my friend Herb Strock, with a screenplay by Kenneth Langry. God, how I could have used some of that talent!

And now, for the first time ever, I wish to reveal a delicious phenomenon about the work I was doing over those years. However innocently, I was running a retreat for clinical psychology! Although the treatment was for many of the young stars I brought from Hollywood, I hasten to add that I too might just as well have been a patient. We were experiencing film as therapy.

11. The Eye Creatures

My first contract picture for AIP was a remake of Ed Cahn's *Invasion of the Saucer Men*. The studio suggested (read demanded) John Ashley as the lead. John had wet his feet quite often in AIP beach party pictures. As we raced through the tight schedule, it became apparent to me this was no bimbo. Good looker, good voice, no Mickey Mouse beach bum. The worst lines I gave him emerged absolutely believable. He was driven. By the end of the first week, we were ahead of schedule.

Then John asked permission to fly out Sunday to Arkansas. I had to say no as motion picture cast insurance forbids such a reckless trip in most cases. Since we had established a great rapport by then, he fessed up. His wife and the mother of his beautiful child was divorcing him. She was on a publicity tour for the studio and would be stopping Sunday in Arkansas.

When he revealed the name of his wife, I melted. Deborah Walley was one of the most beautiful of the young stars emerging from the AIP galaxy. John was hoping and praying for a reconciliation. To hear him talk of Deborah and the baby was heartbreaking. He was especially morose about the child. It was moving to hear this onscreen swinger talk only about "the kid." No beach blanket bimbos, Hollywood watering holes, babes, or yuppie exploits; he just missed his family.

I made him vow silence and sent him off to the airport. When he returned on Monday, I knew by the look on his face that it was over. I believe John finished the film without a second take on any scene.

Unsurprisingly to me, John Ashley went on to successfully produce films in the Philippines and other venues. He is most widely known as a producer of the television series *The A-Team*, *Raven*, and Chuck Norris's *Texas Ranger*. I think we both helped each other through a trying time.

The Eye Creatures was remembered years later by Brian Curran in *Fear of Darkness*, Vol. 1 issue 3:

> Imagine my youthful culture shock, thrust from the grace and style of the "classics" to the blunt, stark bad-truth of Larry Buchanan. . . . *The Eye Creatures* is basically a scene-for-scene remake of the old A.I.P. schlocker *Invasion of the Saucer Men* (directed by Edward L. Cahn, 1956). The original film, first intended as "serious" but transformed on the spot deliberately into a campy comedy, is a simple tale of teenagers vs. alien invaders on Lover's Lane. The Paul

Top: On location for *The Eye Creatures*. I'm at right with bullhorn in hand, directing and playing a role to save the cost of an extra. My aide-de-camp is Warren Hammack, a Broadway-trained actor.

Bottom: The Eye Creature fells actor Bill Peck.

Blaisdell–designed bug-eyed little green men have deadly, alcohol-dripping switchblade claws but turn out to be easy to destroy: they just blow up when hit by the light from car headlights!

Saucermen was an entertaining little movie and scenes of little bug-eyed aliens scuttling about in the woods, fleetingly lit by headlights, may have even influenced the opening scenes of *E.T.*, but *Eye Creatures* did not do for Buchanan what *E.T.* did for Spielberg.

12. High Yellow

Happy with my remake of *Invasion of the Saucer Men*, AIP wanted me to take on a remake of Roger Corman's *It Conquered the World*. I balked, for reasons I'll detail later.

It was time for one of my personal projects.

During my years in New York City, one of my favorite haunts was the main branch of the public library at Fifth Avenue and Forty-Second Street. An author I admired greatly was Octave Mirbeau, a French master of plot structure. I was especially drawn to *The Torture Garden* and *Diary of a Chambermaid*. Satisfied that the latter was in the public domain, I adapted the story to a contemporary frame. In my adaptation, the maid in the piece would be a beautiful mixed-race girl who passes for white in a Bel Air mansion. The son in the family falls for her. The reckless and wild daughter is murdered by a jealous, demented caretaker. The black chauffeur, who has befriended the "high yellow" girl, is falsely accused of the homicide. The young lovers struggle to help the chauffeur against bigoted police interests.

Cynthia Hull, who had been John Ashley's leading lady in *The Eye Creatures*, was a natural for the title role. Although she was not of African ancestry, she had a dusky and expressive quality that made her ideal for a girl "passing." Cindy made the role hers and exceeded all expectations. I have worked with very few actresses who had her instincts in approaching truth on film.

For the entire shoot of *High Yellow*, I wanted to find an antebellum mansion with a haunting quality. We found it but got more than I bargained for in the spook domain. When I first saw the mansion, I knew it was perfect for our film — and it was empty. I thought nothing of the fact that it had been on the market for an inordinately long time. Locals under questioning called it "unrentable." Yet there it stood, a huge two-storied mansion, its architecture somewhere between antebellum and Georgian. It was in a secluded place miles from the little town of Frisco, north of Dallas.

Prospective buyers had avoided the old place, I thought, because of its scary quality — the very thing I sought. Then I learned the story of its builder and the grisly murders that still haunted the rooms. I could not believe my ears when the story had many parallels with my screenplay.

The legend of the Frisco house is classic. An elder landowner, a wealthy cotton grower, brought a young bride to his Xanadu in the 1930s. He gave his bride a servant, a light-skinned young black woman who, unbeknownst to his wife, was in fact his own daughter. The wife,

Newspaper ads for *High Yellow*. No newspaper in the Cotton Belt would run the ad at right.

who only married the wealthy landowner to help her impoverished family, was lukewarm to his advances. He turned to the servant, but she had become involved with a black grounds-keeper. With him she plotted to kill the landowner, while at the same time she plotted with the husband to kill the wife. Before the twists and turns played themselves out and the ghosts evaporated, they were all dead.

Since that dark beginning, the house had sheltered a continuing cast of bedeviled characters. In World War II, a young soldier on leave took his bride to spend his furlough at Frisco Mansion, as it had come to be known. They were found dead the next morning by a grocery delivery boy. The cause of death was never determined or recorded.

One morning, hunters taking a shortcut through the property found all the graves in the graveyard uprooted, the bodies gone.

Long after my crew had come and gone, the producers of the new television drama *Dallas* chose the Frisco Mansion as the ranch of J.R. Ewing and renamed it Southfork. While the expert crews were making the place camera-ready, locals came forward and warned the new lessees that no good would come of the decision to shoot on the estate.

Indeed, from day one of the first episode of *Dallas*, the shooting schedule was jinxed. Animals died. Unseasonably bad weather plagued the crew and cast. There were reports that camera negative sent to the lab in Hollywood carried only ghost images. The professionals from Hollywood dismissed the incidents as bad timing and coincidental. But the setbacks continued. Finally, the team of producers and directors called a meeting to address what was clearly no longer imagination and old wives' tales. The Ewings had to find a new home. So, shortly into the shooting of the first episodes of the show that would climb to the top of the charts, the decision was made to pick another permanent location for Southfork.

I had discovered how peculiar things were around the Frisco Mansion a decade before the television crews. To test the sound recording quality and ambiance of the rooms in preparation for shooting *High Yellow*, I decided to sleep over at the empty house alone. The electricity had been off for some time, and I lit candles in the main rooms and kitchen. After I had eaten my takeout Kentucky Fried Chicken, I tried to read by the candles and a single lantern. This proved futile, so I started my battery-powered Nagra recorder and got to work. I would test the huge living room first. A large walk-in fire-

Our heavy, Billy Thurman, taunts Cynthia Hull with her secret.

place loomed up. While the Nagra reels turned, I set the logs afire in the fireplace. There was a bolt of lightning followed by thunder, and a light rain began falling.

After a few minutes, I stopped the recorder to test the ambiance. I expected to hear effects of rain, thunder and a crackle of firelogs, but there was nothing. I had a dead track. I was sure that I had started at the zero point on the counter, but nothing was coming off the iron oxide magnetic. I was about to do a fast-forward to spot check farther in, when suddenly there was a surprise. Chants, not Gregorian but more West Indian, started filling the room. Then there were voices. It was like one of those old radio plays of the thirties before the advent of television. But these were not Gothic histrionics; the voices were definitely in Southern dialect. What I was hearing sounded like whispered utterances that rose from time to time as if in a quarrel.

Then it hit me like the bolts of lightning that struck the oaks outside: I was hearing the plotting of the principals in the Frisco massacre! The signals of the tape were strong at times, then would fade, but I could reconstruct the actions of the four doomed players in the drama. I had not imbibed any alcohol with my fried chicken, and there was no one else in the old house.

There I was, miles from the small town of Frisco, with no electricity and no telephone. I was shaken up enough to decide to go home. I braced myself and ran to the car where I had a mobile telephone. The battery would not turn the engine over and the car phone did not respond to my dial. At the end of the drama, I rewound the tape to hear it again. Now there was nothing, only dead track through the whole reel. If I had been hallucinating or having an out-of-body experience, at least the sounds of the storm should have been on the tape. Bewildered, I blew out the Coleman lantern and went to bed. The rain stopped. I chalked it all up to exhaustion from preproduction on the forthcoming picture, which is always tougher than the location shoot itself. I drifted off.

Billy Thurman in a threatening pose.

It was still pitch dark when I was awakened by an intense light playing across the room, never resting in one spot. It was as if someone were playing tricks with a five-cell flashlight. My first thought was prowlers. I got up and searched the house, the light following me from room to room. I found no one, heard nothing. The lights played out their terror through the night, never allowing me to really fall asleep.

The next morning the crew arrived to begin prelighting the house. Of course, I told no one of my night of terror and simply tried to forget it.

Weeks later, there was a wrap party that lasted until late at night. Everybody left, pleased with a shoot to remember. I stayed to settle with the caretaker who would clean up the place and put out the familiar "for sale" sign.

I ventured to tell him of my experience of the night of the big storm. He chuckled at first, then let out a big burst of laughter. Telling me to follow him, he threw the main switch and plunged the place into darkness. With a small flashlight, he then led the way up the circular stairs to the second floor. In the big master and guest bedrooms he cut his light and waited.

The lights began to dance and play their spooky patterns on the walls. The caretaker guided me to the veranda and we looked across the valley toward the little town, some miles distant. We waited. Then a car with its lights on high beam crested a hill and disappeared. Minutes passed and another bright beam penetrated the dark valley and was lost. A perfectly logical answer had been supplied for the lights of terror.

But what of the whispers and screams heard on the Nagra? What of the dark, mid-thirties drama of incest, deceit, murder, miscegenation and greed? How to explain the millions of iron oxide particles on the tape forming localized polarities to recount the story, then rearranging themselves to leave nothing?

There is a postscript to the Frisco Mansion story. A few years ago, a mysterious fire swept through the rambling old rooms and halls. Today a skeleton of the former glory sits like a nightmare out of *Gone with the Wind*.

Early in the release of *High Yellow*, I discovered a tactical error, too late to remedy it. It seems that in the Southern United States and in the West, the title *High Yellow* was actually too high-toned for the bucolics, who knew the expression as "high yaller." We were even blasted for our casting of Cindy Hull, who played her part so convincingly that some racist patrons were furious that we had used "that little nigger" in a leading role — even though our promotional material clearly defined Cindy as a Caucasian. I was all

On the set of *High Yellow*. By the black Lincoln is Billy McGee. By the fence, from left to right, are Cynthia Hull, Kay Taylor, and the couple who owned the house. By the camera is cinematographer Shields Mitchell.

too aware of the mindset of the time, having had firsthand experience with this problem on the 20th Century–Fox lot when lovely Jeanne Crain was cast in the title role for *Pinky*.

Ironically, even while the rednecks were spouting off their nonsense, we were taken to task in more upscale markets for *not* casting the part with a black actress!

With all the controversy, *High Yellow* was a big success. It played the popular houses and drive-ins. It even found a niche in art houses and returned the nut to the backers with a sound profit. It opened at the Fox theater in Detroit and garnered $42,000 in its first week as reported by *Variety* (August 18, 1965).

There was another bonus. I had taken pains with the picture, even with its petite dollars and black and white film, and I established a promise to myself which I have carried through more than 30 years in "good-bad" filmmaking. I vowed that no matter how strained the budget, how precious the time allotted, how untutored the cast, I would have one day on every picture that was mine, a day when I would do things exactly as I wanted. Buchanan's Day. That is the day when a baffled crew is told, "Instead of thirty-five setups today, we do ten. You will not be hurried. We will actually *rehearse*! We may even have a 'take two.'"

I have kept that promise to myself these years. Cinéastes and college students studying for exams and being babysat by one of my good-bad efforts actually look for the sequence that was shot on Buchanan's Day. An example is the scene in *Hughes and Harlow, Angels in Hell* in which Howard and Jean stop at a Mexican adobe near Tijuana to see one of his old

For the first time, one of my modest pictures was on the top of a double bill with Hollywood product on drive-in screens everywhere.

Mexican friends. Not one word of English is spoken, but after that early sun-up near the beach, she discovers the real Hughes behind the notorious legend. This film is available at the UCLA film archives. I am unabashedly proud of the big look we achieved in that scene with no money.

13. *Zontar, the Thing from Venus*

The respectable if modest returns from *High Yellow* were a factor when Sam called from AIP. "Have you reconsidered remaking *It Conquered the World*?" I had.

Roger Corman had been given three times the budget we had. His version was in black and white, and he had as his leads Peter Graves, Beverly Garland, and Lee Van Cleef of spaghetti western fame. And the running time was only 71 minutes! For $30,000, I was expected to shoot 80 cut minutes of color and bring in three young stars from Hollywood. Their board, hotel, and air fare alone would be $15,000!

On long distance, I demanded what I thought would be a deal breaker: I would choose the cast this time. Sam paused just long enough to remove his Havana from his mouth. "Done deal." The receiver slammed against the cradle of the telephone.

With the help of a writer friend, H. Taylor, I deep-sixed all of the rambling plot structure of *It Conquered the World* with the exception of the alien pods penetrating the necks of the victims.

Casting presented a more sobering challenge. Good-bad filmmakers know this stuff is treacherous without actors who understand the difference between camp and unblinking sincerity, regardless of how contrived the dialogue.

I had always admired John Agar. What critics don't understand about this artist and his unique place in cinema history is quite clear to me. The reason he has been used over and over again through these decades is this: he can take the inane, the trite, and the ugly and somehow bring his own alchemy to the lines and make them work. Years ago, both John Ford and William Wellman, each a giant of cinema, told me Agar will be remembered as an unfairly underrated actor.

John had been the first husband of the Princess herself, Shirley Temple. He was not only an Aquarius, he was born on the same year, day, and hour as yours truly. How could we lose with big John?

For our leading lady, I recruited the loveliest creature in my Dallas stock company, Pat Delany.

The most difficult decision was casting the part played by Lee Van Cleef in the original *It Conquered the World*. This is an "on the edge" role, and I knew of no young actor in Hollywood who would understand the demons that haunted the role of Keith.

Enter Anthony Houston, a.k.a. Enrique Touceda III. Finding Tony was a blessing. Not only did he emerge from the film as a cult figure in the fanzines and science fiction journals,

John Agar sent me this photo from John Ford's *Fort Apache*. To me it was like getting something from Mathew Brady. There sat my first movie-love, Shirley Temple, by her husband-to-be Agar. Behind them stood the pristine, distant Henry Fonda. Last, there was Western icon John Wayne. During the shooting of *The Alamo* at Bracketville, Texas, Jane and I were invited to the location for a ranch breakfast with Wayne before we watched the storming of the Alamo under his direction. A bonus was the visiting director John Ford, who couldn't resist trying to direct the picture. Characteristically chewing on the linen hankerchiefs made for him in Ireland, the giant got in the way of the shot. Wayne picked up a pebble and threw it at Ford, saying "Get out of the way, old man!" The memory is delicious.

he developed into an inventive screenwriter. We would subsequently work together on a number of projects. Today he is a successful lawyer in Los Angeles. On more than one occasion, he has represented me successfully in my attempts to retain some small portion of the fruits of my labors.

When Pat and Tony met on the set for the first time, sparks flew. They were later married and now live in Studio City, California.

We started with a working title of *Zontar, the Thing from Venus*. This was an inside joke, but the name stuck and *Zontar* became one of the two most infamous of the quick flicks I made for American International. I was as surprised as anyone when *Zontar* became a cult favorite of college students trying to cram for exams in the wee hours. The film even spawned a fanzine called *Zontar, the Magazine from Venus*. It is edited by brilliant young minds who understand the nuances of the subtext that flows from all of my AIP pictures. In fact, to fully savor these pictures, one should read the in-depth vivisections by these Young Turks. The following is an excerpt of a September 1982 *Zontar* article by Brian Curran titled "Art and Alienation: The Terrible Terror Films of Larry Buchanan."

The scaly bat-like, umbrella-like monster looms up in the shadow of the dark cavern. The woman, hysterical, pulls a gun and exclaims: "So that's what you look like —*Zontar*! You're ugly . . . horrible!"— she points the gun— "You think you're going to destroy my world? I'll see you in hell first." BANG! BANG! Bullets have no effect as the flimsy Venusian closes in for the kill . . .

[That's a] scene from *Zontar, the Thing from Venus* (AIP-TV), directed by Larry Buchanan.

It is a measure, perhaps, of the crisis of our "culture" that we have experienced a swelling wave of interest in "schlocky" and "bad" films. In a time when our so-called real world is increasingly plagued by war, crime, suicide, and economic collapse, mass audiences turn ever more to seemless escapist fare in movies, music, TV, etc. Certainly the new-found fashionability of the "bad" can be viewed as at least a partial antidote to the smotheringly slick product of today.

John Agar, the only actor to play three leads for me in as many films. And they were of three genres: science fiction (*Zontar, the Thing from Venus*), horror (*Curse of the Swamp Creature*), and action-adventure (*Hell Raiders*).

This cultural/critical phenomenon has led to best-selling "worst" books, a "worst" films festival, revivals of notorious "bad films"— on TV and in theaters nationwide — not to mention articles on "bad-film" aesthetics in both serious "cinema" and fan-oriented "monster" magazines. Although this has brought attention to the work of a number of neglected geniuses of the American cinema, particularly Edward D. Wood, Jr., of *Plan Nine from Outer Space* and *Glen or Glenda* fame, the most superficial and trend-conscious comments seldom penetrate any deeper than derisive snickering at the obvious technical shortcomings of Z-grade films.

But, to die-hard devotees, Zontoids, and other would-be cultural dictators of tomorrow, the truly great "bad films"* are a source of hope and inspiration that can be heartening in these troubled times when movies are more corporate deals than works of art. These misunderstood and despised geniuses whose determination to make their statement and get it shown will overcome any obstacle: lack of money, experience, encouragement or skill.

Unlike the spoiled whiz-kid directors, who with all their time and money have limitless options (in film jargon, "takes") with which to construct their illusions, the Z-budget, schlockfilm-maker must rely on what he can get, pretty much on the first try.

The "bad-film" director's impoverished working conditions permit the discerning viewer

---

* "Bad film" is a useful phrase coined by the Rev. Ivan Stang and Douglas St. Clair Smith (high priest of the Church of the Subgenius and a noted Larry Buchanan scholar) to differentiate between the true subconscious masterworks of overlooked prophets like Buchanan, and the merely inept, or worse, the intentionally "bad" parody-cheapies.

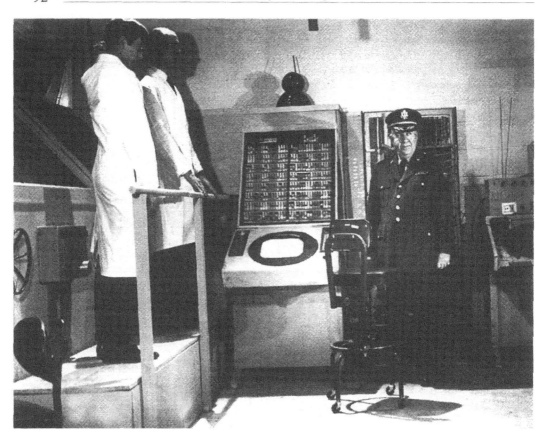

From left to right, Warren Hammack, Jeff Alexander, and Neil Fletcher.

to observe not only the fictional content, or intended "style" of the artist, but the actual circumstances of the filming. The film-maker's own environment is usually the movie's setting; actors are often the director's friends, as are the "art-directors" and "effects men" who use whatever is available to achieve their illusions. The actors' embarrassment, or misunderstanding [of] the "meaning" of the dialogue unintentionally reveals their relationship to the director — the man who is making them say these things! It helps us appreciate what a great country America is! For these brave masterworks can be seen today, shown by the very people who need and appreciate them most. The burnouts, the weirdos, the horror-movie fans.

There exists a hard-core horror/SF/monster audience which will see *any* "horror" movie which shows up on TV, [in] theaters — anywhere. Not only the "classics" of the thirties and forties, but most of the big-bug/space-alien films of the fifties as well were shot in black and white. This was until the mid–60s when color TV began to become more prevalent. TV programmers began searching for more "competitive" color fare. AIP, whose '50s films especially were due to low budgets, in black and white, needed color films, quickly and cheaply, to make their packages more "attractive."

. . . The phone calls were made, the papers were signed. A trifling amount of money was spent. And the result was the creation of the most consistently and truly "bad" series of Z-grade "monster movies" of all time . . . the Terrible Terror Films of Larry Buchanan.

It was an old 1950s Roger Corman script, *It Conquered the World*, itself a derivative of *The Day the Earth Stood Still*, that unleashed the fully developed Buchanan universe on the world. It is the only film he "re-made" whose notoriety may even exceed the reputation of the original.

Anthony Houston became the darling of the fanzines with his over-the-top performance in *Zontar, the Thing from Venus.*

Zontar, the Thing from Venus* exploded across TV screens and into the hearts of millions in the late '60s — completely redefining concepts of how bad a movie could be. The first time I saw it, I turned off the set before it ended.

But I couldn't stop thinking about *Zontar* and mentioned it to others. They remembered it with enthusiasm or disgust.

Larry Buchanan's re-interpretation of the overwrought living room arguments from *It Conquered the World* are the secrets of *Zontar*'s success. His casting helps. The role of Kurt, the idealistic scientist-hero, was played stolidly by Peter Graves in the original, but in *Zontar*, John Agar enters the Buchanan universe. This and his later "good-bad" Buchanan films, by their very transparency, tell us more about Agar than all his professional, bland-hero performances of the 1950s. At least in *Zontar*, Agar tries harder. (He even stands up sometimes.) Perhaps he sensed the higher plane Buchanan was striving for in this production.

But even the strangely re-animated Agar must take second place in the annals of Buchanan lore. For in Anthony Houston's portrayal of the embittered, "too-advanced" scientist, Keith, we have the definitive Zontoid performance — which must literally be seen to be believed. He raves though his incredible monologues as the modern-day anti-Moses, whose dreams of vindication and revenge on those "little minds" who spurned him mix with his idealistic hopes for a new era of world peace. He seethes and stutters as he communicates with Zontar over the little radio he keeps in a closet/cabinet just off the livingroom. Of course, only he can hear the voice of the Venusian redeemer — all anyone else can make out is static. He constantly relates the latest Zontar news to his skeptical wife and insists on spoiling dinner with

Zontar harangues. Even at bedtime, he ignores his beautiful wife to stay by the radio for late-breaking details. Alone, he discusses his problems with the understanding invader.

It soon becomes clear to Kurt that Keith's ravings are more than hallucinations.

Zontar strikes, sending out injecto-pods to subject key humanoids to his will, shutting off all power and making people run around screaming. Zontar's reign of terror soon touches even Keith as his wife is killed trying to destroy the Venusian in his cowardly hideout (a cave just out of town). He learns his lesson too late.

The secret of *Zontar* would appear to be that, through the dialogue and the character of the misunderstood genius who hears a voice no one else can hear, Buchanan found a voice through which he could vent his deepest ambitions and frustrations. He and Houston certainly give the material a more "serious" and passionate reading than did Roger Corman and Van Cleef. (Lee Van Cleef, a great actor and cult star, seems too strong a personality to be deceived by the Venusian's seductive promises. Houston, a slighter and wimpier type, is also hyperactive and quirkily neurotic — and far more "convincing," as well as funnier.)

Buchanan reshapes the old script to emphasize the insane dialogue. The result serves to heighten the paranoid atmosphere of domestic isolation which is the very essence of *Zontar*.

At first, Zontar is looked upon by Keith's wife and close friends as a variety of imaginary playmate. One can easily imagine the young Buchanan may have had just such a secret "friend" in his lonely childhood, or less speculative, was used to having his artistic ambitions dismissed as silly dreams.

Does Buchanan foresee his own fate, dying forever typecast as a "bad" director — his dreams of glory shattered by the very works he has so earnestly spawned — in Keith's final suicidal confrontation with his monstrous counterpart, dying in the arms of the monster he created as he destroys it?

As Buchanan found his poetic "voice" in *Zontar*, so did he also find his surest sense of "style" — particularly a talent for absurd understatement.

Buchanan takes the tongue-in-cheek Corman style of scoring scenes of total banality with "scary" music and does it straight. This, of course, makes Buchanan's films even funnier than Corman's.

A highlight of this style is a scene in *Zontar* where a big-finned car pulls into an ordinary driveway as melodramatic music pounds on the soundtrack. The fact that these are real locations and not sets adds to the hilarity and terror. (The effect is like seeing these things for the first time, presented as strange and weird in an Alien's eye-view.) Buchanan further extends this style, attaching "significance" to such mundane occurrences as lamps turning on, a hose running water, cars starting, etc. You see, Zontar has de-energized the world's power — these appliances only function because *Zontar is our friend.* These must be the most outrageous and lowest-budgeted "special effects" in cinema history!

With *Zontar, the Thing from Venus*, Buchanan seems secure in having "found a style" in ultra-localized "Sci-Fi". . . . a cinema of alienation.

Roger Corman and Larry Buchanan, acquainted since Larry's explosive *Free, White and 21*, were "fast and furious" young Turks who provided thousands of miles of celluloid to the American International pipeline but never worked together. There were two close calls in the late sixties.

Roger had a sensitive, racial drama script to star Jim Brown. The director was already set: Monte Hellman of *Two-Lane Blacktop* fame. Larry, who speaks Texan fluently, was asked to come aboard as co-producer or line producer, an unusual move for the "in-control" Corman and an unusual decision for the independent Buchanan. Roger, Larry, and production manager Jack Bohrer met in Houston to scout locations. Although they found the perfect town for the script (Halletsville), AIP, under pressure, felt the material too explosive and halted production. This, from the distributor that initiated the Blaxploitation cycle with Buchanan's *Free, White and 21!*

In 1972, Corman had a script that he felt was Buchanan's material: *Boxcar Bertha*. Buchanan recalls the screenplay as excellent and true to the "hard traveling" subject matter. He also recalls that he wanted the assignment. But the AIP head honchos Arkoff and Nicholson, and eventually Corman, decided the promising Martin Scorsese should get the nod.

These close encounters are certainly more than apocrypha. Corman must have liked what he had seen of Buchanan's work. In a 1975 *Photon* magazine interview (Corman, *Photon* #26 1975), when told that the Buchanan remakes (which included two of Corman's scripts) were "horrible," Corman replied: "That's strange, because Buchanan's a talented guy." He attributed the purported low quality of Buchanan's films to lack of budget.

The epitaph for the career of Larry Buchanan should come from the stirring closing speech of his greatest film, *Zontar, the Thing from Venus,* as intoned by the voice of John Agar over choppy cuts of dead bodies, burning cars, and old rocketship footage.

"Keith Ritchie came to realize — at the cost of his own life — that man is the greatest creature in the universe! He learned that a measure of perfection can only slowly be attained — from within ourselves. He sought a different path and found. . . . death, fire, disillusionment, loss. War, misery, and suffering have always been with us, and we will always strive to overcome them. But the answer must come from within — not from without. It must come from the very heart of man himself." Music rises. The end. Commercial.

14. Curse of the Swamp Creature

The American International Pictures contract deal continued. The studio was so pleased with *Zontar*, they thought it would be good to have another John Agar starring vehicle. Tony Houston had by now become a permanent member of my stock company, excelling in acting and screenwriting. He delivered a first draft on *Curse of the Swamp Creature* and asked for a few days for a polish. I carefully explained to him that a polish would lose the immediacy of the drama and that a solid structure of the libretto would leave us nowhere to go in improvisation. He looked bewildered but was beginning to understand "badfilm" and guerrilla cinema.

We shot *Creature* at Caddo Lake, a huge swamp on the Texas-Louisiana border. The small cast and crew were put up at the Fly 'n' Fish lodge, set among the green cypress trees. The nearest town was Uncertain, Texas. The Fly 'n' Fish would not take our black cast members, so we had to shuttle them from the swamp set to private black families in the little town of Uncertain.

In addition to John Agar, the cast included pretty Francine York, my dependable character man Billy Thurman, and the late Jeff Alexander.

Francine later did a lead for my friend Ted V. Mikels in his 1973 film *The Doll Squad*. She was always a joy to work with but really broke up the company when we introduced her to illegal "mule" whiskey, a cash crop for the natives. The mud catfish is quite good in those parts, too.

We were plagued by the humidity, cottonmouth snakes, and mechanical troubles throughout the shoot, and John made me promise that the next time we worked together, it would be a cakewalk.

As for the picture, it was merchandise delivered as represented, and it took its place in the genre. Brian Curran, in an article for the magazine *Fear of Darkness*, called it "seedy and depressing" but seemed sympathetic to John Agar:

> None of his confrontations with gillmen, giant tarantulas, mole people, puppet people, or evil brains from Uranus prepared Agar for the ultimate horror film: appearing in a Larry Buchanan production. The horrified Agar spends most of *Curse* in an alcohol-induced stupor which thinly disguises his disgust and embarrassment. He's seated most of the time and constantly smoking cigarettes. Meanwhile, unbearably undynamic suspense and incoherent subplots build up to the most spectacularly anti-climactic "shock" monster revelation ever filmed — the Swamp Creature is nothing more than a guy in a putty-smeared cheap fright-

96

The irrepressible Francine York. On location for *Curse of the Swamp Creature*, she was fearless of gators, gar, and gill monsters created by my special effects man.

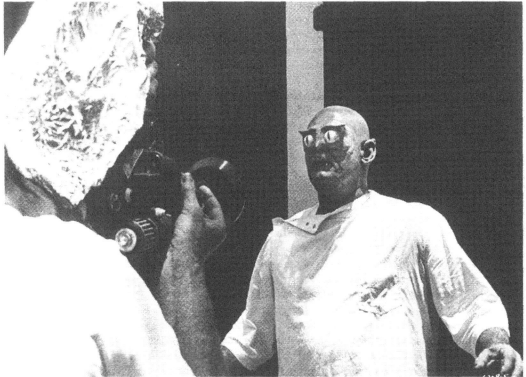

Top left and bottom: Bill Thurman as the Swamp Creature prepares to feed Jeff Alexander to the alligators but takes time out to pose for a closeup.

mask with ping pong ball eyes. Buchanan films all this with a grim seriousness, which, combined with his murky camera work and Agar's alcoholic resentment, makes this one of the more interesting of Buchanan's epics.

Freddie Mertz offered further commentary in an article that appeared in the eighth issue of *Zontar, the Magazine from Venus*:

> The credits for *Curse of the Swamp Creature* are dispensed with quickly over a repetitious tape-loop of pounding jungle bongo-drums that will continue with little interruption throughout the film. This "musical" element, perhaps inspired by a similar "scoring" technique employed by Sam Katzman in *Voodoo Man* (1944), soon transforms itself from a mere irritant into the very essence of pain, becoming a concrete metaphor for the film's uncanny stretching of time into a tortuous infinity. Within minutes, the viewer comes to understand, indeed to *experience*, the essential meaning of *Curse of the Swamp Creature*. This is not going to be a mere "story" about mutation and failure. This is, rather, the deepest essence of entrapment by the horror of reality as captured by Buchanan's Narcomystical sensibility.
>
> Visually, the camera takes us panning across a characteristically barren tract of landscape until we come face to face with Buchanan's first all-too-real "setting": the Fly 'n' Fish, a sleazy bar-restaurant-motel where sleazoid music always plays.
>
> The atmosphere of cheapness and decay captured in these first few minutes of *Swamp Creature* has all the flesh-creeping seediness of an old "detective" magazine, with grainy half-tone photographs of "re-enactments" by cruddy actors, that you might expect to find with its cover torn off in a box in some old fart's garage. The combined obtrusiveness and poor quality of the camerawork acts to *reduce* the level of narrative detachment one usually expects in a movie. The result is an incredible simulation of real time, so intensely felt as to seem stretched out, held still, as it were, as if in a time warp. This is the essence of the "documentary" element that is essential to all great badfilm. Not only does the film became more an examination of the actual fact of these people *making* a "film" than a narrative, but it also forces one to consider oneself, in the act of watching this thing. The miserable facts of life that one is trying to escape from for a few hours actually fuse with the non-events that transpire on film, inducing soul-searching and blemish-intensifying effects akin to those experienced in the throes of a bad hangover or acid trip.
>
> Of course, even the worst films have their merits. The performance of the actor who plays Dr. Trent is surely one of the delights of the Buchananoid cinema. His hissing, over-the-top villainy is in the classic Buchanan tradition. Dr. Trent is just the sort of sniveling pervert that a real mad-doctor would be. And the film itself will serve, if nothing else, as the extreme example of LB's mastery of a certain sort of mind-numbing, time-stopping, cinematic boredom that would make Stan Brackhage green with envy.
>
> *Curse of the Swamp Creature* can probably claim two major distinctions that set it far below even the *worst* cinematic atrocities of all time. First, the Creature itself must be the least convincing creation in monster movie history. I would rate it far worse than the *Robot Monster* and at least as bad as the *Creeping Terror*. The master director actually compounds the failure of his creature by withholding it for so long. By building to his epic anti-climax, Buchanan makes the Swamp Creature itself the very essence of disappointment and failure . . . translated into cheap rubber and ping-pong ball eyes. The Swamp Creature's scaly rubber frightmask is composed of the very substance of despair.
>
> Perhaps more horrifying in the end than the Swamp Creature itself is the dismal and endless tape-loop of bongo-drums that pounds throughout the film. Strangely, we never see the source of all this drumming. What do these drums mean? Are they symbolic of the terminal boredom of the film itself . . . or a formal device to drive the audience mad, like the abominable Dr. Trent? Are the drums in the characters' minds or in ours? This is unclear, but the pain induced by the "Tape of the Unconscious" (to use critic Gregg Goodsell's term) in *Curse of the Swamp Creature* is not easily endured, or forgotten.

15. Mars Needs Women

I had reached my pain threshold in the remaking of bad scripts, and I told the heads of AIP that, as a breather, I wanted to do my own script, *Mars Needs Women*. Had they balked, I would have walked. Almost weekly, I was turning down Pasadena Money (offers from little old ladies from Pasadena whose family story "would be a winner") from outsiders. So I posited what could have been a deal breaker. But they loved the script.

Sam Arkoff of AIP would not bend, however, on the leading Martian. It had to be Tommy Kirk, former child star of Disney films including the classic *Old Yeller*. I have called many of my flicks "Film as Therapy" and although I did not know it at the time, Tommy qualified as a patient. (I hasten to add that this is by his own admission.) For the record, I have never worked with a more prepared, professional, eager, and courteous thespian. Some measure of my respect for Tommy's talent is that I asked him back again to do the lead in *It's Alive!*

Almost every "star" farmed out and sent to me in Dallas by American International Pictures was suffering from some crisis of emotional trauma or sexual identity. These difficulties took the form of alcoholism, homosexuality, substance abuse and a panoply of ills, real and imagined. My operation came to be known by some cruel wiseacres as "Buchanan's Clinic"— much like that named after Betty Ford, only my facility covered the whole spectrum of the human condition. On reflection, and armed with the clarity of hindsight, I now know that my nickname of "Dr. Buchanan" was a compliment.

In short, I was sympathetic to their concerns. I was totally unfettered with the mindset that is uncomfortable with homosexuality, or the narrow hypocrisy that some have toward the alcoholic. With one or two minor exceptions, my actors and I have remained friends.

Tommy Kirk and I shared one common ailment: We both were the issue of strict Southern Baptist upbringings. We both moved to Hollywood in the same year, I as an adult from Texas on the prowl for a career in films, he as a child from Louisville, Kentucky, beginning his acting career at the Walt Disney Studios. His work as a youngster at Disney made him a star. *Old Yeller*, *The Absent-Minded Professor*, and *Swiss Family Robinson* secured his reputation as a talent of range and sensitivity. But Tommy, like so many child stars, had trouble with the crossover into mature stardom. Perhaps his case can shed some light on the curse of child celebrity and its emotional fallout.

Although I had liked Tommy's work for Walt Disney, I knew him only as an adolescent on the screen and did not particularly wish to meet him. But in 1964 Gentleman Jim Nicholson of AIP had insisted I at least watch him work. I had nothing in mind for him and *Mars*

Needs Women was two years away. He was at that moment shooting *Pajama Party* with co-star Annette Funicello. I balked until I heard that two guest stars on the flick were Dorothy Lamour and Buster Keaton. I was magically transported back to the balcony of the Capitol Theatre in Dallas and Dorothy singing to Ray Milland.

I couldn't wait to meet her, no longer as a threadbare orphan, but as a fellow professional. And I would be introduced by director Don Weis. The magic was still there.

And Buster Keaton? What can you say about this original? The youthful energy was gone but the sparkle was still in his eyes. You could see the cavalcade of Hollywood in those pupils only slightly hidden by the drooping eyelids. At lunch, he brought laughs by just *listening*!

I watched Don direct Tommy Kirk and suddenly realized that this was no Disney Mouseketeer; this mature young man could act! He was holding his own with Keaton and Lamour. Meeting him prompted me to start thinking of some vehicle for Tommy. This idea came to fruition two years later in *Mars Needs Women*.

When Kirk stepped off the plane in Dallas in 1966 to start production, I knew three things about him: he was a disciplined actor, he was into drugs, and he was a homosexual. If film was truly therapeutic, he seemed a classic candidate.

He was a cool customer, clinically focused, letter-perfect, patient, willing. I do not recall ever having to do a second take with Tommy.

Although we were working fast and furious, I found time to listen and reconstruct his story. With the Walt Disney machine behind him, his career had taken off. He grew into a handsome property. He put on a brave front as a bon vivant dancing the night away with lovely young contract players on Sunset Strip. But alone, he was in turmoil with his repressed sexuality. When it became common knowledge that he was having a back-lot affair with another actor, Disney had fired him. This was a time of hush-hush in matters of what was then called "deviation," so he was not welcomed by the other major studios. Losing his envied place as the young prince of the Disney empire, he turned to pills, pot, and heavy drinking.

In this state Tommy reported to me. I told him that I had heard, without soliciting it, all of the gossip about his lifestyle from the American International camp. Then I talked to him of Robert Flaherty, the father of the documentary film, and his thesis of "non-preconception." We struck a bargain, acknowledging that we are all flawed and vowing, like Flaherty, to start the clock at zero. Nothing in our pasts would enter the equation. We would learn and work together. I gave him my philosophy of work in any field, my "band of brothers" speech.

The production of *Mars Needs Women* proceeded like a fine watch from Benelux. I know it wasn't easy, but to my knowledge Tommy Kirk never ingested anything stronger than Gatorade. His work became a joy with the arrival of his AIP associate, Yvonne Craig, my favorite of the beach party players.

After the television run of *Mars Needs Women* and *It's Alive!*, Tommy was quoted as follows: "What I was doing in those pictures, I don't know. The only thing I can say is that I had a drug problem. I was an idiot. Buchanan is like a cinematic killer and he's got to be stopped before he kills again!" But I was never convinced that he meant those unhappy sentiments; in fact, I was reassured of my thesis. The therapy was a success. I took the same kind of sting from quotes by John Ashley, John Agar, and later Fabian Forte, but without exception, they retracted their early statements after learning more about good-bad cinema. As of this writing, the results of filmmakers working under duress and pitiful dollars are beginning to be heralded and honored; consider the 1994 homage to Badfilm director Ed Wood, Jr. The players find themselves pleasantly remembered for their work in my pictures as much as for some of their major studio titles. In the April-May 1993 issue of *Filmfax*, Tommy Kirk had

Delightful leading lady Yvonne Craig and featured player Byron Lord in *Mars Needs Women*.

this to say: "Larry Buchanan was one of the nicest, most gracious men I ever worked for. He paid me well, he was generous and he was decent."

Even as I had worked on the script of *Mars*, I pictured the perfect female lead who would be the principal woman of the five Martian targets. I knew Yvonne Craig only on film. She is widely remembered as the original Batgirl, but she had grabbed my attention when I saw her starring with Elvis Presley in *Kissin' Cousins* and playing the lead in AIP's *Ski Party*. Yvonne embodied the totality of what woman can be when approaching perfection. She combined an incredible face and body with great attitude, camera sense, talent, humor, and, most importantly, sensuality coupled with quiet intelligence, a rarity in film.

Our effects budget for *Mars* was zero, zip, nada. But with characteristic enthusiasm, we plodded on. In one scene, we actually used a Frisbee as a spaceship. It was thrown up into the fog and the camera was overcranked to give the movement a threatening reality. It worked.

Tommy, Yvonne, and my regular stock company of actors gave it all it needed and more. The reader must remember that this was a time when making movies was fun. Sure, there were crises and problems (which I choose to call "challenges"). Major studio practice is to carry the disruption to a trailer or to a corner of the sound stage, leaving those not consulted bitter and hostile. Our solution was to open everything up to the entire company. Not to sound mawkish, but we were truly a family.

Mars Needs Women was the most talked about of the series and the most successful of

A dramatic moment in *Mars Needs Women*. Years later, a comic book satire played off our title with "Mars Needs Velcro." Our space suits were bargain basement wetsuits, and the radio gear was from a toy store. From left to right, Larry Tanner, Anthony Houston, and Star Tommy Kirk.

my sci-fi horror films. It was syndicated by American International and Filmways Corp., and is now distributed by Orion Pictures.

Several real power players have optioned the underlying property for either a remake or a sequel. The most interesting proposal was for a Broadway musical. At this writing, the latest to option *Mars* has been the team that successfully brought *Fried Green Tomatoes* to the screen, Jon Avnet and Jordan Kerner. It was to be a Universal Picture. The option was renewed several times before they passed and the property reverted to me.

It finally occurred to me that, a finely tuned conceit aside, no one could do a sequel of this material better than the creator. It is now one of my works in progress.

Below I quote, warts and all, the words of two young film critics who to my mind seem to have grasped the subtext of the science fiction and horror films that I produced and directed for American International Pictures. Greg Goodsell and Brian Curran pierced the veil early on. They realized that I had no choice but to deliver the banality, crude structure, rough editing and in many instances bad acting to satisfy my contract. With the pathetic monies given me, I could do no better. They saw that with persistent determination, I defined a theme that only now is being appreciated and vivisected at home and abroad.

In *Zontar, the Magazine from Venus*, Greg Goodsell wrote the following:

> The series of science fiction and horror films Buchanan made in conjunction with American International Pictures in the mid to late sixties, define, if not give a new meaning to, the term *banality*.
>
> If you've swallowed the party line that *Plan Nine from Outer Space* is the worst movie ever made, you've obviously not seen many movies and certainly none from Larry Buchanan.

The reason Ed Wood Jr. has endeared himself to camp movie mavens was in the manner in which he conveyed wacky Hollywood fringe life and personal eccentricities to his projects. If anything, Buchanan imbues his epics with a feeling of desperation, boredom, apathy, and resentment that lingers long after the last commercial has faded along with the majority of the film's plot.

And Brian Curran offered detailed commentary in his article "Art and Alienation: The Bad Horror Films of Larry Buchanan" (*Fear of Darkness*, Vol. 1, Issue 3).

> Buchanan, secure in having "found a style" in ultra-localized "sci-fi," served up *Mars Needs Women* (1966), an original script by the director. Ex–Mickey Mouse Club star Tommy Kirk took the role of the lead Martian. The beautiful Earth girl he falls for is played by Yvonne ("Bat Girl") Craig. . . .
>
> *Mars Needs Women* is probably Buchanan's most twisted and formally adventurous effort. He shows total contempt for cliched audience expectations as he indulges his anti-visual object-fetishist style to its furthest extreme. In an extended opening scene depicting the alien spaceship invasion, Buchanan puts a similar sequence in *Plan 9 from Outer Space* to shame, presenting all "action" as described in dubbed "radio messages" accompanied by endless static, close-up shots of a wall-mounted loudspeaker, spiced by occasional tattered stock footage of old jet fighter planes, and that's it! Most of the rest of *Mars Needs Women* transpires in a motel room and has something to do with a "mysterious" suitcase. I challenge readers of *Fear of Darkness*— do you have the nerve to actually study and decipher this neglected cinematic landmark?

Mars Needs Women made a list of "Fifteen Sacred Cinema Classics" in *Zontar, the Magazine from Venus*. It tied for third with *Curse of the Swamp Creature*; first place went, predictably, to *Zontar, the Thing from Venus*. The editors had this to say:

> *Mars Needs Women* is, essentially, a trancelike meditation on the parking-lot exteriors and motel-room interiors of low-rent Dallas, which seems to *these* reviewers to be photographed with the loving care of a hometown boy who wants to put his world on the map. Regardless of whether we are "reading too much" into this film (as if *that* were even possible!), there is no doubt at all that *Mars* is one of the most formally daring of *any* films. Here, Buchanan boldly takes the outmoded concept of "narrative coherence" and throws it into the trashbin of aesthetic history. Moving beyond the wildest and most pretentious "theories" of the most avant-garde "art" filmmakers, Larry provides the stunned viewer with so-called "scenes" whose minimalist aesthetic is so extreme as to call into question, at times, the very existence of a film known as *Mars Needs Women*. The opening scene is perhaps the most celebrated example; it consists almost entirely of alternating shots of (1) a loudspeaker shot in clinical closeup, and (2) some incredibly shaky and tattered Air Force stock footage. This perplexing and alienating montage is accompanied by overdubbed conversations — apparently taking place over radio— involving contact between U.S. forces and an invading force of Martians seeking to mate with Earth women. The scene is long and seems even longer, even *endless*! The brutality of Larry Buchanan's "concrete cinema" makes the so-called "structuralist" montage films of Stan Brakhage seem, in comparison, like the made-to-order and predictable art-poop that they really are.

16. *Sam* (a.k.a. *The Hottest Fourth of July in the History of Brewster County*)

After the rigors of *Mars Needs Women* and *Curse of the Swamp Creature*, it was time for a "therapy" picture, something totally removed from the material I was regularly churning out. So, naturally, when a trio of Dallas lawyers wanted a spin on the cinema crap table, I put a shine on my Lucchese boots and had my Stetson hat cleaned and blocked.

Sam was my first western since *Apache Gold* 14 years before. Jody McCrea, the son of frontier icon Joel McCrea and Francis Dee, was part of the American International family. He was doing the beach party films along the sands of Santa Monica and Malibu Beach with Frankie Avalon, Annette Funicello, John Ashley, Fabian, and my favorite, Yvonne Craig.

I thought Jody had promise, and he was eager to get off the beach and into real movies. I wrote a simple frontier drifter story and called in my family of cast and crew. They too were delighted to go on location to Alamo Village, an authentic looking western movie town near Brackettville, Texas, that was originally built for John Wayne's *Alamo*.

The shoot went well, and there was a lot of barbecue and Lone Star beer. This time around, we *were* close to the border of Mexico, and the cast and crew spent some quality time in Villa Acuña, across from Del Rio, Texas. I really wished Jack Klugman could have joined us; we would have played catch-up as I would have honored an old debt. But by now, Jack had his richly deserved acclaim for his performances in the stage and film versions of *Twelve Angry Men*. His agent wanted $50,000 for Jack, exactly what we spent on the whole enchilada: horses, wardrobe, guns, laboratory, sound, and talent. I hasten to add that Jody McCrea dispatched the leading role with grace and humor. Later, Jody would take me to spend time with his parents on their ranch in Camarillo, California.

For the peanuts budget, the finished film was technically fine but lacked energy and was a rehash of western clichés. Even so, it should have had a release. When it didn't, I blamed myself until I learned that the project was a tax shelter and the three investors had never planned to release it. In other words, the flick was more valuable as a write-off than being unspooled in a theater. This time around, the news didn't hurt, but there would come a time when this same spectre would stop a film which I really cared about and which some have declared my best film. More on that later.

On location for *Sam*. From left to right, producer-actor Caruth Byrd, actor Bob Harris, actor Billy Thurman, owner-manager of Alamo Village "Happy" Shahan, actor Jack Carney, actor Ross Thompson, and actor Bud Breen.

I enjoyed one major benefit from the making of *Sam*. Jody McCrea, via his giant of a father Joel, was a friend of director William Wellman, a filmmaker I greatly admired. Jody and I drove out to Brentwood for a lunch with the aging Wellman. It had been some time since he had helmed *The Ox-Bow Incident*, *The High and the Mighty* and other important films.

The feisty Wellman was now slowed by crippling arthritis, but as he recounted story after story, he seemed to shed his years. He was a young man again, making silk purses out of sows' ears. The arthritis seemed to dissolve. He was suddenly a big man, up from his short stature. He was truly one of the giants. I would witness such a transformation once again when Jane and I drove to Palm Springs in 1977 to visit director Howard Hawks.

17. In the Year 2889

With *Sam* put on the shelf for tax reasons, I had to return that other Sam's call. Arkoff was sending me a script that Roger Corman had directed called *The Day the World Ended*. The script by Lou Rusoff was a minimal effort and I asked if I could throw it out. No dice. I then demanded that this downer about post-nuclear fallout have some comedy and sex relief added. The response was permission to introduce anything I wished to relieve the oppressive pallor of the property. I called my friend and ex-partner Harold Hoffman, whom I had worked with on *Free, White and 21*. He agreed to breathe some life into the script. He embellished a character in the show and tailored the role for Quinn O'Hara, a pretty redhead who was approved by AIP without delay. Audiences had loved her in two-piece bathing suits in the beach party pictures.

The leads, who turned out to be very good, were Paul Petersen, Quinn O'Hara, Charla Doherty, and my regulars including dependable standby Bill Thurman.

Petersen was best known for playing Donna's son on the successful television series *The Donna Reed Show*. A Tom Cruise type, he had real talent, great male looks, and brains. I expected him to soar; I don't know what prevented that, but then people expected great things of me too. Paul gives of himself and his time today, helping actors through drug rehabilitations and other crises.

We rented a large Dallas mansion and with the control that comes with that location exclusivity, production moved smoothly at first. But then we began to have problems.

Quinn O'Hara, through no fault of her own, was sabotaging the show. Quinn was a stunning sexpot with a comic temperament. While the crew should have been focused on the horrors of the nuclear story, they were in stitches from Quinn's antics and mesmerized by her measurements. We were at an impasse.

In major productions, the director can work through a long line of underlings to deal with any problem that arises, but in guerrilla cinema, the buck stops with the man calling "action." So I had to confront the redhead.

"Quinn, we've looked at everything you've done and it's great, really great," I started. "But . . ."

Quinn winced. "I've let you down?"

"Not at all! I said your work is fine. But my whole crew is crazy about you. They can't wait for me to call 'cut' so you can all exchange jokes. Paul and Charla can't get into character without cracking up!"

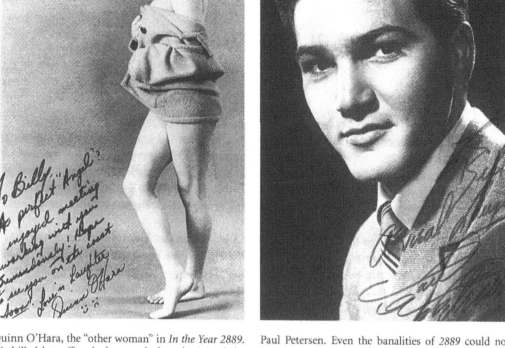

Quinn O'Hara, the "other woman" in *In the Year 2889*. We killed her off early, but not before she joined the growing Billy Thurman fan club, as this autographed shot demonstrates.

Paul Petersen. Even the banalities of *2889* could not hide his remarkable talent.

She made it easy. "Okay, chief. How do we fix it?"

I remembered from the AIP beach party puff articles that she had bemoaned the fact that she had never had a serious scene and that she would love to do a death scene before she threw in the towel. With some hesitation, I dropped the idea on her. "We're gonna kill you off! The heavy is going to drown you in the pool. We'll let you choose the most daring bikini you can find at Neiman-Marcus. We'll pull out all the stops. It'll be Chekhov time!"

She got her death scene. I got my crew back. The going-away pool party we threw for Quinn could have gone into the *Guinness Book of World Records*.

18. *Creature of Destruction*

One of the great perks of being one's own producer/director is the ability to exercise whims. The summer of 1967 in Texas was lovely and I yearned to break out of the cloistered rooms of the *Year 2889* experience. Sam Arkoff and Jim Nicholson suggested a remake of *The She Creature*, a wild tale of a hypnotist in love with his assistant, a future incarnation of a prehistoric monster. The original had a respectable cast of Marla English and some very good 1940s names like Chester Morris and Tom Conway who were just coasting in their golden years.

I cast Pat Delany in the Marla English role and veteran Les Tremayne as the hypnotist. Pat had made a positive impression in *Zontar, the Thing from Venus*. As for Tremayne, I had admired this gentleman with the great radio voice since I was in high school. Every Friday night at the orphanage, without fail, we would gather around the magic wireless to hear Les introduce *The First Nighter*. After describing the week's play and its stars, Les would intone "And now, the first nighters are entering the little theater off Times Square." It was magic. Tremayne's voice made the face of the radio a proscenium arch with characters on a screen. Rounding out our cast was the young lead, Aaron Kincaid, one of American International's beach party regulars.

The flick was shot entirely in and around the Tanglewood Lodge at Lake Texoma on the Texas-Oklahoma border. It was a picnic for crew and cast. Remember, this was when making pictures was still fun.

In *Filmfax* No. 38 (April/May 1993), Gregg Goodsell had this to say about the film in his article "The Weird and Wacky World of Larry Buchanan":

> *Creature of Destruction* (1967) is a re-make of *The She Creature* (1956). Familiar radio voice Les Tremayne plays a carnival hypnotist who cases a spell over his lovely assistant Pat Delany. The monster, this time a shabby third-removed cousin of *The Creature from the Black Lagoon*, is a modified wet suit with scissor-cut fins, in addition to the ping-pong ball eyes. *Creature* is full of distinctive Buchanan day-for-night scenes — a blue gel slapped across the camera lens. [Not so; we had no money for special filters. For "day-for-night," we simply *removed* the Wratten 85 correction gel and underexposed by two full stops.] The noonday sun is clearly visible on surfaces of water and car bumpers.

19. Comanche Crossing

Redemption, how sweet thy song! I now filmed my third western, and not a bit too soon. Finally I had a welcome hiatus from monsters with ping-pong ball eyes. Those few short weeks, vacation from tattered, recycled horror figures, did me a great deal of good. Most important, I could return to my beloved Big Bend Country where Texas dips into Old Mexico.

Caruth C. Byrd, last in a long line of Dallas movers and shakers, loves the West and its lore. We had talked often of working together. When Caruth asked if there was time between my contract pictures to do a simple, sympathetic drama of the Comanches of Texas, I said I would make time.

I quickly examined my contract with AIP to make sure the expression "exclusive services" was not a part of the deal. Free to do as I wished, I went to the typewriter and plunged into a lean story of a young Comanche warrior, his betrothed, and their anguish when the lovely innocent is savaged by a party of mountain men. Like an avenging ghost, the warrior tracks the brutes and destroys them.

No actress from Hollywood or any other talent pool on earth could have been a better choice for the maiden than our own Cynthia Hull. In *High Yellow*, she had broken our hearts with her sensitive performance as a black girl passing for white. Now she would play a Native American. She did so with a convincing grace and simplicity.

For the Comanche warrior, my choice was capable and dependable Anthony Houston, who had drawn much attention in *Zontar, the Thing from Venus*. He, too, was the perfect Comanche.

The Western setting was stunning. The music, wardrobe, editing and, to my mind, the story and direction were at least journeyman quality. But *Comanche Crossing* did not have a significant distribution.

This was not puzzling to me. Recall, please, that this was 1967. For five decades, since the days of Bronco Billy Anderson and even Cecil B. DeMille, such pictures as *The Covered Wagon*, *Stagecoach*, and *The Plainsman* had pictured the Native American as savage, cowardly, given to sloth and fond of torture. Into our culture and language were imbedded misguided phrases about their nature: "drunken Indian," "Indian giver," and "filthy redskin."

Now here came a portrait of an Indian couple who touched with affection. They laughed. They cried. They suffered. How dare they?

Texas has a large Native American population. When it was settled in the early 1800s, there were large camps of various tribes dotted across the territory. There were the Coman-che, spread from what is now the bayous of Galveston, up through the Big Thickets of what is now East Texas, and on into the Panhandle and the Staked Plains.

Hollywood got it right on the Comanche at least once. John Ford's *The Searchers* (1956) starring John Wayne and Natalie Wood, brought an uncharacteristic integrity to the por-trayal of Native Americans. Of course that was the firm and sure hand of John Ford, the only director who could ever stop Wayne from trying to act and just "be." Even so, Ward Bond, one of Ford's stock company of players, almost stole the show.

The Caddo, a peaceful Indian nation, were food gatherers and farmers. They were vir-tually vegetarians, growing corn and planting pecan trees and baking bread in mud ovens. They moved from their tidy camps only in time of famine or drought. Little pockets of Caddo could be found throughout the southeast of the territory and along what is now the state line between Louisiana and Texas. Hollywood has never dealt with the Caddo expressly be-cause they have never been violent, let alone savage. But of course my little filmmaking tribe got into the act, shooting several films on and around Caddo Lake on the Texas-Louisiana border.

Very few Pueblo or Cliff Dwellers could be found in Texas. They were well up into the Panhandle and the Llano Estacado or Staked Plains, close to the present New Mexico. Since they too were gentle of manner and family, Hollywood has shown very little interest in telling their story. The same could be said of the Kickapoo, Tigua, and the Alabama-Coushatta in both East and West Texas.

That leaves only the Apache, and in particular the Mescalero Apache. These were the warriors, the nomads, the proud who resisted encroachment onto their hunting grounds. They bristled at the white man's barbed wires.

Now *there* was something Hollywood could deal with. The bloodbaths began on film, and international movie audiences got their "education" and perception of the Apache from the end of a Winchester rifle.

John Ford did much to correct the image but died before he had a chance to film the ma-jor works he planned. These would have rewritten the script.

That brings us back to *Comanche Crossing* and one glimmer of the change in mindset about this people.

Upon finishing the film, we had a few bucks left over from the budget. I asked producer Caruth Byrd's permission to give a powwow for the Indian community and show the film for their impressions. Would they come? The Native Americans of Texas have their own grape-vine system of spreading the word about happenings and gatherings, and I was not prepared for the pilgrimage that resulted.

They came from all over the state, even some Tiguas from faraway El Paso and Kicka-poos from Eagle Pass. We had to move the screening from a little theater in Dallas to an out-door screen in the little town of Cedar Hill nearby. Even though it was still the "Magic Hour" in filmmaking terms, with light still in the sky, a bonfire was lit.

The caterers with the barbecue could not find us and were late, so we had to start the film without them. *Comanche Crossing* unspooled. It was met with total silence. I suffered.

The end title faded from the makeshift screen. My audience sat, rigid and without a murmur. Young Indian boys started to build up the bonfire to chase the darkness. They were stopped by an elder. He turned to me and put his finger to his lips as I was about to express my bewilderment.

"Shhh," he whispered, "they are seeing the pictures again."

We waited. After a few mystical moments, the elder raised his hands above his head and clapped, not in the manner of the white man's applause. All responded, hands above their heads. As they clapped, the high beams from the barbecue truck swept over the scene. What was only a whim on my part had turned into a genuine powwow. The morning light was reddening the sky before the last of the crowd left the grounds in pickups and old cars.

Years later, I relived that moment and understood it only when I read the moving 1988 best-seller *She Who Remembers* by an old Texas friend, Linda Shuler, for whom I had once directed some short documentary films on Texas ethnicities. We had talked of the cruel and ignorant spin that Hollywood had put on the Mescalero Apache, the Comanche, and the Cliff Dwellers of the Southwest. Now, 25 years later, that same Linda Shuler was being applauded for her superb novel and the sequels that followed.

Producer Caruth, who also did a very good acting job as a mountain man, was very understanding of the somewhat less than lustrous box office potential of the film. Perhaps, in time, this morality play and unfettered parable will find an audience in home video.

20. Hell Raiders

My next effort was a classic tale of World War II and a platoon of explosives experts caught behind enemy lines in Italy. It was my third and last feature with my now good buddy John Agar. Also in the cast were Richard Webb, Joan Huntington and my old standby Billy Thurman.

Italy? World War II? In Dallas? Why not?

In North Dallas, there is an old shopping center, Highland Park, whose 1930s architects replicated the arches, tiles, and bell towers of an Italian village. It was convincing enough for our purposes, so for two weeks in the spring of 1968, Highland Park became Foggia, Italy. From an army surplus dealer we rented a Sherman tank, ten rifles, uniforms and other gear. Presto! Siamo in Italia! It worked.

We had a close call with the powder. Our team was to blow up a munitions factory by the lake. We found the shell of an ancient, abandoned pickle factory known as the Vinegar Works that would serve well. Our special effects man, Jack Bennett, who was performing his first powder assignment of many, wanted to please me with a real blast. When the overloaded charges ignited, you could hear the report miles away. The ground shook like a quake from hell. Within minutes, the local gendarmes were on the premises. Pajama-clad farmers and their wives with hair in curlers stared at this apparition in understandable horror.

Although on many locations we would "steal" the shot if it looked dangerous, we had obtained a permit this trip out. But no one could find it. I was told that I was under arrest and was being led to the squad car when the night sergeant arrived.

We stared at each other for a moment, then I recognized him as a classmate from Buckner Home. We had been crazy about the same girl in graduating year, and we both remembered rabbit hunting together in these same fields 20 years before. He dismissed his officers, and I called a wrap to the company. My old Buckner mate and I retired to the nearest Mexican café and ordered tamales and Lone Star brew. What began as a quiet reunion between friendly rivals over Texas brews and spicy fare turned into one of the strangest encounters I had experienced in a life in film.

The place was quiet for a honky-tonk. The juke box was playing one of Eddy Arnold's old numbers — "Candy Kisses," if I recollect right. Only one couple slid around the floor to the beat, in no hurry.

Upon graduation from Buckner, the girls could count on a job at Southwestern Bell, and the guys were welcome to join the excellent Dallas police force and enter the training academy. "Freckles," as I'll call my friend, had done just that and had moved up in the ranks.

We had finished the tamales and were on about the third cold beer when I sensed that Freckles wanted to talk about something on his mind. He wasted no time in small talk.

"I saw your picture show about Lee Harvey Oswald." (Yes, even as I write, some Texans still call films "picture shows.")

I didn't see how he could have seen the picture since we were suppressed so early after the premier in Milwaukee. But in a few minutes I discovered he not only had seen the picture, but he knew a great deal more about the Kennedy assassination than any cop or city official I had talked to during those dark days in 1963.

"You and Harold [Hoffman, my partner in the crime] got it right when you did the show, but hell, you were shooting just weeks after the hit. You couldn't have known what came out later."

I asked Freckles if I could make some notes.

"Why not? Hell, it's been five years now and the whole mess has been swept under the rug. Anyway, I'm retiring this year. Come May I don't have to answer to anybody but the missus."

Later, when I reconstructed my penciled scribblings, the following facts emerged:

Harold and I had been right that there had been absolutely no police conspiracy in the Dallas ranks. Sure, Freckles and his pals spent a lot of midnights at Jack Ruby's Carousel Club, but they were just lonely guys trying to get connected. The first beer was free to anyone on the force and the cover charge was waived.

What about the top dogs in Big D? Mayor Earl Cabel, District Attorney Wade? "Don't make me laugh," Freckles responded. "These guys were too dull, petrified, or too close to retirement."

Oswald? We know he was in the sniper's nest, but did he have the expertise to make that shot?

"No," Freckles interrupted, "he was just a dumbass who was recruited and who was expendable. Hear this, the rifling on the gun was shot — worn out. And where did those Warren people get the idea that he could hit a barn door at noon? Hell, just remember, he had a perfect target in General Walker. Walker was just standing in a well-lighted living room and Oswald could take his good old time to sight in on him. Oswald was hidden by the bushes so there was no panic. He missed. Whereas, up in the Texas School Book Depository, the adrenaline must have been pumping like a new oil gusher."

Then I looked Freckles straight in the eye.

"All of us who have spent any real time over the years on this horror know that the fatal bullet came from the front right, grassy knoll. Why can't we make them see that?"

"Because," he continued, "that would put the collar on the right pony . . . or rather the right asshole."

I took a deep breath. "We're talking LBJ here?"

"You got it. Lyndon Baines Johnson. You know, he and his buddy J. Edgar Hoover coined that phrase 'crazy conspiratorialists' just to silence any real inquiry into the 'hit.' So everybody backs off so's they don't look like friggin' idiots."

Freckles was reaching for his cap and gear. But he wasn't about to go until he tied some pieces together. "Someday, somebody's gonna put it all together," he went on. "Lyndon's first election to the Texas House of Representatives. 'Landslide Lyndon!' Box 13 down in Duval County. The 87 votes that put him in office turn out to be dead Meskins under tombstones. But hell, that was just for openers. Check out the story on the dead pilots of the private plane out of Austin the night of the storm, the running of the greyhound dogs on the border, the Billie Sol Estes scandal, the meetings at La Grange until 'the best little whorehouse in Texas' got too popular with the Aggies from Texas A&M. As senator, he ran the state of Texas like a chess game. Money? This good old boy from pisspoor roots with cowdung on his shoes? Hell, nobody in politics got richer faster. But that was all just a warm-up for what he was gonna get, whatever the cost: the presidency. Nobody had more to gain with JFK dead. Nobody hated the president more than that ol' mealy-mouth snake oil salesman from the Pedernales River country."

The music coming off the box now was "Slippin' Around." The bartender stepped over to a microphone near the juke to announce, "Last call for alkeehol." Freckles and I stood up as if on a cue.

"The word was out to the right people. Lyndon was to be dumped. Even though JFK was a shoo-in, he wouldn't tolerate LBJ as a running mate."

In the parking lot, Freckles was heaving his big frame into his squad car. "Another thing. I was on the detail to Love Field where Air Force One was waiting for Johnson and the JFK corpse. All the way to the airport, ol' Lyndon was hunched down in the seat where we could hardly see him. He wasn't taking any chances. After all, there were some real marksmen out there. When he finally appeared on the tarmac, I swear to hell he had that shit-kickin' toothless smile on his face." With that Freckles pulled away into the Dallas night.

21. The Other Side of Bonnie and Clyde

My next project was a personal, out-of-pocket send-up of Arthur Penn's classic *Bonnie and Clyde*. Well, "send-up" might be a little harsh. Long before Warren Beatty and Faye Dunaway came to Dallas to work on their film, Sam Arkoff and I had discussed a remake of AIP's *The Bonnie Parker Story* with Dorothy Provine from 1958.

Penn or Beatty had to have seen AIP's *Bonnie Parker Story*. You can bet on it. In Penn's

Copyright 1968 Dal-Art Films

Bonnie and Clyde (1967), Clyde (Warren Beatty) and his brother Buck (Gene Hackman) come together at a roadside tavern. Clyde has been in prison in Huntsville, Texas. They are overjoyed at the reunion but, typical of male behavior patterns of the time, have no way of showing their affection. Rather, they begin the familiar ritual of a mock boxing match. Thus they're touching without being too close.

In AIP's *The Bonnie Parker Story*, the same characters come together and engage in the same jousting. That in itself could have been a mere coincidental director's whim. What is of interest cinematically is that the fisticuff exchange is, *cut to cut*, an identical sequence! The similarity is remarkable.

Folk singer Burl Ives narrated my *The Other Side of Bonnie and Clyde* (which I had originally planned to title *Bonnie and Clyde: Myth or Madness?*). His agents had dismissed my calls after I told them I had very little to pay Burl. They demanded $50,000, which was more than I had ever had to make a

The final campaign for *The Other Side of Bonnie and Clyde*. I had demanded the removal of Burl Ives' name and a tasteful press book.

115

whole movie. What they didn't know was that Burl and I had been acquainted since World War II. We spent many hours watching football games on Sunday afternoons at his apartment at the Chateau Marmont and later at his place on Sweetzer in Hollywood. At halftime, we would reach for our guitars and "noodle chords" and swap stories about blues greats Leadbelly and Blind Lemon Jefferson. Burl did the narration for a small fraction of the agent's demand.

What I didn't plan on was the distributor's using Burl's name misleadingly to promote the film. The first ads, done before we arrived at the final title, contained only the following copy: "I Killed Bonnie & Clyde. With: Burl Ives. In Color." I protested, but the distributor apparently misunderstood, for the next effort described the film, in large type, as "Starring Burl Ives." Under threat of litigation, the posters were eventually recalled. The final campaign omitted Burl's name altogether, much to my relief.

Libby Booth, as the Naked Witch, returns after a hundred years in her grave. She will kill the descendants of the villagers who drove the stake into her heart. Since our shoot was only at night, the people of Luckenbach, Texas, in 1957 didn't know what to make of us.

Top: The Gill Monster of *Creature of Destruction* clowns for the crew. Behind the ping-pong ball eyes and rubber suit is one of my cinema stock company regulars, Byron Lord. This was not a demotion from his memorable role in *Mars Needs Women*; we were an ensemble group. Arguably, the only ego was mine. *Above:* Me with my longtime collaborator Lynn Shubert.

Top: Misty Rowe and costar Terrence Locke in *Goodbye, Norma Jean.* This scene was later used in *Goodnight, Sweet Marilyn.* The chemistry was undeniable. *Bottom:* Paula Lane as Marilyn Monroe during her last hours in *Goodnight, Sweet Marilyn.*

Top: Famed artist Boris Vallejo's key art for *Mistress of the Apes. Opposite:* The building of our monster for *The Loch Ness Horror.* Clockwise from upper left: running the control lines in the workshop; welding the mechanicals; the hydraulics crew practices; Nessie finally takes a dip; a dress rehearsal.

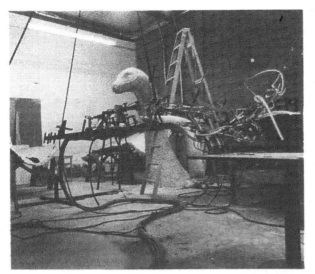

THEIR MUSIC GOT THEM KILLED ... YOUNG!

Opposite page: Paula Lane as the doomed Marilyn in Goodnight, Sweet Marilyn *(left); campaign poster for* Down on Us *(right). Above: Jacket for the Australian videocassette of* Goodnight, Sweet Marilyn.

Clockwise from top: With Jane (left) and Alice Faye at a charity fund-raiser in Dallas; pondering a shot at lakeside for *The Loch Ness Monster;* signing the last of many contracts with Samuel Z. Arkoff; a recent publicity photo.

22. It's Alive!

Six years before that other Larry (Cohen) made his *It's Alive!* (1974), I made mine. A quarter of a century before *Jurassic Park*, my *It's Alive!* begins with the principals entering a dinosaur theme park. To quote critic Greg Goodsell, "As the credits roll, we see prehistoric dinosaurs eerily peeking through the trees, masterfully foreshadowing the bizarre drama which is about to unfold."

Tommy Kirk returned for his second starring role for me, as did the monster suit from *Creature of Destruction* (now worn by stalwart Bill Thurman).

Goodsell is one of the few writers, along with Douglas St. Claire Smith, who are able to fathom the subtexts of my films. Because his vivisection of *It's Alive!* is imprinted with an almost spiritual cognizance of *all* of my work, I would like to let him speak, chapter and verse, warts and all. What follows is the full text of his article "Tape Loop of the Unconscious: Plumbing Buchanan's 'It's Alive!'" from *Zontar, the Magazine from Venus*, Vol. 4, No. 2.

> A couple is seen driving in their car. The camera stays in one continuous take as they drive endlessly on a two-lane highway through a densely wooded area. There is no soundtrack. The shot continues like this for what seems like at least ten minutes without sound or any cuts away from the windshield.
>
> "What's going on?" asks the befuddled television viewer. "Isn't this supposed to be a movie, called *It's Alive!* (1968), starring Tommy Kirk and directed by dreck auteur Larry Buchanan? Surely, I haven't stayed up past two in the morning for naught?"
>
> Just as abruptly, rain dots the windshield, to which the intrepid driver flicks on the wipers. A voice, probably Buchanan's,* recounts an old wives' tale that says "When it rains while the sun still shines, the devil is kissing his wife!" These profound words usher in the great Buchanan's most nebulous and minimal film to date, a story fraught with infidelity, cruelty, poor relationships, and prehistoric monsters.
>
> *It's Alive!* is the most enigmatic of Buchanan's sci-fi canon. For once, the technical short-comings in the series produce unintentional results that strike ominous chords within the viewer. Those who have seen the film, the faithful that stay up until the wee hours of the morning to insure they have seen every monster/horror flick ever made, remember the film vividly even though few recall the plot *or* title.
>
> The film is atypical Buchanan. An original script in lieu of a remake of an old AIP monster picture, it seems at this early point in Buchanan's career that he was under contractual obliga-

---

* It was indeed my voice.

My good luck charm, Billy Thurman, plays the horror in *It's Alive!* Even though Hollywood had now discovered him, he put on the gill suit and ping-pong ball eyes and worked for scale.

tion from AIP for product. I have little doubt that a great deal of the film was improvised on the spot.* As such, there is little of the philosophical meanderings in his earlier works. *It's Alive!* is ridiculously cheap even by Buchanan's standards; a cast of five with around half of the film played out in silence. Muffled monster movie soundtrack music is the only connecting thread between scenes. The old master has given up all hope for quality at this point.

But *It's Alive!* is by far the most powerful example of the director's work. The film connects with the subconscious mind unlike any avante-garde effort I have seen. It strikes a responsive chord to those who can recall dreams that occur midway between slumber and consciousness.

A repressive husband and his wife stop at a rural reptile exhibit presided over by a drooling madman, played with relish by Billy Thurman. He begs them to see his pride and joy located in a nearby cave . . . an offer which they foolishly accept. Once there, they are thrown behind bars, along with meddlesome "paleontologist" Tommy Kirk, to be later fed to a dreaded prehistoric monster — mainly the ping-pong-ball-eyed, scissor-cut, rubber-finned creature previously featured in Buchanan's *Creature of Destruction*.

Those who are into monsters will find very little to interest them in *It's Alive!* In Mississippi seconds (in effect, "one Mississippi, two Mississippi,") the monster is on screen for no more than fifteen throughout the film. Buchanan follows the tested domestic formula where his characters talk out their existential despair.

The high points of the film are the digressions of the crazy man's prisoner/housekeeper, a little old lady school teacher who took the wrong turn on the road and wound up under

---

*Again a correct assumption.

the geezer's power. Her flashback sequence takes up roughly more than half the film's ninety-minute running time and is told solely through narration accompanied by that beloved library monster music. We see her kept prisoner in her rented room. The old man denies her food and drink, wakes her up from her infrequent naps with a police whistle, and feeds her rats with garnish in *What Ever Happened to Baby Jane?* fashion.

It is here where Buchanan becomes his most uncomfortable. Having wandered through this film halfway, the audience waits for something meaningful to happen. It never does. We begin to empathize with the old lady, left with nothing to do but rock in a chair and stare at the sparsely furnished room. We all know that the sets in a Larry Buchanan movie have all the warmth and charm of a doctor's office. We are treated to ponderous shots of a clock, a ceiling, a lamp, a desk, a bed, a chair . . . the old lady is the only Buchanan figure acutely aware of the limitations of the Buchanan universe. Without distractions or diversions, she is left with the blank horror of the non-existence of the Buchanan vision that is ultimately the end product of civilization.

Similarly, David Lynch in *Eraserhead* tries to convey a society devoid of character and energy by focusing on banal objects such as radiators, coathooks, dressers, window sills, etc., but redeems them with beautiful black and white photography.

Buchanan films his objects in inimitable television "bad" color, brightly lit and blandly framed. This induces claustrophobia in the viewer; we WANT OUT OF THAT ROOM. We want to turn off the set and go to sleep, but hope the film will improve, or at least add meat to the non-plot. It never does.

Therefore, when the old lady throws cleaning fluid in the madman's eyes while feigning sleep, Buchanan films the scenes so devoid of inspiration we realize the old lady's flight from the house will avail to nothing. Buchanan doesn't give even one diddly towards integrating the library music to the action on screen, so the droning monster movie library plays on without highlight.

The old lady flees through the woods pursued by the madman. She trips and falls over a tree stump as the madman whips off his cardboard and vinyl belt and beats her with it. It is only here that the film becomes even the slightest bit unintentionally funny. Buchanan wants the sequence to be in slow motion but doesn't have the necessary setting on his cheap 16mm camera, so he comes up with the next best thing; have the actors act in slow motion! Their grotesque gestures and exaggerated pacing add up to the surrealistic tableau as the old woman intones, "I was trapped. Like one of the creatures he kept in the cages."

It's Alive! reaches a predictable conclusion with the monster confronting his madman keeper with Kirk producing a stick of dynamite to seal up the cave. For the climactic explosion, Buchanan throws handfuls of dirt on the ground and drops a rock on the concrete cavern floor as a monster movie library music explosion is dubbed over the ever-droning soundtrack. Kirk and the honey exchange "what is the meaning of art and science in the view of mental illness and desire for short term gain" dialogues, and we get the impression they will return to their estranged mates. Fade out.

It's Alive! would do Edgar G. Ulmer proud. The film is note-for-note the depressing, nihilistic viewpoint held in his likewise no-budget cult favorites *Detour* (1946) and *The Cavern* (1966).

Buchanan is similar to Ulmer in his ability to create within the viewer anxiety, despair, hopelessness, and the feeling of a genuine raging bummer.

The real reason for the obscurity of *It's Alive!* is the more famous (and later) film of the same name, the Larry Cohen mutant baby picture. The confusion between the two (whenever you order from mail order movie still companies for samples of Buchanan movies, one is always deluged with pictures of mutant babies) is both ironic and tragic.

Both *It's Alive!* (1968) and *It's Alive!* (1974) share a strong anti-creative anti-art stance. *It's Alive!* (1974) draws its power by setting its story of bloodthirsty infants in suburban tracts and shopping malls while a great deal of the action is talked away in domestic settings,

Buchanan's non-aesthetics note for note! The irony here lies in the fact that the Cohen picture was embraced with semi-legendary cult status because of these very attributes, resulting in a lot of moolah for Cohen and a money-grabbing sequel, *It Lives Again*. Other things, besides sheer ineptitude, have conspired towards Buchanan's current obscurity.

It's Alive! taps into the subconscious power of the viewer with a hazy, narcoleptic power that cannot be denied. When it debuts on your local station at two o'clock in the morning, you owe it to yourself to catch it . . . Videodrome be dammed!

23. A Bullet for Pretty Boy

Making *It's Alive!* was all anguish and no fun. The studio, AIP, was not prepared to increase the laughable budgets. I was ready to walk and prepared to risk everything to stop the madness. My crews and the Texas talent had gone to the wall with me and would have continued had I said the word. But, alas, I could no longer face them in good conscience, knowing they were now carrying me instead of the other way around.

I served notice to Sam Arkoff that I could no longer produce a feature film in color for $35,000; nor I asserted, could any other filmmaker in the world. I was not prepared for Sam's reaction.

He laughed, long and hard. Then, in a most jovial mood, he confided that he was not surprised and that he wanted to take our deal to a new plateau with more money!

"What do you want to do and what is *your* bottom dollar to do it?" How sweet those words were.

I had approached Sam years before with a screenplay that I had cowritten with my team player Anthony Houston, actor and scenarist. It was *A Bullet for Pretty Boy*, a thirties gangster flick on the exploits of a contemporary of Clyde Barrow, Charles Arthur Floyd. He had earned the nickname Pretty Boy by his prepossessing manner and looks when he approached pretty bank tellers to suggest that he could relieve them of those "dirty ol' dollar bills."

Sam, who hated to read scripts, insisted I pitch the story again. I had only gotten through the description of the country boy turned killer when Sam got That Look.

"Fabian!" He slammed his hand on the table and never let me finish the step outline.

It seems that Fabian Forte, the teenage singing and acting idol, owed AIP a picture. They had been unable to find anything for him and were faced with the "play or pay" clause in Fabe's contract. This meant they would forfeit the money for his services although he would not face a camera. You may not believe this, but the sum involved was $35,000 — the same amount they were paying me to turnkey a complete production, with cast, crews, editing, lab work, et cetera!

I told Sam no dice. I wanted to use a young actor who was making some noise with some of Roger Corman's pictures, Jack Nicholson. Sam felt Nicholson was good enough for bits in *Little Shop of Horrors* but not yet seasoned enough for a real lead. This was before Nicholson would play a small but career-making role in *Easy Rider*. Too, it was a full year before he would do *Five Easy Pieces* for Bob Rafelson. I stopped dreaming and, with some uneasiness about Fabian, started to work.

Stars Fabian Forte and Jocelyn Lane take time out from robbing banks.

I needn't have worried. Fabian couldn't have been more cooperative. Although the Texas heat was oppressive and the double-breasted wool wardrobe smothering, we pumped the teen favorite with salt pills and branch water and he came through it all — sometimes sullen, but always the professional. Incidentally, Forte ("Fabe" to his friends) is an Aquarius like me.

Also in the cast was one of my favorite actors, Adam Roarke. He had done leads in such films as *Play It as It Lays* and was a favorite of the late Howard Hawks.

The girls were talented and quite pretty. Jocelyn Lane played the gun moll. The country-girl wife of Floyd was Astrid Warner. And there was a young actress making her film debut in the role of another moll. Behind her casting lies a tale.

Early in the story, Pretty Boy Floyd waits at a thirties filling station where a slick gangster is to deliver him his first machine gun. He tries the tommy gun repeater out on the gas tanks, which explode. But the scene was not working. I had Fabe hold the gun in the "phallic" position which should have conveyed the sexual connotations of the scene, but it wasn't working because our moll wasn't there. One of our leading ladies had been literally snatched by the Mob. I will detail that shortly, but for now suffice it to say we were without the "juice" that the scene needed.

I called the very capable actor's agent Peggy Taylor in Dallas, 40 miles to the south of the location. I told her my situation and said I needed a replacement. She promised me the best she had would be on the location before we were through with lunch. "I don't have to send anyone but her — you'll like this one."

I did. She drove the big 1934 Buick convertible like she had just stepped out of Howard

Morgan Fairchild as gun moll in *A Bullet for Pretty Boy*. In her small first role, she showed a radiance that reached to Sunset and Vine. People looking at the dailies in Hollywood wanted to know who the "fox" was.

Hawks's *Scarface*. When Fabian Forte fired the gun until it jammed, then looked at the blonde behind the wheel, her reaction told cast and crew we had the right girl. Her name was Morgan Fairchild.

The budget should have been $900,000, but I was given $300,000. The result I consider a testament to what can be done with even a small margin for error. The flick opened big, and it had "legs."

The studio had timidly opened the film in six cities for a test run. The grosses started coming in and at the end of the first seven days, house records had fallen and there was a gross of $126,000. The film then went wide and was held over everywhere.

As they said in *The Hollywood Reporter* and *Variety*, "Pretty Boy Floyd is still killing 'em!"

But one of the most memorable things about making this film had to be our little brush with the Mob. One of our gangster molls from Hollywood, playing an important lead, had an indelicate problem that soon became mine. (As if I did not have ample concern winning Fabian over to the Texas ethic.) "Lana," let's call her, was just starting to "happen" when we signed her for *A Bullet for Pretty Boy*. She was a stunner, she was talented, and she was in trouble. Not yet "married to the Mob," she sure as hell was engaged.

Let's give her guy an alias too; I like to sleep nights. "Al" didn't like the idea of Lana being 1700 miles from Beverly Hills where he held court and pushed people around. He was baffled that she wanted a career when he could give her anything she wanted, however

tainted. I have always been chagrined at this phenomenon. These hoods and their blood brothers in white collar crime simply don't understand the hungers their girlfriends suffer in wanting a career in show business. The necklaces, the Mercedes and the dinners at Morton's are all welcome, but what the girls really yearn for, and will put out for, is that small part in a megabuck feature. The formula is as old as show business.

Al wanted his Lana to spend at least weekends with him in Beverly Hills. And since he had a large block of stock in a major airline, it was only natural that she would have the posh treatment on her weekend jaunts.

But I couldn't let her go. The insurance carriers for motion picture cast protection will not, for whatever reason, cover "above the line" players (read, those important enough that their death would put a picture in the commode) if they are on location and insist on flying out on weekends. There are exceptions to this rule, but the deductibles are humongous. So I firmly told the mobster's intermediary calling from the coast that Lana had to stay put.

But there was another complication. Lana didn't *want* to make the trip, and for a very good reason. She had fallen head over heels in love with the hotel's night manager. Burt was a bright, handsome kid just out of *Southern Methodist University* in Dallas. As usual in these matters of the heart, the buck stopped with Buchanan.

After a long, overtime Saturday in the third week of our shoot, I returned to my room beat and hungry. The largest fruit basket I had ever seen was on the dresser along with a bottle of champagne. The note said that a friend

A sample of the ad campaign for *A Bullet for Pretty Boy*.

was waiting in the bar to "pay his respects." The writer had a sense of humor. "I'm the only guy in the place without a tie." The note was signed merely "A."

Walking through the lobby I noticed that Burt was still on duty. I remembered that he was off at midnight and that he would be heading for room 405, where a tired but willing Lana would be waiting.

Although I had in the past experienced many close calls with the fraternity, I had never actually known a member of the Mob. With some fear and trembling, I approached the pleasant-looking man at a far table who was wearing no tie. I had suddenly stepped into my own Film Noir. But I needn't have worried; "A" was a pussy cat.

Over corned beef sandwiches and lager, he talked of everything but Lana. Then: "There's this kid at the desk, the manager . . ."

"Yes, that would be Burt. Just out of SMU." What in hell's name was I doing? This guy had snookered me with his fruit basket and corned beef and here I was feeding him information!

The numbers speak for themselves. And they loved our 1930s pin-up kid in Europe too.

"He wouldn't let me put through a call upstairs."

I countered, "He has explicit instructions. When there is a no-calls order, he can't make exceptions."

"But how about you? You're the producer. She works for you!" There it was. No more games. "She" was Lana.

I would have to embellish. "SAG — that's the Screen Actors Guild — they could make a heavy penalty case against me if I override her request. It would have to be a critical emergency."

He chewed this over for a few moments.

"That's what this is, what you call a. . . ."

I helped him. "A critical emergency."

"Yeah. And it's got to be settled now." Oh God, he suddenly had that hard look. A waiter approached with the bill. Al picked it up with a practiced flair. He dropped a C-note onto the platter and said, "Keep it." Then he leaned toward me.

"I didn't want to hurt the kid," he whispered. "A phone call? Forget it. I owe her; she's never asked for much. But now. . . . It's like this. My kids and their mother are back home. It was my idea. I kinda missed their noise and, well, Mom's all right, putting up with a lug like me."

He picked up the hotel stationery on which he had written a note. "Here, see what you think of that." The penmanship was in a fine Italian hand, almost feminine.

"Sorry Lana, I can't ask you to put up with my stupid life anymore. It's funny but your goodness makes me want to try again with her and the kids. Like that Pretty Boy Floyd . . . Go out there and kill 'em, kid.   Al"

He stuffed what looked like three thousand-dollar bills into the hotel envelope and pushed it into the pocket inside my coat without sealing it. "Take good care of her," he said. Then, with a smile, he added, "If she don't look good in your movie, we'll have to talk."

He then asked if I would see him to the front for a cab to the airport. Burt was the only one on duty that late. He blew a police whistle and called up a Yellow Cab. The two never spoke. Al did not leave a tip.

24. Strawberries Need Rain

One sweet pleasure of having a hit picture is that one can choose at the very least the next project.

In my serious reading days, I had found a Scandinavian folk tale of a 16-year-old girl who is visited by the Grim Reaper. She is given 24 hours to live. She spends this precious time seeking out those who had expressed a love for her in hopes that before her departure, she can know the sensual wonders of the fragile thing called desire.

The simplicity and directness of the tale so moved me that I wrote *Strawberries Need Rain*. The influences of Ingmar Bergman are unabashedly obvious in the script.

The big state of Texas has limitless opportunities for locations that resemble other parts of the world. One such happy place is Luckenbach, the quaint village in the German hill country west of Austin where I had filmed *The Naked Witch* in 1957. Settled by immigrants from Scandinavia and Germany in the mid-1800s, the area provided the perfect setting for *Strawberries*.

The girl I found for the lead, Monica Gayle, was the perfect match for the girl on paper. My favorite heavy, Bill Thurman, came aboard. Rounding out a dream cast from Hollywood as the Grim Reaper himself was Les Tremayne, my old friend from *Creature of Destruction*.

The shoot was also a dream. I had a small cast and a small crew headed up by my inventive and dedicated director of photography Bob Jessup. We had great weather, there were bluebonnets in full blossom, the mill race was full of spring water, and even the catering was superb. Every facet of this surreal experience made it, like *High Yellow*, a most rewarding venture in a long career.

The art houses loved the film. The drive-ins and big hard-tops couldn't wait to cut short the engagement and ship the prints back to the exchange. I remember it with a wistful nostalgia.

Filming in Luckenbach again, I couldn't help thinking of Miriam, the ambitious local newspaper editor who wanted to be a screenwriter. Recall that I said I never saw her again after the wrap party. She had wistfully walked barefooted to her beat-up Volkswagen, unhappy at our departure. Had she gone to Hollywood? Made it? The odds were unimaginable. Failed? Likely. Had she returned home?

For me as director, the schedule for *Strawberries* was a piece of cake compared to the frenetic antics of *The Naked Witch* years before, and I was blessed with some time for remembering. I made up my mind to find Miriam if at all possible.

127

For *Strawberries Need Rain*, I had Les Tremayne as the Grim Reaper and a jewel of a beginner in Monica Gayle.

The newspaper staff had not seen her since her departure the day after we wrapped *The Naked Witch*. All they could provide was the address of her mother; they had no telephone number. There was something familiar in the street name: Lang's Farm-to-Market Rd.

Could it be this easy? The old grist mill which we used in *Witch* was known as Lang's Mill. The mother's place would have to be one of the stone cottages nearby.

Leaving my car, I walked to the mill, which was almost hidden by the big oak and mesquite trees. The mill race was dry, loaded with leaves, the big wheel fallen on its side. It was apparent that it was being pillaged for firewood. As I moved around this bleak setting, I kept encountering ghosts from the first film we had shot there — our witch Libby Booth with those great cheekbones, cameraman Ralph Johnson long since gone to join the heavenly choir, actor Howard Ware, who was the first to have his blood spilled by the avenging spectre. I could almost see the water turn red with our "blood," a mixture of Karo syrup and food coloring. I was snapped out of my reverie by the sound of a screen door slapping shut.

The woman at the door stared for a long moment, her hand shading her eyes against the

Opposite: Evolution of an ad campaign. The distributors didn't like the title *Strawberries Need Rain* (one actually snickered, "I thought they needed horse shit!"). They came up (*top left*) with "Why Me!" and a sultry poster proclaiming "starring Monica Gay [*sic*], star of Nashville," which she was not. I insisted on more taste, so they took away the tennis frock and added a clock (*top right*). I blanched. Now they got rough (*bottom left*); my sensitive picture became "Teenage Bait" and the art was even more lurid. Finally a compromise (*bottom right*): my title, their art.

sun. Her suspicion vanished when I introduced myself and gave her Miriam's name. We sat on the uneven porch in rockers and sipped iced tea with real mint leaves from the yard. I had made up my mind not to rush her. She had the classic reaction to my being from "that there place Hollywood." I didn't have to wait long.

She disappeared into the house for a moment, making sure the screen door didn't bang, and returned with two letters. They were the only things she had left of Miriam. The first message was short, saying little more than that she had arrived safely and that she had found a place in the old Studio Club, a home for Hollywood extras and professionals.

Then she handed me the other letter. It was worn with creasing and handling although the postmark was only a few weeks old. I read to myself. I'm reconstructing it 25 years later, but I remember it so vividly as to be certain that it read very much like this:

Dear Mama

Not much new to tell. I've moved again but I won't send the address because I don't think I will be here long.

From my apartment window, I can see up into the Hollywood hills. There it is, big as life, the famous Hollywood sign. Remember, I showed you pictures of it before I left home. I got so interested in it I'm writing a screenplay with the sign as a background. Lots of hours at the library. The best book on it I found at the gift shop at Grauman's Chinese Theater . . . you know, the movie palace where all the stars have placed their hands in the wet cement when they make it to the top.

There was a newspaper clipping in the book that got me working on the screenplay. I call it "H is for Heartbreak." You'll know why I call it that when I tell you more.

But first . . . the sign was built way back in 1923 by some real estate people. At that time, it read "Hollywoodland" but the "land" part fell in a storm and they never put it back up.

My screenplay about the sign is part of what they call here "Hollywood Tarnish"; you know, the other side of the dream.

My story takes place in the early 1930s and it's about an actress name Peggy Entwistle. It is sad but true. Her real name was Lillian Millicent Entwistle but she knew that would be too long to put on the marquee (that's the big sign outside the theatre, mama). So, she chose the name "Peggy."

She had nearly starved to death in New York where she had gone to be in the theatre. Then, like a Tinseltown fairy tale, she got a part in a new play. The critics loved her. When the play closed, armed with her "notices," she took the train to Hollywood. Her high hopes were dashed when she found she was just one of thousands of young girls who were starstruck and made the rounds daily looking for work. Anything in the movies, even extra work. Soon, even extra work was hard to come by. Then came waitressing or posing for cheap, pulp magazines. As the years passed even those call-backs stopped. You can guess what followed. I don't have to tell you, mom, about the depression years. It was the same here as it was in the dust bowl of the southwest. Sometimes Peggy wouldn't eat properly if she didn't sleep with some unsavory oaf or humor a geriatric stranger.

The rejections were taking their toll. She was crying out to anyone who would listen, "Touch me . . . heal me." But all she got back were her own echoes. She tried religion. One foggy night she saw the big electric sign "Jesus Saves" above Aimee Semple McPherson's big tabernacle. She joined the choir and seemed to get some solace for a while. She idolized Sister Aimee. Then late one night, she was alone, ironing her cap and gown at the temple. She went to put her things away and stumbled upon Aimee and her lover in a naked embrace.

Peggy took the "Red Car" home. That's what they called the old electric trolly that ran between Hollywood and downtown Los Angeles. She dreaded that ride. It was always lonely. That night it was an ordeal. In her conjured mind, it was a ride through Hades, symbolized by the swaying, clacking Red Car.

When she reached her pitiful room, she did not turn on the lights. She opened the blinds and the moonlight that flooded the Hollywood sign spilled onto her face.

In the half-light, she showered. She dressed in her best dress and shoes with Cuban heels. She carefully made herself as pretty as she could but this had become difficult lately.

Peggy, without looking back into the room, closed the door and began a long walk up into the Hollywood hills toward the sign. The white bulbs that brightened the sign in the evenings had been turned off for the night. But the letters glittered with the moonlight as if lit by big arc lamps. The kind of lights Peggy had seen on all too few movie sets.

The letter "H" seemed especially brilliant. It was taller than she had expected. She had heard the signs were forty-five feet high but didn't believe it until she lifted her head. But from her little room, "Hollywoodland" had looked like a child's playsign. The "H" beckoned.

From somewhere down in Hollywood, music drifted up the hills. It could have been one of those late night radio shows with a big band or maybe a small bar where lonely people comforted each other.

Peggy recognized the tune: "I've Got a Pocketful of Dreams." Peggy kicked off her shoes with their Cuban heels. Then, hitching up her tight skirt, she stretched to reach the first rung on the service ladder running up the letter "H."

It seemed to take forever to reach the top. But she smiled through her panting breath. She was amused at the irony of it. The top of Hollywood! Rising to her full height, she drank in the sparkle of the few lights left along Sunset Boulevard below. Now, the music seemed closer and she recognized the singer. It was Bing Crosby. Der Bingle! She had seen him once when she went to Paramount to read for a low budget western. He was finishing up "I've Got a Pocketful of Dreams."

Silence. Peggy felt a chill. But the thin smile never left her face. The climb had been long. But the fall was forever. Of all the images that flashed before her in her own personal movie, the brightest was the cover of a book she once saw in a window. "Dreams Die First."

That's all for now. Love you Mom.   Miriam.

Before I had finished the letter, the sun was on the porch and Miriam's mother had drifted off for her afternoon nap. I sighed and leaned back in the rocker. The squeak woke her.

She folded the letter and smoothed the creases with a practiced hand. I thanked her. As I walked down the hill to the car, she wanted to know "Thanks for what?" I had no answer for that. Life writes dirty scripts.

25. The Rebel Jesus (a.k.a. Live from the Dead Sea)

As I had approached graduation from Buckner Academy so many years earlier, I expressed outward eagerness to accept the ministerial scholarship I was offered to Baylor University at Waco, Texas, even though privately I was counting the days until I could take the Greyhound Express to Los Angeles. I felt I owed those who had encouraged and nurtured me the courtesy of at least considering a career in the ministry. "Doctor of divinity" did have a nice ring to it. After all, this was a time when "evangelist" was not a four letter word. Evangelists were revered and more important, they drew crowds, which appealed to the actor in me. But during my matriculation at Baylor University, I was woefully unprepared for the onslaught of the strict constructionists. The campus was crawling with these innocents. Eager to impress anyone who would listen, they locked horns in ecclesiastic debate at every opportunity, pausing only to wipe their bifocals before pointing fingers again.

I was no stranger to the religious passion of would-be Southern Baptist clerics, but this was a downright bore. All their arguments consisted purely of a literal reading of scripture with no margin for exploration or dissent. It was "John says," "In Matthew we find . . . ," "He said" this or "He said" that. So with no hope of real unfettered debate or even the right to question, I let the cacophony about me fade in my ears. I'm sure they were all sincere and acting properly within their experience, but this was no place for me. I hitchhiked to the wicked city of the Angels, palm trees and Aimee Semple McPherson.

But I had developed an abiding, even obsessive interest in the historicity of the man from the ancient Roman province called Galilee, and that interest has continued to this day. I have devoured the works of Dietrich Bonhoeffer, Malcolm Muggeridge, G.B. Shaw, H.G. Wells, Albert Schweitzer, and other scholars on the Nazarene. Mine is a magnificent but frustrating obsession. Like the giants mentioned above, I believe that 2,000 years ago, in Judea, there lived a man who knew God. I do not believe his was a virgin birth, nor that he struck wine from water, nor that he raised the dead, nor that he experienced an embodied resurrection from his death.

Rather, he was an Essene who spent much of the period known as his "lost years" studying at Qumran by the Dead Sea and traveling to distant countries such as India and China. I do believe he gave his life to punctuate his mission and his message: "There is one God; all men are brothers, love the worst of these." I was driven to make a film that explored what happened during those unknown years of Jesus' life between the approximate ages of 13 and 30. Thus was born *The Rebel Jesus*.

We filmed the picture in Technicolor's new wide-screen system Techniscope. Shooting in Israel was out of the question — not because of the Arab-Israeli conflict or even because of our slim budget of only $170,000, but instead because in modern Judea there are no villages without a forest of television antennas reaching for the signals that flow through the atmosphere. Even at Khirbet Qumran by the Dead Sea, the cradle of Christianity, one finds tour buses, pilgrims, and a snack bar, not to mention the intense below-sea-level temperatures. All these factors and more dictated another location. My Lady Jane and I continued our search. After arranging for film laboratory work at Technicolor in Rome, we booked a jet for an hour's flight across the Mediterranean to Tunisia.

This incredibly backward country in North Africa was a director's dream. The villages and towns some 300 miles south of Tunis and Gafsa are an art director's mother lode. No TV, the sands of the Sahara, camels for $1.00 a day, lush, unspoiled oases with tall singing palms, and government-sponsored luxury hotels and meals at bargain prices. Here is where we would shoot *The Rebel Jesus*. What followed was a surreal, Byzantine dreamscape of sometimes nightmarish activity. I wired my trusty cinematographer, Bob Jessup, to round up a small but dedicated crew. My very few Hollywood actors had already been secured; the rest would be hired locally. Things looked bright and scouting proceeded smoothly — perhaps too smoothly. By now I was no longer naïve in matters of negotiation or bureaucratic whim. So, feeling expansive, we met with SATPEC, the *Société Anonyme Tunisienne de Production et d'Expansion Cinématographique*. This was the government agency that oversaw all filmmaking activities in Tunisia.

The location of our confab couldn't have been more beautiful or serene. It was on the north coast of the Mediterranean in the little town of Sidi Bu Said, not far from the famous Roman city of Carthage. The view across the turquoise sea was breathtaking. Our SATPEC liaison, Hamida ben Amaar, and the committee smiled as strong tea and a tray of assorted goodies were served.

With each request we made to ensure a troublefree shoot, they nodded politely and smiled. "No problem." I was particularly emphatic about the need to clear customs quickly. Again, "No problem." Filmmakers are very wary of this expression — and for good reason. Our equipment, costumes and props, rented out of London and Rome, were in customs at the Tunis Airport for nine days! Only when we parted with *baksheesh* of $1,500 (750 dinar) in American Express checks were we able to load our cameras and lights and gear.

We had not shot a foot of film but we were behind schedule nine days and $5,000 (2500 dinar) in hotel bills and covert payoffs. For a major film company, this would have been a small, expected nuisance, but for a guerrilla filmmaker with a budget of less than $200,000 it was scary.

Because of our enforced stay at the Hotel Africa, our cast and crew had spent much time in the souks and bazaars of the old city of Tunis. They were ready to head south into the Sahara. When the company left Tunis before sun-up, I recalled another caravan departure in Texas. It had been almost 20 years to the day since we ventured into the wilds of the Big Bend National Park to begin *Grubstake*.

The Tunisian desert views and the welcome oases were stunning, and the villages unspoiled. We settled in finally at the village of Nefta, 350 miles south of Tunis in the mystical Sahara. Words are futile when one tries to describe the mystical vibrations that pervade the Sahara. Nothing and no one is hurried. A kind of measured slow motion seems to define the crew and cast. Our camera motors are set and run at 24 frames per second, controlled by

Tunisia offered a fabulous variety of locations, from desert to lush oases.

Jesus at Galilee with disciples.

crystal synchronization, but deep in the desert it seemed suddenly that we were all moving and acting at 48 frames a second. This is not to say that all was turgid and tedious. On the contrary, the phenomenon seemed divinely inspired.

My cast featured Gene Shane, who had been brilliant in *Strawberries Need Rain*, as the Nazarene. As the Centurion who pursues Jeshua Ben Joseph through the desert, the role fell to stalwart and dependable Garth Pillsbury, a member of my permanent stock company. The part of the harlot Mary Magdalene was to be played by Lee Zagon.

My small crew of six was led by my dependable and artistic Robert Jessup, director of photography. His operator was Don Reddy, who was working his first feature. Today he is one of the most sought-after cinematographers for professional feature films. His credits include *Lonesome Dove*, Clint Eastwood's *A Perfect World*, and many other acclaimed successes.

Our Tunisian coproducers weren't exactly forthcoming in laying out the parameters of shooting in this Muslim country. We were well into the first day of shooting when I observed that the Tunisian crew was not partaking of the great feast before us at noon. Then I was informed that the Muslim holiday of Ramadan had just started and the devout would not eat until after sundown! I was baffled, having checked into the possibility of this very conflict as I was planning our schedule. I had been told that Ramadan occurred in the ninth month, and it was now late November. Little did I know that November is the ninth month of the Islamic calendar. Imagine the heat of the Sahara, sparsely spaced oases, and grinding, 14-hour days, with the extras and our cast in their camel-hair cloaks. But there was nary a whimper or complaint. Our company, composed of Anglos, Arabs and Jews, patiently worked and waited for the orange disk to slip into the horizon, bringing the "magic hour."

Then, from out of what seemed a barren Sahara, the "blue people," their faces and hands glowing with the dyes from their cloaks, appeared like ghosts. They carried large pans of steaming couscous, pomegranates and dates and olives sauteed in wild honey. A feast of sweet citrus followed as tambourines and claves echoed on the dunes. The dancers were barefoot but wore layer after layer of clothing.

Our Tunisian liaison explained that these women were known as "savage." Here they would expose only their ankles. Later, with anonymous partners, they would slip under cover of the night to an oasis flooded by the moon. I was reminded of the "boys towns" on the Tex-Mex border. The girls, most of whom were mere children, who came to the mud villages by the Rio Grande were sisters under the skin to these "savages." These young Tunisian girls, these bedouin of the "blue people," also traded their favors for a short while in a mystic oasis to save up for a dowry and return to their village to marry their waiting beaus.

I have shot film in the deserts of West Texas, New and Old Mexico, and now Tunisia. They all have a spiritual kinship. It is written that "man is born of water and he cannot be saved lest he return to it." Puzzling, until we remember that the fossils tell us that most deserts were at one time the floor of large bodies of water.

At precisely the halfway point in our shooting schedule, the point of no return, the trouble began. We were at a large oasis far from our home base, shooting a camel caravan, when in the distance we saw a sleek Mercedes 600 speeding to the location. The car stopped and two aides emerged with folding canvas chairs and a folding table which they set up under the tall date palm trees. They spread linen and from a picnic basket laid out silver and Arab delicacies including cold couscous. A small burner was lit. Then the chauffeur opened the door of the air-conditioned limousine and Monsieur Hamouda ben Halima emerged. Halima was the representative of SATPEC, which made him in effect the film czar of Tunisia. Enjoying the cakes and breads and the tea now hot from the burner, he took a very long time to tell me and my key people that SATPEC was taking charge of the production! We were paying too much for props and other purchases, he explained. By doing so we were disrupting the balance of the local economy. I didn't dare but I almost laughed out loud at Halima. We were paying a dollar a day for each camel! Hollywood would have considered a hundred dollars daily a steal. Halima then told me to sign off on all of our American Express checks, a total of $126,000. He gave me a receipt. Then he informed me that our liaison Hamida ben Amaar would make all the deals and negotiate all accommodations for the company.

With a courteous handshake, Halima turned to the car. The aides loaded the picnic items and the big Mercedes headed back to Tunis, 300-plus miles away. I remember a big red ball of a sun was dropping into the Sahara as the car sped away. The desert night cold seemed somewhat harsher than usual. We were being held hostage by the authorities!

But the arrangement actually seemed to work well, and we wrapped close to the expected finish day. Then we returned to Tunis for the real surprise. Halima's messenger was waiting for us at the Hotel Africa. There would be a meeting that evening. Halima entered late with his entourage. He dispensed with the usual annoying preliminaries. His liaisons, he informed us, had miscalculated the rigors of producing a film. (This was another way of saying they had screwed up.) In fact, he smiled, we owed SATPEC 7,741 dinar. This converted to $15,482!

I protested that they had assumed control of our funds and that we could not be held responsible for their mismanagement. Halima smiled again and reminded us that the authorities had our passports and our return plane tickets to Rome. We could wire for the funds or go to jail. The officials would meet us at breakfast for our decision. Then Halima and his aides were lost in the large lobby of the luxury hotel.

Our little movie company was caught up in a scenario that rivaled *Casablanca.* Humphrey Bogart's trials in that great classic could not hold a candle to our dilemma. Before we left Hollywood, my friend and cowriter Rick Touceda had met me for a farewell dinner, and

The baptism of Jesus.

it was he who planted the *Casablanca* analogy. "I can see it all now. You and some swarthy Arab in a white linen suit. He is smiling and using Mid-Eastern homilies to cover his devious plans to fleece you. I see a ceiling fan turning ever so slowly, zip, zip, zip."

I called upon everything I had learned of guerrilla film tactics but seemed blocked at every turn. Then, praise Allah, the principle of "what goes around comes around" invoked itself.

There she was, approaching me in the Hotel bar, Cécile Decugis. Cécile Decugis is a lovely, redheaded French film editor who had edited, among other pictures, *Claire's Knee* for Eric Rohmer.

Cécile was just finishing cutting a film which had been shot in Tunis. That very afternoon Cécile had come to me with a problem. She was flying back to Paris and had lost her return trip ticket. She had been helpful to me with her French when there was a need for interpretation around the hotel, and I was more than happy to give her the price of the fare to Paris.

Without speaking to me, she snapped her finger to the bar waiter and handed him some francs. Then she grabbed my arm and rushed me to a side exit of the hotel. All the way, in broken English, she explained my precarious situation. I was to be put under house arrest until the affair was settled. She kidded me not. The "chaperons" were already on their way to the Hotel Africa. "Don't hesitate," she urged me, "There is no time." George, my production manager, was waiting in a cab. The American vice consul was a friend of Cécile's, as it happened. "You must get behind the walls of the embassy before you can negotiate this mess," she said. "Phillip will handle everything — just tell him the truth."

By the time our cab got to the embassy, it was already late evening, and Phillip H. Ringdahl, the vice consul, was on the telephone with Hamouda ben Halimah. It was midnight before an agreement was hammered out. But Phillip would not let us leave until the proper signatures were dry on the papers which were covered with an array of impressive bureau-

Mary Magdalene and the madam.

cratic stamps. I remember distinctly, when Halimah signed off, the shadow of a ceiling fan brushed ever so slowly over the negotiating table. Zip, zip, zip.

We returned to Hollywood for the editing and more shooting and finally to the good fortune of working with Alex North. Therein lies an anecdote that I cherish. To fully appreciate the serendipity, we must go back to 1952 and the shooting of Elia Kazan's *Viva Zapata!* with Marlon Brando. The location was Roma, Texas, and "Gadge" Kazan had put me on as an assistant. I had no illusions. He didn't need or want my film experience. What he needed was someone who spoke "Texas" and Spanish but who also had studio experience since the crew was all from New York. Their grunts of "dem" and "dose" were somewhat out of place amongst the lilting rythmns of the local Latinos and soft-spoken Anglos.

Then Alexander North arrived. (Later he would ask his friends to call him simply "Alex," and so his name would appear on his screen credits.) Alex was to compose and conduct the score for the film, which would be his first major credit. He had asked Kazan for permission to visit the set for inspiration, and the director had brought him in for a few days' observation.

Alex was an introspective and gentle artist. He was never at ease with the chaos of a film crew at work and was totally bewildered by the simplicity of the laid-back natives. So I inherited the unofficial job of looking after the shy and soft-spoken composer. We spent many hours talking, mostly about folk music. He was surprised to find I liked, as he did, Kurt Weill's *Down in the Valley*. We even mused over the idea of talking about a film adaptation of it when we got back to New York. Later Alex introduced me to Lotte Lenya, Weill's widow. She was excited by the prospects, but the lawyers, as they are wont, killed the idea.

My acquaintance with Alex would come in handy on *The Rebel Jesus*. By the time my creative partner and collaborator Anthony Houston and I had finished the edit on the film, we were out of money for a score. One day Tony sighed wearily, "What this film needs is a score by Alex North and seventy musicians."

"Then we'll get Alex and the seventy," I answered, only half joking.

Tony's response was predictable. "Stop dreaming and finish your tacos. We don't have enough budget for a zither score." After all, by that time, Alex had 11 Academy Award nominations, his share of Emmys, and a list of works that included *Spartacus, A Streetcar Named Desire*, and many others. But I told Tony about meeting Alex during *Viva Zapata!* and soon set about the task of finding Alex. I discovered serendipitously that he lived with his new wife in Pacific Palisades, the very same upscale community near the beach where my family and I had been living for the last couple of years. I knew Alex did not drive an automobile, so I made an appointment to go to his house a few blocks away. My passion for the project and the subject could not be contained. Never once did we talk of the Nazarene's Jewishness, only his humanity.

Alex asked me to slow down and enjoy my coffee. Then I dropped the bombshell: We had no money! Alex did the most wonderful thing. "Arrange an interlock,* I'll find a driver for me, then we'll see!" He was firm but he was smiling.

I set the interlock screening at Technicolor's biggest room in Hollywood. After all, we had shot the film in Tunisia and Israel in panoramic Techniscope. We were set for ten o'clock. Alex and his driver arrived at ten sharp.

I was flabbergasted when I saw who the driver was. It was a suntanned, smiling, robust, slightly balding Max Youngstein, the United Artists executive who, 20-odd years before, had looked at the screening of *The Cowboy* and made it possible for me to see my work on the big screen at the Victoria Theater in New York.

The picture unfolded. There were a few breaks in the work print, but my guests were professionals and knew how to look at a work in progress.

As the last frame faded, there was an embarrassed quiet. Oh, dear Jesus, I thought, there goes that dream. Max and Alex whispered for a brief moment. Alex, without elaborating, stood with Max. "I'll call you tomorrow morning" was all he said. Yes, I thought, it was that old kiss-off—"Don't call me, I'll call you." Well, I had given it my best.

The next morning, the sweep second hand on the kitchen clock rose to high noon. At precisely twelve o'clock, Alex North called with a plan. It seemed his new wife had recently been a musical contractor in Munich, Germany, and enjoyed a first name professional relationship with the best musicians in that musical city. She missed these old friends, and they all continually asked about Alex, who had endeared himself to them on an assignment there. Christmas was only a few weeks away.

If I could muster up first class air tickets, hotel expenses for the couple, and studio time charges, Alex told me, he was sure the artists would be glad to play the score! Alex had by now become one of the foremost film music composers in Hollywood, and the musical Germans clamored to be a part of this gig. I had to continue the editing, so I placed Alex, Mrs. North, Tony Houston and his new wife Pat Delany on the plane to Munich. They enjoyed the holiday of their lives and brought back a beautiful score played by (you guessed it) seventy musicians. It was one of the wilder events of my career.

The picture won in its class at the Atlanta Film Festival in 1972, but I was not content with this child of mine. A test engagement in Amarillo, Texas, was sold out, but I still was

*For definition, see glossary.

unhappy with the fragmented theme. I continue to work on this personal passion. The ecclesiastic climate is, I believe, slowly inching toward the thesis expressed in the film.

In 1988 I was dismayed by Martin Scorsese's treatment of a somewhat similar topic in *The Last Temptation of Christ*. I even composed a rather frank open letter to Scorsese, which went as follows:

Dear Martin:

Thanks for nothing. It gets worse so let me preface this little missive with my admiration of the work you did in your film *King of Comedy* (1982). I do not buy into the dominant popular vote of *Raging Bull* (1980).

With the release of *The Last Temptation of Christ* (1988), I experienced a second flurry of negative Scorsese fallout. The first was when I lost the directing assignment for *Boxcar Bertha* (1972) to you. I was originally pegged to direct *Bertha* with Roger Corman as producer. It was my thing: rural South, bucolic settings, Depression angst, hillbilly idiom, country music. But your prowess won out and you did an overlay of Bronx-cum-Italia-cum-*Mean Streets* veneer on *Bertha*. It just didn't play. My spies on the crew confirmed your own personal grievance on the shoot.

But these things happen in show business. It goes with the territory. You left for the Arkansas location with my blessing.

No Martin, my disappointment with you — along with millions of filmgoers around the globe — was the shambles you made of *The Last Temptation of Christ*. Critic after critic has enunciated your excessive indulgences therein. Let's not chant the litany here.

It isn't as if I don't understand your need for this personal exorcism. If the puff articles are correct, you were an altar boy in your borough of New York. Although our denominations were alien, we were as youngsters kin. We have both heard the chimes. But we chafed at the disciplines. We heard the call of the wild. We have no quarrel here.

So what is my beef?

Your vision of *The Last Temptation of Christ* has spelled the finish to an ageless exploration on film. Since David Wark Griffith's *Intolerance* (1916) and Cecil B. DeMille's *The Ten Commandments* (1923), until Hugh Hudson's *Chariots of Fire* (1981), daring filmmakers have ventured into the spiritual nature of man and his relation to God.

In 120 vicious minutes, you murdered that genre, certainly for our generation and perhaps for all time. I am not speaking of your not-so-subtly placing the man from Galilee at the end of a line of patrons waiting to couple with a known harlot. I was not even disturbed when you had this master of the spirit making coffins for the crucified.

What saddened me was the moment you decided one bloodletting on the cross was not enough. You had to shoot your "Crucifixion II: Return to Golgotha!" The same overkill that is your trademark slashed away *without mercy* (the very essence of that Master's mission). On the "hill of the skulls," we choked on the blood, dust, and venom when they should have been our salvation. Too, we should have been prepared given that same overkill we witnessed in some otherwise great cinema: *Mean Streets* (1973), *Raging Bull* (1980), and *Taxi Driver* (1975).

Whatever happened to *Alice Doesn't Live Here Anymore* (1974)?

Since your spin on the novel of Nikos Kazantzakis, no filmmaker dares submit an uplifting drama with Biblical origins. *Any* script on the Nazarene is rejected out of hand. The reason given? "Scorsese has cast a long shadow on that kind of film. At least until the Millennium!"

Did the cinema of Jesus die at your Golgotha?

Were you there, Martin?

Cordially,
Larry Buchanan

26. Goodbye, Norma Jean

In 1975 I made a film that remains my box-office champ to date. It was a "career picture," and after its debut at the Cannes Film Festival, I was no longer "Larry who." Good friend Lynn Shubert and I wrote the heartfelt script that told the story of Marilyn Monroe as a young girl trying to make it. The setting was Hollywood in the early forties.

The financing was peanuts again, but I *had* to make this film. My passion for the subject won over an Australian distributor and an American real estate broker. The best they could come up with was $180,000. Bear in mind this was a period picture, with vintage automobiles, period dress and settings, and a cast of 30 speaking parts — and as if all that were not a formidable enough deterrent, we were going to have to "steal" the picture in true Guerrilla fashion. That meant no permits from the city, no releases on extras, no payments to establishments which are photographed in the many sequences, no money for cops and firemen for traffic and pyrotechnic control and very little time for rehearsal and retakes. In short, madness.

I innocently thought that finding our Norma Jean Baker would be a piece of cake, given the many Marilyn look-alikes who prowled the streets of Hollywood and agents' offices. But they turned out to be shamefully superficial and, for the most part, without a shred of histrionic subtlety.

Enter the old standby, the talent contest — in particular a Marilyn Monroe look-alike marathon held at the Hollywood Palladium as a salute to the many fond memories of big band dances during World War II. There were cash prizes for runners-up and a screen test for the winner that would lead to the top role in *Goodbye, Norma Jean*.

Sitting on the judges' panel with me was my friend Andre de Dienes, a professional photographer who was much in demand. Andre and I had renewed our friendship when I was researching Marilyn's young years. No one then or since had a keener emotional connection to the girl than Andre. He was the first to take her on a road shoot that took the couple from the Mojave desert through Las Vegas and Yosemite and up into Portland, Oregon. There they visited Norma Jean's mentally ill mother in a depressing hotel room. Norma Jean's attempt to gain some emotional contact with her mother ended in a shambles.

Andre talked often of this photo shoot and the incidents that filled their days and nights together. Long before their joining in sex, Andre had fallen in love with the ambitious Norma Jean. When finally they shared the same bed, it was bittersweet. Andre knew that when the trip was done, their relationship would terminate. Many times when Andre and I would meet,

Our Marilyn look-alike contest. Lindsay Bloom is fourth from right.

even for coffee or a quick lunch, the talk turned to Norma Jean. His slightly Hungarian-accented voice would soften so that nearby diners would not share what we had to say.

If the pamphleteers and pulpiteers had really cared to know the innermost mystery of Marilyn Monroe, they had only to turn to Andre. But he was largely left out of the hype and puff articles that filled the magazines and inundated us with lies about her.

Andre died in April 1985, but he left us with a most intimate and truthful view of the tragic soul of Marilyn. His photos and his confidences to me of his trip with Norma Jean tell us all we need to know. (I will return to this subject shortly.) I miss Andre de Dienes.

In the Marilyn look-alike contest, Andre and I both liked a beautiful blonde named Lindsay Bloom. She had been a runner-up in both the Miss America and Miss Universe contests. But Lindsay was quite tall and we felt the earliest scenes of Norma Jean in foster homes would not ring true.

Reluctantly, we voted for another blonde who was a page at the ABC television network. We dutifully gave her the prize money and scheduled her screen test the next day. Her reading was impossible. To give her credit, she had warned us that she lacked training.

But the real shock and the deal breaker was when we read the crucial scene at the end of the script. In that scene, Norma Jean has gained entry into a projection booth where, unknown to the executives who are present, she will see her screen test projected. During the scene, the cigar-chomping "suits" make obscene gestures at the screen. In the booth, the

The first day of shooting *Goodbye, Norma Jean*. Playing Norma Jean's war plant buddy is Jean Sarah Frost at left; Misty Rowe is at right.

character of Norma Jean leans against the wall and whispers tearfully but firmly, "That's the last cock I'll ever have to suck!"

Our choice for Norma Jean refused to read the line. My first impulse was to try to reason with the girl with honest explanations of the scene's integrity to the pain and abuse that plagued the young Marilyn, but over her shoulder, I saw Andre shaking his head over the hopelessness of casting this girl. I flashed on the many times Andre must have tried to make some bucolic prude see the artistry of the human body in his nudes. We dismissed the girl and returned to our search for Norma Jean Baker.

We had a start date that could not budge. Even in guerrilla cinema, there are some absolutes. Equipment had been loaned with specific return dates, actors had signed on for open days from other shoots, and Myron's Ballroom, a 1940s-style downtown Los Angeles dance hall, had reserved certain evenings for shooting that could not be moved.

We were tired and downcast. I remember the evening well. Buddy Lynn Shubert, two other members of my team and I slouched into our chairs at our modest office on Cahuenga in Hollywood. Through the window, we were watching the traffic at the red light as the nine-to-fivers rushed home to warm living rooms, understanding spouses, children, and warm dinners.

The light changed and there she was. Norma Jean Baker, in cut-off jeans and high heels, swinging a hat box, was walking toward the office.

In reality her name was Misty Rowe. She read a scene. Although Lynn Shubert and I had written the lines, we were hearing them for the first time! We would have been happy with

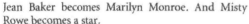

Jean Baker becomes Marilyn Monroe. And Misty Rowe becomes a star.

At the world premiere in Atlanta, my cowriter Lynn Shubert introduces Misty Rowe to the sell-out audience.

Misty purely on the basis of her dead-ringer looks, but here was an intuitive actress reading her heart out. We had found our Norma Jean. Truth to tell, if we had seen every actress in Hollywood, we could not have been more blessed. Out of the Hollywood night, like a *film noir* with Bogey, Misty Rowe jump-started our little picture *Goodbye, Norma Jean.*

Shooting any film is fraught with anguish and setbacks. Shooting any film with no money is a nightmare. But shooting a film with no money and intending to go head-to-head with major works costing ten million plus!—that comes from hunger.

We did it! I won't attempt to tell you how because a film's evolution is fraught with a zillion instinctive changes in people, dialogue, and locations. There are backers to calm, lovers' quarrels to referee and contracts that don't mean what they say. But even today, I remain optimistic because with each disappointment there seems to be a pleasant surprise. For the novice or first-time filmmaker, I would like to recite some anecdotes from the shooting of *Goodbye, Norma Jean.* Some of these were joyous, others chaos. But they point up the need for the beginner to fight tooth and nail for creative control and artistic immunity. In the passion to make a film, reason takes flight.

I was going to start production without a script supervisor (in those days generally called a "script girl") because we simply didn't have the budget for such a luxury. Then one evening, just before we closed the office, a pretty young thing walked in and announced she wanted to be our script girl. I was firm in my resolve to rid myself of this applicant, but she was not easily deterred. In fact, she didn't seem to know the meaning of "no way." She had come down from San Francisco and was green to the picture business. She was stubborn, not deterred by the fact that we had no money for the position. "I'll work for nothing. I can stay at a friend's house and I'll bring my own lunch!" Her tenacity was at once fetching and reasoned. She looked me straight in the eye and asked, "Haven't you ever known that feeling?" That did it. I couldn't let her work for nothing, so I said we might find $75 a week for her. She was thrilled.

No one worked harder than Debra Hill. She showed up early and stayed late, bombarding me and the crew with questions about every move we made. Twenty years later, she is a major player in production. Among other works, she produced *Halloween* and its first sequel, coproduced *The Fisher King* starring Robin Williams, and continues to make successful waves in this cockeyed, competitive business.

1975. On the Croisette at the Cannes Film Festival. How sweet it was. Mark Josem, our Australian "Angel" for the picture, and Misty bask in the Riviera sun. Like Marilyn, Misty was electrifying when she heard a camera shutter.

We shot *Goodbye, Norma Jean* in February 1975. We were into March and cutting the film when our backer and the executive producers decided they wanted to have the film finished and offered at the Cannes Film Festival. Cannes was only seven weeks away! The task was of course impossible. But they seduced me with a promise of a new deal and a new picture and the Moviolas worked overtime. It was 1600 Broadway all over again.

We squeaked in just in time. Exhausted and bleary-eyed, Jane and I settled into our coach seats for the ten-hour flight to the most prestigious film showcase on the globe.

Misty Rowe, we learned, followed on the next plane and was met at the Nice airport by one of our Australian producers. Unknown to her, he instructed the cab driver to deliver Misty's luggage to his suite at the upscale Carleton Hotel on the Croisette. The Carleton is where much of the action is when one goes to Cannes. The establishment saw action of a different kind when Misty learned of the presumptuous act by our producer. Didn't all actresses sleep with their producers? Well, not this one.

Fortunately, against this Goliath, we had two Davids: David Winters and David Blake. Both were friends of Misty and young professionals in film; Winters was a director and Blake a distributor. When I was given a blow-by-blow account of what happened that evening, I was reminded of those popular old live road shows like *Getting Gertie's Garter* and *She Lost It in Campeche.*

Blake, pretending an interest in distributing *Goodbye, Norma Jean*, lured the Aussie down to the Carleton bar for a drink. Winters, with his legendary charm and, I am sure, a promise of a screen test, snookered the maid to let him into the "assignation suite." There, he removed Misty's luggage and left a note purportedly from the management elaborating on France's laws dealing with the abuse of minors.

Our producers, ignorant of the niceties of a first trial or answer print, had arranged for a screening the following night. But they could not take my word for the quality of the print and insisted on looking at the print in a small, shabby room designed for 16mm projection. Light poured onto the screen as the rude Cannes "lookers" popped their heads in the door with curiosity. The short throw of the image produced a disastrous, washed-out image as the timing of the colors and density were set for theater projection. My explanations fell on deaf ears.

The producers panicked and insisted that I cut the film to the juiciest parts and call it a product reel. Jane and I, already reeling from jet lag, went to an ill-equipped cutting room and spent the entire night trimming the print to 40 minutes.

The next night, in the big theater, our product reel unspooled. The throw was long and the carbon arcs in the Projection booth sizzled. I watched from the booth high above the screen. Our Norma Jean, Misty Rowe, smiled, wiggled her behind and walked into the story. The impact was thrilling. Within minutes both of our producers were in the booth praising the look of the film and apologizing, somewhat belatedly. In spite of this and other snafus by our producers, the story has a happy ending.

The first indicator that we had a hit was an invitation from a major player to discuss a healthy advance and a distribution deal. He was Jennings Lang. He was with Universal Pictures and was in Cannes looking for "pickups." Lang had been a central figure in one of Hollywood's juicier sex scandals. Years before, he and forties star Joan Bennett were enjoying a covert relationship. There was one gnawing problem: Bennett was married to Producer Walter Wanger, and he found out about the affair. Enraged, Wanger waited in the bushes near the Lang-Bennett love nest. Placing a bullet into a critical zone between Lang's legs, he put an end to the near-fatal attraction of Jennings and Joan.

Lang arrived at our Aussie's suite on his way to a prestigious screening at the Palais de Festival. He was direct and did not try to hide the fact that he intended to make a deal on our flick. He pulled open his black tie and opened the first button on his dress shirt. He was ready.

Then the two clowns calling themselves producers blew it. Lang suggested an advance of $800,000 or the cost of a negative pickup (an advance for the total production cost of the film), whichever was most, plus all other expenses to date and distribution terms of 30 percent — a generous deal for this modestly priced little picture.

Rising with self-importance, our Australian producer blurted out what he thought was a power move. "Too little. We won't discuss anything less than a million and twenty percent distribution."

I will never forget Jennings Lang's classy response. He quietly buttoned his dress shirt, faced an armoire mirror and neatly tied his black tie, and walked to the door without a word. Jennings was a class act.

Even with the crude exploits of our executive producers, there was no lack of distributor interest in our film. The first person to see its potential was a regional distributor from Cincinnati, Ohio. Later, I felt very comfortable with him and his associates when they flew into Los Angeles for a working dinner. The vino flowed and the pasta was Old World. Terms were agreed to and the excitement was sealed with a handshake. Our new friend flew back to Ohio to complete the details.

Then "Laurel and Hardy" struck again. They were offered a better deal from a New York City source, so instantly it was goodbye Ohio, hello New York. I railed against this unethical turn but was ignored.

The gentleman from Ohio was just that. He didn't blame me but let me off the hook with a remark I will never forget: "Even in this business, sometimes called a whore's Eden, a man's word is his deed. I don't wish to do business with anyone who will break that bond." His name was Robert Rehme. He later moved to Los Angeles where he distinguished himself in every facet of the Hollywood scene. Bob is a past president of the Academy of Motion Picture Arts and Sciences and is held in high esteem by the biggest players in the industry. This unpretentious Midwesterner is now one of the most successful producers in Hollywood. At this writing, he was enjoying the applause of the industry for his *Clear and Present Danger* with Harrison Ford. A vast gulf separates us in prestige, but he is always

After a series of battles over sleazy ad copy and bad titles (first "The Naked Marilyn," then the more passable "The Young Marilyn"), we get a campaign that sells with a modicum of salaciousness. The papers love it.

genuinely friendly when we meet at trade functions such as Show West in Las Vegas or the American Film Mart (AFM) in Los Angeles.

Goodbye, Norma Jean opened in a wide multiple release (i.e., with more than one theater per community showing it) in the Southeastern United States. House records were broken in Columbus and Atlanta, Georgia, and several other cities. We were a hit! I've had losers and I've had hits and hits are better. I know of no euphoria more intoxicating than that which was triggered when I answered the phone in my Atlanta hotel room. "They had to turn 'em away in at least a dozen houses!"

When the film opened in October as a multiple in London, the Brits fell in love with Misty Rowe and we had some more record grosses to enjoy. We opened against *The Outlaw Josey Wales* with Clint Eastwood; its average gross per theater for the first week was $3,970, and ours was $5,034. The second week was *Wales'* $3,678 against our $4,360. The same story prevailed at the other houses in the multiple where we outgrossed *Picnic at Hanging Rock* and *Logan's Run*, among other first-run Hollywood products (see *Weekly Variety*, Oct. 19 and 26, 1975).

While films which cost five, ten, and even fifteen million dollars slip into oblivion after an initial run, *Goodbye, Norma Jean*, can still be found on the shelves at video stores after more than twenty years in distribution. Our cost to make the little gem: $180,000.

By now, the reader will have determined that I remember this film with some degree of pride. But all is not vanity. I truly feel that the billions of words written about Marilyn and Norma Jean fail to get at the essence of this icon, and it was out of this belief that I made *Norma Jean* and a follow-up, *Goodnight, Sweet Marilyn*, about which I will say more later. If you would really yearn to know Norma Jean Baker/Marilyn Monroe, you could spend time with Andre de Dienes, my friend who helped judge our Marilyn look-alike contest. But sadly, Andre died in the spring of 1985.

The next best effort would be to look at the exquisite photographs he shot of her in 1945 when she was only 19. They reveal a young creature in love with whoever is snapping the shutter. When I first saw them in the mid-forties, I wanted to know the photographer, but Andre had moved to New York City where he was enjoying success in commercial photography and portrait work for actors and actresses.

So it wasn't until 1950 that I met him on a still shoot in Central Park. The Thornton agency sent me over to the location without giving the name of the shooter. Our trails crossed then as they would again. Behind on the clock, we worked through lunch and when we finished at sundown, we were both famished. We walked the short distance to Macario's Italian restaurant behind the St. Moritz hotel, Central Park South. After ordering, I led the conversation quickly to the waifish shots he had made of Norma Jean. That was a mere five years before, yet on Manhattan screens she was already playing in *All About Eve* and killing 'em.

"It's been only five years," I said. "She's come a long way."

"Yes, finally, the right makeup, lighting, hair . . ."

"*All About Eve!* Jesus, she walks away with it," I exclaimed.

"Yah, she's no longer tough little Norma Jean."

"Lost her?" I asked.

"Don't misunderstand me," Andre answered, "I'm happy for her now. And once in a while she'll call me — maybe I will shoot a few rolls on her — but the other, in affairs of the heart, five years is a long time. I know what can happen to her."

"Too much too soon?"

"Oh no, no, not that cliché," Andre objected. "She has earned her success; it is long overdue." Andre rarely used contractions such as "She's" or "It's." It was "She has" or "It is" with a pointed emphasis which, along with the Transylvanian accent, gave a kind of purity to his already unquestionable sincerity. He wanted to talk of that other person, Norma Jean. I wanted to hear that.

"The first time I saw her approaching my place, she was stumbling on high heels. She was carrying a hat box. I had some years already as a photographer in Europe and the first impression was that the agency had sent me the wrong person. I had asked for a model who would pose in the nude and be willing to travel. Then she was at my door. Through the curtains I saw her take a deep breath before ringing the bell. She wore a pink sweater and a ribbon to match was tied into her hair. She shook her hands as if to calm her nerves. She even practiced her smile before I turned from the curtains to admit her. 'My name is Norma Jean Baker.'

"Once inside, I made small talk to cover my disappointment. So awkward, naïve, so young. Then her magic began to work on me. I reminded myself that this very innocence, freshness, this unspoiledness was what I wanted in the nudes. Also, with that rinky dinky voice, she had just told me she was married but was getting a divorce. Her husband was in the merchant marine service or something like that.

"Suddenly, she had me captivated with her gushing, trusting voice. With that came the fear that she might not accept the conditions. I could only pay her a hundred dollars a week and I wanted to start on the road right away. There was no negotiation. She accepted, jumping up and down like a twelve-year-old.

"There was no need to have her take her clothes off now. I had developed a sixth sense about a model. I had told my friends I am a camera. I know instantly if this a photogenic subject with style and sex appeal. I was able to really observe her as she relaxed, knowing she had the job. She started walking around my print room. She stopped at my portrait of Ingrid Bergman in a field of ripe wheat. Then there was winsome Dorothy McGuire on a cliff top, her hair blowing in the wind."

I was surprised. I had thought Andre was a just an untried immigrant when he met Norma Jean. "So, you were doing all right?" I interjected. "Bergman? Studio portraits?"

"Yah, but listen. She saw my portrait of Shirley Temple and moved closer as if she had vision problems. They were so much alike — the curls, the child-woman, the giggles. Then, she seemed to be suddenly intimidated by the oversized matted stills. She turned and the giggles were gone.

"She confessed that this would be her first job. Could she ever hope to be a star like those wonderful women on my walls? I reassured her that once she appeared in magazines around the world, she would no longer be scared of anything.

"Even as we piled her things into my Buick, she didn't ask where we were going. I liked that trust. It was December and I pointed the car toward Death Valley and the Mojave Desert. Norma Jean was good at improvising. If we found roadside diners few and far between, she would gnaw on an apple or spoon peanut butter or cottage cheese into her pretty mouth. Then, she would curl up and go to sleep."

"Were your feelings still totally professional?" I asked.

"I had lost that the moment I saw her," Andre replied frankly. "When a photographer and a model work together alone, especially on a location shoot, something happens. Intimacy is very easy. When the job is over, the closeness is over. You shake hands and say goodbye. But with Norma Jean, I knew that could not be the case."

"Say it, Andre, you were in love," I prodded.

"No, that came later. All I wanted then was to hold her in my arms, protect her, explore her, *make* love to her." Andre seemed lost in his reverie. Returning suddenly, he asked, "Where was I?"

"You were heading into the Mojave."

"Because I was thinking of how things would be when we stopped for the night. I wanted to reach Furnace Creek before dark. Then we had a flat tire. While a young fellow from the station worked on the car, Norma Jean and I walked up the highway. It seemed to stretch forever and into infinity. She was wearing jeans and a halter. The skin around her belly button and on her forehead was dotted with beads of sweat. The late crosslight backlit her curls. A half-moon was just starting to rise. I took out one of my cameras. I told her to pretend the long empty road was her highway to the stars. 'Reach,' I said 'reach, for the moon.'

"She reached. Now uninhibited, it was as if she had been waiting for this. She radiated sex. In my viewfinder, some kind of magic was taking place. This was not the nervous girl of nineteen who had rung my doorbell. All the elements of nature seemed to rush to her and do her bidding for the shots I was taking. Tireless, she reached for the moon."

"She was larger than life?" I asked.

"Exactly. Another person. I wanted her. It was dark when we reached the little tourist village in the middle of Death Valley. Trying to appear nonchalant, I asked her if I should ask for one or two rooms. She was not embarrassed or shocked, she just said that she was tired.

She wanted to get a lot of rest. She wanted to look her best the next day. She did. With the first light, I bounced out of my room and ran to wake her up. To my surprise, there she was, dressed and waiting for me. We plunged right in. Alone with the rocks and the cactus, we finished roll after roll of negative. There was nothing she wouldn't try. She skipped, danced, twirled until she fell in the sand laughing. I cradled her head in my lap and toyed with those wonderful curls. Although I was only thirty, she seemed so young and vulnerable now that she trusted me.

"That afternoon we were heading towards Yuma, Arizona, when we had our second blowout of a tire. A weatherbeaten old woman who ran a gas station gave me the kit for patching the tire. I worked with the inner tube while the old girl took Norma Jean into the screened porch for lemonade.

"When they came out, I knew the old witch had been bending Norma Jean's ear. She had found out that Norma Jean's mother lived in Portland and was on her own after a long time in a psychiatric hospital."

"That would be Gladys Baker?"

"The old girl at the gas station said I was crazy, taking pictures in this god-forsaken desert, and that I should take the girl to see her mother. The witch was putting a spell on me. She said there would be 'signs.' I paid her off and we took off for Yuma. There was a sandstorm and many times we could not see the road and found ourselves in knee-deep dunes. Norma Jean sat quietly through it all. She seemed to be somewhere else.

"I turned the car around and we headed north to Portland."

"That must have been at least a thousand miles away," I said, surprised.

"Easy. I drove night and day. We stopped only at special places like Yosemite National Park. The cabins there were near freezing cold. This was an irony after the blistering heat of Death Valley.

"Gladys Baker lived in a dilapidated small hotel in the center of Portland. When we walked into the room, there were no happy exchanges at seeing one another. The reunion was a pitiful failure. Gladys did not want to know anything about me or my relation to her daughter. She seemed ancient and even disturbed at our interrupting her noon nap. Norma Jean unpacked the presents she had brought her. The mother never noticed. There was a long silence. Then Gladys buried her face in her hands and refused to look up. She was obviously a very sick women.

"Driving south from Oregon, I stayed at the wheel until after dark. Concerned, we looked for cabins, fearful that we would be caught in the cold night without a room. Finally, the sight of an old motor lodge brought a sigh of relief. There was one room left. One double bed. Strangely, this did not phase her for a moment.

"The dining room was cozy. Over a good dinner I reassured Norma Jean that she had done all she could for her mother and she should not feel guilty for something beyond her. This seemed to help. Back in the room, we flipped a coin to see who would get the shower first. She began to sing to herself. She ran to the bed, naked and laughing. I couldn't wait to join her. I had waited so long. But it had to be this way."

I guessed at his meaning. "She had to be willing?"

"For such a long time I had imagined what it would be like. But the reality far exceeded my wildest dreams. She had put me to the test with her trust. I had not failed her. Her surrender was mixed with gratitude and respect.

"The cabin fireplace gave out the only light as we discovered each other. Exploring, reaching, clinging, ours was a shared pleasure and excitement. It was as if some pressing guilt had lifted and drifted away like a big balloon. We could not get enough of each other. Then, in the half-light, I noticed tears on her cheek. At first, I was beside myself. What had I done? Then I saw that she was smiling."

The waiter at Macario's stood too close, waiting for us to pay the check. I reached for the tab, but Andre was having none of that. "That's mine. The client will reimburse me," he said.

"You left me somewhere up in Oregon."

"I am sorry. When we got back to Los Angeles, we stopped at Schwab's drugstore [a famous actors' haunt where many were discovered over the decades]. I left her for a moment to write out her check which I knew she needed. When I returned she was talking to a photographer I knew. He wanted her for a shoot and she was cheerfully giving him her telephone number. A chill passed through me.

"I had an assignment here in New York and didn't see her for two weeks. When I returned, I learned she had taken an apartment in Santa Monica. All I had was the address. That evening, I had hardly stepped out of my car when I saw a young man leave the apartment building. I sensed this could be someone she knew. After he had driven away, I knocked on her door. I could hear bare feet running to the door. She opened the door and her face told me everything. She was in a black lace negligee which revealed her young but full body. She had expected the visitor had returned. She let me in, shut the door. The room was untidy, cluttered. Clothing was scattered about and the bed was unmade. Dirty glasses and an empty bottle were on the table." Andre fell silent.

Eventually I broke the silence, gently asking, "Reality time?"

"I was determined not to show my jealousy," Andre said. "She was crying softly. I knew the only solution was to treat the moment lightly. I told her I had no right to expect her to marry someone like me, a vagrant photographer working with beautiful models all day long. She should stay away from sex-mad Hungarians."

"Did she buy it?"

"Hook, line and sinker. I kissed her like a friend. But what I thought was the end was only the beginning. We never were intimate like that night in the cold motor lodge. But every few months, I get a call for a session with her. Sometimes she will call at three in the morning, forgetting the time difference in New York.

"By the way, remember I said I had an engagement?" I nodded. "It is at the Stork Club — she's in town on some kind of promotion. She always asks for me at these crazy things."

Then Andre was off, leaving me with my Cointreau and coffee. We would talk on the telephone from time to time, but I would not see Andre de Dienes again until 25 years later when we were casting for the lead in *Goodbye, Norma Jean*. During our preproduction, we saw each other over lunches at the Shack, a cinemaland hangout near the Technicolor plant. Much of his wisdom and insight found its way into the screenplay. He could talk freely about Marilyn Monroe, but had difficulty when the subject turned to Norma Jean Baker.

I wonder if, when Andre left me that night in New York to go to the Stork Club, he saw my friend Mesquite. It was almost a certainty that Mesquite would have been put on as a bodyguard for Marilyn. I first met Mesquite in the fall of 1951 in New York City. We were both very young actors, both natives of Texas. I was making a film (as actor and assistant director) at the Signal Corps Photographic Center in Astoria, Long Island. One of my jobs was to hire actors as day players in these Army training films.

When I learned this fellow was from my state, I put him on for the day. When I discovered that, like me, he had a real acquaintance with Marilyn Monroe, we became good friends. When Marilyn had promotional junkets to New York City, Mesquite was called in as one of two bodyguards for her stay. Although Mesquite told me that he was bisexual, it was obvious he had a strong attraction to Marilyn.

I had first met Marilyn in 1945 or 1946. I was a contract player at the Fox Studies on Pico Boulevard in West Los Angeles, what is now Century City. She was about to start on her bumpy ride to world stardom. I was not the only actor who was ready to hock his watch in the hope he could date her, but this was not in her game plan and any poor guy, young at that time, who tells you he dated Marilyn is lying.

Strangely, when she learned that I was reared in a Texas orphanage, she suddenly was responsive to me. She couldn't get enough of my stories of being punished with epsom salts and castor oil or of being locked into the "wet-bed" closet for some minor infraction of the harsh rules (usually my questioning a passage of Holy Scripture). Our acquaintance, never close, continued over the years and was usually confined to chance meetings at some studio commissary. With that great smile, there was always a breathless "Hi, Tex."

Back to Mesquite. His driven goal was to get out of Texas as soon as he could leave school. He actually joined a carnival as a "sketch" dancer. When he swirled in a Polynesian grass skirt or as a Parisian "Apache," the yokels on the midway whistled and stomped their approval, giving "her" dollar bills tucked away in cotton candy. When there were enough of these, he made for the Greyhound terminal in Dallas.

In New York, Mesquite had a bartender's license which really kept him alive. He tried hard to be an actor but could only get work on the features that came to New York from Hollywood. I got him work on the film *The Marrying Kind* starring Judy Holliday and Aldo Ray. The director was George Cukor, who liked Mesquite's good looks with more than a professional eye. When Mesquite came to me for advice on how to handle George, I coached him. After all, I had faced the same problem with George. If an actor said the wrong thing to an aggressive, homosexual director, the word spread and the jobs weren't there. I warned Mesquite not to embarrass George, a cultured and proud man, and to tell him, "I'm sorry, Mr. Cukor, but I'm engaged to this girl in Westport." The dodge must have worked because Mesquite worked on many shoots with me in those early years of the fifties: *Kiss of Death*, which introduced Richard Widmark; *On the Waterfront* with Marlon Brando (and Elia Kazan directing); and many others.

He wanted to work on *The Seven Year Itch* with Marilyn and Tom Ewell, but the production manager thought it best he stay in the background as her bodyguard. I was not on the picture in any capacity but was with him on a certain hectic night at 52nd St. and Lexington. Director Billy Wilder made Marilyn walk over a subway heat exhaust again and again to get her white skirt to blow just so. It was probably the only time in her life she wore two pairs of underpants. The evening produced one of the ten most recognized photographs in the history of hype. Mesquite kept watching Marilyn's husband Joe DiMaggio, who in turn watched Marilyn from the circle of spectators. On about the third take, Joe DiMaggio angrily turned and walked to a waiting limousine. Mesquite abruptly shook my hand and ran to protect Joe, saying "Meet you later at P.J.'s." P.J.'s was an actors' hangout. Mesquite helped the fuming Joe into the car and the limo sped away from a cheering crowd.

I left New York shortly after that night for my new job in Dallas at Jamieson Film Co. For the next six years, I saw very little of Mesquite because of our separation in miles. When he paid infrequent visits back to his hometown of Mesquite (about seven miles east of Dallas), I would meet him at Love Field, which was then the Dallas airport, located north of town.

The next to last time I saw Mesquite was in that same airport, Love Field. I was in the cutting room at the studio when my script girl broke in with a whisper that Mesquite was on the phone and that it was important. You could see Love Field from the studio. We were so close that many takes were ruined by aircraft passing overhead in the sixties.

Mesquite would not take no for an answer and insisted I meet him at the airport lounge.

A "friend" was on her way to Juarez, Mexico, for a divorce. The border town was across from El Paso and a popular stop for quick separations. The layover would be two hours, and Mesquite wanted me to have a drink or two with the "party." I was to meet them at the bar.

In January 1961, Texas was still a dry state. You could only get a drink of hard liquor if you were a member of a private club or you knew the bartender. Some sophisticated suburbs voted "wet" under what was known as local option. As a minor celebrity around town and an acquaintance of the barkeep, himself a would-be actor, I had no trouble ordering booze. There were only a couple of "railroad ladies" at the bar. Otherwise, the place was quiet.

Mesquite walked into the bar carrying a large canvas bag and holding the arm of Marilyn Monroe. She wore no makeup and was wearing sunglasses and a scarf around her unkempt hair. Marilyn was resisting the idea of meeting anyone and was turning away when she saw me. "Tex! Buenas días!" The haunted, dour look disappeared and that bright smile glowed.

So this was the "friend." Marilyn was on her way to divorce her husband, playwright Arthur Miller. The bartender turned on a black and white television set. The two hookers had failed to attract any business, so in an otherwise empty airport bar at Dallas' Love Field on January 20, 1961, my friend Mesquite and I sat with a very lonely and disheveled Marilyn Monroe and watched the inauguration of John F. Kennedy as president of the United States.

In less than two years, Marilyn was dead.

I lost track of Mesquite, but the grapevine revealed that he was trying Hollywood again and was in with the "rat pack" made up of Frank Sinatra, Sammy Davis Jr., and Dean Martin. He supported himself bartending, working as a bodyguard, and driving for a limousine company.

The last time I saw Mesquite was in 1975 when I was casting for *Goodbye, Norma Jean.* Mesquite heard about our contest to find our leading lady and called me. I was at a sleazy studio on Cahuenga Blvd. in Hollywood. Everyone but me, tired from the endless search for good actors who would work for scale, had gone home. I met him at a movie hang-out on Cahuenga near the old Technicolor lab. He thumbed through the script quickly to the end and tapped his fingers nervously on the checkered cloth of the table, an old habit. He turned to me. "That ain't the way it was, L.B." He never called me Tex, nor I him. Few Texans do that.

After extracting my firm oath that I would not betray his confidence and put his words in the script, at least for the time being, Mesquite proceeded to tell it "the way it was." I kept my promise, but what he told me that night made me drastically change the script in a matter of hours. I had planned a triology on Monroe: *Goodbye, Norma Jean, Norma Jean Wakes Up Screaming,* and *Goodnight, Sweet Marilyn.*

Mesquite began, "Just days after our meeting in Dallas [January 20, 1961], Marilyn was admitted to the Payne Whitney Psychiatric Clinic in New York City. She was signed in under the name of Miss Faye Miller. When the press penetrated the cover, they were told her problem was exhaustion. But those close to her and I knew it was her mental health — madness if you must. Madness ran on both sides of the family. The worst fear of Marilyn was to wind up like her mother. She had told me that her mother had, with unthinkable cruelty, told her that if Marilyn ever saw her mother in her makeup mirror and strapped in a straitjacket, she was 'going over the edge' to insanity. Just like her mother before her.

"At first they wouldn't allow her a telephone in her room. But when the knock-out drugs could not put her to sleep, she was given a private line out of the hospital room. I was the first person she called. She was sedated and slurred in her speech when she blurted out, 'I saw her!' The person she had seen was her mother in the bathroom mirror of her room. She was in a straitjacket. She repeatedly warned her that 'This is the way you'll wind up.'

"She made me promise again our pledge. She called me her 'pledge buddy, Tex.' Simply, that pledge was that when she could no longer function mentally, I would help her across to what she called 'the Grampian Hills.'" I later mentioned this expression to my friend and co-writer Lynn Shubert, who is better read than I. He informed me that it was an expression used by the great theatrical actor John Barrymore when speaking of death and the hereafter. Lynn sent me scurrying to Gene Fowler's biography of Barrymore, *Goodnight, Sweet Prince*, to find the passage about the Hills. I would later use Fowler's book to suggest the title for *Goodnight, Sweet Marilyn*.

Mesquite continued, "I promised, of course, but only to quiet her pain and tears. You see, I loved her. But never, not once, did I touch her except in affectionate reassurance.

"In July of 1962, she was admitted to Cedars of Lebanon hospital in Los Angeles. There, they performed the last of many abortions. I don't think she ever recovered from that. Her calls to me became incoherent. She told me I was one of a very few friends left now that the megabucks had dried up. Nobody, certainly not George Cukor, expected her to finish the film being directed — or, as I later discovered, misdirected — by the famous 'women's director.'"

Mesquite referred to his notebook. "August fourth, 1962. I was in L.A. still trying to connect in films. I was working barkeep when I got the current issue of *Life* magazine which carried the last of her many cover shots. I called her to express my good wishes on the *Life* cover. She interrupted me in tears. 'He's in town — Malibu. [She was referring to the attorney general, Robert Kennedy.] They're all here. This whole town's crawling with people who want me dead! I was supposed to be picked up by Peter [Lawford] and taken to the party. But they say I'm smashed and stoned. I think he has someone else.'

"Later that night, she called. She could hardly speak the few words. 'Bring something . . . I mean something for the Grampian Hills.'

"I called a friend of mine who worked as a photographer for the L.A. police department. I told him the need. He, in turn, called a friend of his in the coroner's office. Between them they were able to obtain two suppositories loaded with a lethal substance.

"Late that evening, I parked my car a few blocks from 12305 Fifth Helena Drive, in Brentwood. This was the only home she ever bought. I always thought that odd for the orphan who so much wanted a real home. Especially when the chic thing is for a star to have several homes in Aspen, Beverly Hills, and condos on the Big Island.

"I walked in the dark to her door by the pool. She could hardly speak. There were few words. I slipped the suppository into her. I pulled up the covers. Of that I am sure.

"The story given out by the West Los Angeles Police Watch disturbed me. They said they found her dead and naked, stretched out on the bed without bed-clothes and reaching for the phone! When anyone goes out on lethal drugs, they curl involuntarily into the fetal position. They don't lie out like a *Playboy* centerfold."

Mesquite sat silent for a while. Then he let out a long sigh of relief. "Tell it like it was, L.B."

In 1985, a member of my old cinema stock company called from Dallas. He said simply, "Larry, the great god Pan is dead. It was AIDS." He was talking about my friend and his, Mesquite.

The story of Marilyn's torment in the months before her death would be incomplete without an account of her ill-fated final movie project, *Something's Got to Give*. I learned the details of what happened secondhand, but from reliable sources — mostly gaffers, grips, and best boys whom I had known during my tenure as a contract player on the 20th Century–Fox lot seventeen years earlier and who were still there in 1962. All that they told me was confirmed by comic Phil Silvers, who had been signed for the picture. I knew Phil through his then wife Evelyn Patrick, with whom I had worked in New York when she was a top model.

I also confirmed the story through comedian Wally Cox, who likewise had been signed for the picture. I had known Wally from NBC live telecasts we did together.

By 1955, Marilyn was powerful enough to have a list of "approved" directors from which producers of her films would have to select. One of these was George Cukor. They wanted to work together. The first plans were for Cukor to direct *The Prince and the Showgirl*. This idea fell through when her costar, Laurence Olivier, was offered the directing assignment. Cukor was upset because he coveted the idea of directing the two superstars in a proven play by Terence Rattigan, *The Sleeping Prince*; it had even been Cukor's idea to put Marilyn in the title with the addition of the word "showgirl."

Cukor privately fumed but bided his time. In 1960, he was signed to direct Marilyn's 20th Century–Fox "package" picture *Let's Make Love*. Gregory Peck was to be her costar. Without the knowledge of the author of the screenplay, Norman Krasna, Marilyn enticed her Pulitzer Prize winning husband Arthur Miller to work on the shooting script. Peck walked. Others offered the part, including Cary Grant and Charlton Heston, would not undertake the Miller-Krasna romance. Finally, French star Yves Montand was signed. Cukor was not involved in the decision making. The picture was a debacle, Marilyn's most embarrassing starring vehicle. Cukor's grudge was stronger now, and directed against Marilyn.

By the spring of 1962, Marilyn was a physical wreck. Addicted to drugs, sloshed with alcohol, and mentally disturbed, she managed to hide her troubles from the brass at 20th Century–Fox and they opted to star her in *Something's Got to Give* as one of a package of films she owed the company. They signed Dean Martin as costar.

The fan world has been inundated with truths, half-truths, and rumors about the attempts to make this film. I cannot add to that trivia, but I do hope to shed light on Marilyn's emotional state during the filming. Of the 33 days cast and crew were called to work on the picture, Marilyn reported only 12 times. Since these were sporadic, with long periods between, the following commentary refers only to the days on which Marilyn reported.

Marilyn's Day One: All who saw her said that she was radiant and stunning and surrounded by a glow. (Stills and film released later confirm this description.) The studio had built an exact replica of Cukor's estate and swimming pool on the sound stage. While cast and crew applauded her bubbly excitement, Cukor led Marilyn behind the flats and windows that made up the false front. Above them, on the cat walks, a best boy and an electrician listened. "Irene Dunne played a role like this back in 1940," he told her, probably referring to *My Favorite Wife*. "If you want to be taken as seriously as she was, don't start throwing your ass around!"

She flinched. The witnesses to this confrontation did not recognize this Marilyn. This was not the first Marilyn feature on which they had been assigned as crew, but this was not "their girl." Gone were the breathless wisecracks and the toss of the head and ready smile. She was thin, wobbly, drained in face and body. The eyes were glazed and empty as she suffered the attacks of the famed director.

Cukor bored in. "Take off your shoes; let me see the heels." Bewildered, she removed the shoes. He examined the high heels, having been told that her sexy sway when she walked was aided by having the heel of one shoe shortened. This produced the rolling motion that made her behind jiggle. The heels were even, however.

"One more thing," he continued. "Dean Martin was not my choice for this picture but we're stuck with him. He has a natural, shit-kicking, little-boy act that will devour you if you don't listen to me. Understood?" She nodded, trying to hold her shame. "Now, walk out there quietly and businesslike. No more Shirley Temple innocence with big tits!"

Marilyn could not hold her light lunch and threw up in her dressing room, but Cukor did not let up on her that afternoon. She was shaking with fear when she left for the day, and she did not report the next day.

Cukor instructed those closest to him on the crew to keep an eye on Marilyn, even away from the studio. On more than one occasion when one of Cukor's spies was trailing her, Marilyn panicked with the thought that it might be a star-stalker. One "watcher" parked his car under the big trees on her Brentwood street during late hours, reporting her visitors back to Cukor.

Marilyn's Day Two: Cukor did not try to make up for lost time as any other director would have done. Instead, he ordered repeated takes of the simplest move. Between takes he would berate her lack of concentration. Presumably knowing already that the film was a sinking ship, he made sure the record showed that he was trying to get a performance from the shivering woman.

Marilyn's Day Three: Very late reporting, she was scolded by Cukor. She tried to please him but could not get the most inane line right. She kept finding fault with her hair and her wardrobe.

She turned more and more to her controversial coach, Paula Strasberg, the wife of the famed founder of the Actor's Studio in New York. Marilyn had asked to have Paula present at every take, and each time Cukor would call "cut," Marilyn would look at Paula off camera for her reaction. Paula would signal her approval or disapproval, most often the latter. Marilyn would ask for another take. This infuriated Cukor. (Laurence Olivier, directing *The Prince and the Showgirl*, had ordered Strasberg off the set.)

Marilyn's Day Four: A tug of war between Paula Strasberg and George Cukor began with the very ill Marilyn suffering the fallout of venom. Now Cukor began to speak to Marilyn only in a whisper. Sprinkled with obscenities, his instructions were becoming more and more pointed. What he said to Marilyn was generally not heard by the crew or cast, but the substance was remembered by a sound man through a peculiar set of circumstances.

George Cukor was not a technically oriented filmmaker. He didn't know or care to know the difference between a directional or a shotgun microphone, and he would forget that the highly sensitive mike above him and Marilyn was always open. At least two technicians wearing headphones were privy to the covert abuse. Cukor's failure to curb Paula Strasberg was beginning to chafe.

Marilyn's Day Five: Not one shot was in the can before lunch call. A recurring virus sent Marilyn home before the end of the short day.

Marilyn's Day Six: Cukor's whispers to the leading lady brought on a new dread. He had always been known as a "spitter"; that is, when excited he would salivate, spraying spittle into the face of his cast. This tendency is common among actors in heavy drama. In Shakespeare or Ibsen, it seems to go with the territory. I had observed this phenomenon in Cukor when working with him on *The Marrying Kind* in Manhattan. Now, when there was a spitting close encounter with Marilyn, she would wince and insist on a trip to the makeup chair for a touch-up. A few such interruptions and the day was shot.

Marilyn's Day Seven: Marilyn would not start the day until all press, visitors and guests were asked to leave. Producer Henry Weinstein, knowing the film needed all the promotion it could get, was beside himself. He entered the fray. Marilyn now exhibited mounting paranoia.

Marilyn's Days Eight, Nine, and Ten: Weinstein's pressure seemed to bear fruit. Three days in a row she reported to the studio! But it was all a part of her game playing, a set-up to facilitate her own agenda. She flew to New York and the birthday ball for President Kennedy. Peter Lawford introduced her as "the late Marilyn Monroe." She continued her liaison with Kennedy. Weinstein was forced to shut the production down for two days.

Marilyn's Day Eleven: During the two days Marilyn was in New York, director Cukor evaluated the mess he was in. When he watched the news film of her singing "Happy Birthday" to the president, his keen instinct told him that she was only able to stand at the podium those few minutes with the help of uppers. His leading lady was a hopeless addict. On day eleven, Cukor found fault with every move and utterance she made. He told her what little footage he had in the can could not be shown to anyone, it was so laughably and pitifully unusable.

Marilyn's Twelfth Day: June 1, Marilyn's birthday. The set became a birthday party with champagne, cake and caviar. The hilarity was bitter for Cukor because the festivities took over the expensive replica of his own home. Yet he was not a part of it, fuming on the sidelines. When Marilyn did not report to work the next day, she was promptly fired by producer Weinstein after a meeting with top executives at 20th Century–Fox Pictures. She was rehired with plans to finish the film later in the year, but before "later" rolled around, she was dead.

27. Hughes and Harlow: Angels in Hell

The rhythms of cinema finance continued: losers begat dry spells, winners begat multiple offers and interest. And so it was following the success of *Goodbye, Norma Jean*. This time, however, I had decided that I could no longer stomach the pains of working with no money at all. I determined then and there that I would hold out as long as I could to get a budget of at least $250,000. I knew I could deliver a $2 million look for that kind of small change.

I had to say no to a lot of garbage. Most of the potential backers wanted "girls in jeopardy," horror, or mindless "road" pictures. I was holding out for one particular script I was fine-tuning. I had written it for Lindsay Bloom, the classy blonde whom I had had to turn down as the lead in *Goodbye, Norma Jean*. It was titled *Hughes and Harlow: Angels in Hell*. I knew Lindsay would walk right into Jean Harlow's skin.

Finally, an L.A. clothing manufacturer gave me the green light for the picture, but I could not exceed his limit of $240,000. I signed Lindsay as Jean Harlow and Victor Holcheck as Howard Hughes. I wanted the supporting players to ring true, so I called upon old friends who had reiterated that they were ready to return favors for the old days. Royal Dano would play censor czar Will Hayes, and David McLean would be perfect as Howard Hughes' sidekick and troubleshooter. My friend from *A Bullet for Pretty Boy*, Adam Rourke, would play the part of Howard Hawks.

Although the budget was still laughable by major studio standards, for the first time in my career, I was able to hire some very good people on both sides of the camera. The director of photography, for example, was Nicholas Josef von Sternberg, son of Josef von Sternberg of *Blue Angel* fame. Nick and I had teamed before and would again. He is a dedicated craftsman.

Imagine, if you will, being given only four weeks to shoot a 35mm color picture, wardrobe and vehicle period circa 1928, featuring World War I dogfights!

Now imagine that the crew and cast deliver a slick, professional, entertainment only to learn at the invitational screening at MGM Studios that the whole exercise is a tax shelter — a scam! This meant simply that the product of our efforts would be shelved so that the "executive producer" rag man would convert his $240,000 to a four-to-one write-off, essentially earning a net of $720,000 without one play date.

Some consolation came when the UCLA film archives asked for and got a pristine print of the film after they had praised it for its accurate Hollywoodiana. Guerrilla cinema hopefuls at

As Howard Hughes and Jean Harlow, Victor Holchak and Lindsay Bloom prepare for a blue screen special effect of simulated flight.

Lindsay Bloom as Jean Harlow.

UCLA are able to see the film and see what can be done with nothing if the heart and talent are in place.

A major character portrayed in the script was Howard Hawks. By the time we were making the film, Hawks was over 80 years of age and living in Palm Springs. I needed and wanted his approval on the scenes in which he was depicted, and of course I idolized the man who could move me so with his artistic range from *Scarface* to *Only Angels Have Wings*.

"Who's playing Hawks?" he asked when I called him to request a visit. His blunt tone rocked me for a moment. I replied timidly, "Adam Rourke." Lucky for me, he not only knew Adam but had directed him in one of his lean and mean westerns.

"Come on down and bring a pretty lady," he invited. That was easy, so Jane and I drove down for one of the last visits he ever had with a long line of filmmakers and newspeople.

It could have been a wake. Here was the man who had directed material as diverse as *Red River*, *Sergeant York*, *To Have and Have Not*, and *Gentlemen Prefer Blondes*, and he was "unemployed" (his word). But he was vital, impatient, caustic, nostalgic, and animated as he took us back to his early *Barbary Coast* and his classic 1934 *Twentieth Century* with John Barrymore.

He was having none of our pity. He stalked the room by the pool, pitching his current interest. It was an action-adventure tale of a couple of two-fisted oil workers ranging the global oil fields in search of "honest work, loyal buddies, and old-fashioned women." With unerring prophecy, he had set the climax in the oil fields of Kuwait. Hollywood was not listening.

He told me a story about Hughes and Harlow, two mercurial personalities who had long fascinated me. Fellow Texan Hughes had come up from the Lone Star State with Daddy's money determined to pin Hollywood to the mat, along with a multitude of starlets. But Jean Harlow, even though almost penniless at the time, was having none of that.

Hughes, a crack pilot himself, had a script about World War I airplane dogfights titled *Hell's Angels*. Against everyone's advice, he cast the unknown Harlow in the leading female role. Jean wasn't having any of the casting couch trade-off, so Hughes made a bargain. "O.K., Miss Platinum, this is the deal," he told her. "While we're making this picture show, it will be hands off. But if I pull this shenanigan off and make you a star — if it is not a dry hole but a gusher — we'll tie one on that will make Will Hays crap in his long-johns." They pulled it off and fell in love.

After the cast and crew screening party, when I learned the picture was merely an inflated tax write-off, I pleaded with the investors to give the picture a chance in the marketplace and not pocket the tax-shelter scam money. They wouldn't budge.

One of the saddest days of my life was when I faced those guys and gals who had gone beyond the pale making a heartfelt film. I had to tell them there was no way I could promise any more work soon. I must confess that I choked up a bit when their spokesman rose and announced, "We're ready when you are, L.B."

The line was an old industry joke, and it brought the house down with laughter. The story behind it is worth recounting. In 1923 Cecil B. DeMille was directing his silent biblical epic *The Ten Commandments* near the little town of Guadalupe, 150 miles north of Hollywood. Thousands of chariots, horses, archers and swordsmen were waiting for the order to surge across the sand dunes for a climactic assault. Three cameramen were placed at strategic positions to fully record the action. One of these was some distance from the camp. DeMille raised his bullhorn and bellowed "Action." The hordes swept across the dunes, chariots upturning, horses falling, warriors rolling down the hot sand. It was a one-time shot, and all and sundry wanted to do their best for this moment in movie history.

Just as Pharaoh's armies stormed the gates of the city, DeMille called "Cut!" with a satisfied shout. He turned to speak to the crews.

"Camera A?"

"I'm sorry, sir, our tripod was kicked over by a falling horse."

"Camera B?"

"Our camera jammed before they topped the dunes."

DeMille, glowering and turning beet red, raised his bullhorn to shout at the distant third cameraman.

"Camera C?"

"Ready when you are, C.B.!"

28. Mistress of the Apes

Jane and I traveled extensively after the disappointment of *Hughes and Harlow*, taking a sort of reflective hiatus. Prior to this current dry run, we had confined our trips mostly to the festivals and markets such as Cannes and Milan's MIFED, and domestic destinations. Now we made short trips to Egypt and other exotic stops. For the first time, we took our rented cars into the smaller towns. We especially liked the Luberon area of France, the white hilltop villages of Spain and the old houses of Tuscany in Italy.

I know of no real filmmaker who can travel for long without thinking of a new story possibility or longing for the cutting room. So when John Rickert, an old buddy from the Dallas days, now a distributor, caught up with us in London, I listened. He wanted to know if I had a modest outdoor story that could be done quickly and be ready for Cannes by May 1981. This was January. Sometimes you do a flick just for the hell of it. Putting to celluloid a fanciful idea that the majors would never touch is in itself intriguing.

I told my friend that in my trunk I had a treatment he might like. I had long been fascinated with the female animal behaviorists who had spent months, years, even lives studying the primates in Kenya and the Delta of Africa. Their dedication and fearless spirit would intrigue any storyteller.

"Whaddaya call it?"

"Mistress of the Apes."

Rickert was hooked. "When can you start, and can it be done for less than a hundred thousand?"

Of course I could not do it for a hundred thousand, especially with the trip to Africa. But Rickert slayed me with the oldest chestnut in Hollywood history, one used when the backer will not take no for an answer.

"A rock's a rock, a tree's a tree," said Rickert. "Shoot it in Malibu State Park!"

When he has been too long away from his love and the unopened bills are starting to fall into the wastebasket, a filmmaker's imagination goes into overdrive. Suddenly, Malibu State Park looks remarkably like the African veld. Are those not drums that echo off the limestone cliffs? The prop house people say they can dress the show for a couple thousand bucks. "Hell, we've got stuff left over from *Trader Horn*—the original." And, lo and behold, you've got an outstanding credit at Western Costume!

I called every one of my stock company, cast and crew, who were facing mortgage payments or expecting babies and who might be reeling from the work drought. Not one of them

The final ad for *Mistress of the Apes*, with Boris Vallejo's art.

passed. But the first call produced one question: "Are you using Jenny Lee for the catering?" We were, and that locked them in. From then on I opened my telephone call by announcing that we would have Jenny Lee feeding the company. She was a hard-driving dynamo who worked alone out of an ancient station wagon. She always had beef and chicken for the big guys and vegetarian dishes that appealed more to the ladies and the New Age forward thinkers. But everybody liked her peach cobbler.

In *Mistress of the Apes*, I was able to see another of my instincts pay off. We could take a minimal approach to cast and props, but our apes had to be perfect or they would be unintentionally comic. I called one of the most respected special effects creators in the business. He was tied up but was very quick to tell me he might be able to help. In his work on *Planet of the Apes* (which was also shot in Malibu State Park) he had a new assistant who in his judgment was "destined to be one of the best in film. He's available now but not for long. Grab him, here's his number." Feeling slightly shafted, I called the number for Greg Cannom.

Greg came aboard, and his primates were terrific. I knew I was seeing excellence in make-believe. After many other accomplishments, Greg Cannom won the Academy Award for special makeup in Francis Ford Coppola's *Bram Stoker's Dracula* and picked up another Oscar for his makeup job on Robin Williams in *Ms. Doubtfire*.

The film had a catchy blurb before we even got started: "She found fulfillment in the jungle . . . with the ape that walked like a man." John Rickert and I even coaxed a very sexy piece of poster art out of Boris Vallejo, the cult artist who had been doing sword and sorcery bodies for calendars and magazines for years. We approached him timidly, since there was no budget for a big-name talent, but he was delighted to do what we needed. He had always wanted to do a movie poster, but no one had asked!

I consider *Mistress* the perfect success model for what is known as a sexploitation film. This genre of movie has always been there (*King Kong, Poor White Trash, She!*), is with us now, albeit in pretentious multi-million-dollar extravagance (*Basic Instinct, Showgirls, Interview with the Vampire*) and will be with us as long as images bombard us from theater screens, TV and CD-ROMs. I offer a synopsis of *Mistress of the Apes* as a perfect example of erotic promise and imagination overcoming nonexistent budget dollars.

In the "civilized" jungle called New York City, Susan Jamieson, wife of a famous anthropologist, is rushed to the hospital in the wee hours of the morning with labor pains. While a tired surgeon tries to deliver the premature baby, a trio of acid heads enters the dark hospital to raid the drug reserves. Their assault on the delivery room causes the baby to be stillborn. Hardly has Susan recovered from this traumatic incident when she learns of the disappearance of her husband in the equatorial rainforests of central Africa.

David Thurston, publisher of a popular hunting magazine that appeals to gun lovers, has been hungry for Susan's body for several years. He agrees to sponsor the safari to Africa, much to the chagrin of his wife Laura. So David the macho gun lover, Laura his jealous wife, Susan the ethologist, and Paul Cory, the handsome guide-ecologist and writer for the magazine, make a long flight to Africa and the strangest adventure any one of them has ever known.

West of Bukavu, the party meets Matheson, a dealer in safari bearers (natives hired to carry equipment and supplies) and poacher's booty. We learn in a whispered scene that David has paid Matheson to do away with Susan's husband, hoping that will leave Susan to him.

Paul tries to hire from Matheson some bearers for the trip in the rain forests, but the men are afraid of "the ape that walks like a man." The lovely Bantu maidens have no such fears, and it is left for them to carry the portage. While the party sleeps, Matheson finds his

On the set of *Mistress of the Apes*.

poacher cronies Brady and Pullman and orders them to follow the party at a distance as he feels something profitable will come of it.

Deep in the forests, after confrontations with the poachers and wild animals, the members of the party realize they are being watched. Several incidents occur which confirm that they are dealing not with natives or primates, but with *Homo habilis*, the so-called missing link! The sightings and sounds of the "near men" take a toll on the four. David makes strong overtures to Susan, who rejects him and seeks out her kindred spirit Paul. Laura, jealous of Susan, finds sympathy in Paul.

In a sighting of the "near men," trigger-happy David shoots the only female of the troop, bringing on the wrath of Susan. She responds to this by searching out the "near men" and finding the gorge where they live. She breast-feeds the only infant in the troop, left motherless by David's rifle. This act is watched by the "near men," and they slowly creep down to examine the strange biped.

Thus begins our three-way progression of Susan living with and imitating the "near men," the drunken David back at camp abusing Laura who seeks comfort from Paul, and the poachers trying to find Susan and the "near men." David, now lashing out at anyone and anything in his rage, is caught in one of the poachers' traps, which pulls him up into the air. When the "near men" find him and his gun, they explore the magic club and wind up firing it several times into his body. Back at camp, Paul has become the prisoner of Pullman, the demented poacher. To save Paul, Laura kills the poacher and falls into the arms of Paul, realizing her first unselfish feelings in many years.

At the camp of the "near men," Susan realizes she is truly assimilated into the troop when the two dominant males fight over her and one is killed. She now dedicates her life to educating the "near men" in the acts of affection and communication. She intended to return to her world but now finds herself pregnant. She makes her choice and returns to the small colony of "near men" to devote herself to their welfare.

What made *Mistress of the Apes* work? Great African vistas? No, we shot in Malibu State Park. Thousands of extras? Our cast was four principals and a trickle of extras. Exotic animals? The closest we had were actors in six *Homo habilis* makeup masterfully created by Gregg Cannom.

Sometimes less is more. I choose to believe that somewhere in the collective consciousness all is kindred. All works for all. When we crawled out of the Olduvai Gorge in Africa, one branch of what would become humans went one way, another branch a different way. One, in a rapid leap of 5 million years, is now sipping cappucino and building an electronic highway. Another, in an arrested form of development, is stared at by children in zoos as it stalks its short exercise run in bewilderment.

King Kong threatens us all, then gently puts Fay Wray down with a light caress. Frankenstein's monster terrorizes a village, then softens long enough to lead a lost girl back home. Why is it only children fathom the real meaning of *Beauty and the Beast*?

The producer of *Mistress of the Apes*, John Rickert, is a wise veteran with a keen "take" on audience shifts. He went for a limited run of theater playdates, playing the flagship drive-ins at a loss just to establish audience appetite, then went straight to video cassettes. This was not because of waning response, but the handwriting was on the wall for the drive-ins. Today it's hard to find one standing, and the few that remain are no longer showing sleazy exploitation pictures. For the major studios have upped the ante to tens of millions for what is essentially a skin flick.

29. *The Loch Ness Horror*

By 1982 I thought it was time for a family picture — that is, a film of, by, with, and for the Buchanan clan.

Jane and I, in our footloose period, had enjoyed a stay at the Buchanan Arms in Scotland. Using this as our base, we combed the countryside looking at castles, ruined and otherwise. Our stop at Loch Ness was blessed with unusually warm weather and late spring flowers. Even so, the natives warmed their hands by the wood fires at the bed and breakfast, hypnotizing us with their fanciful yarns of the monster in the loch. There is something mystical about this part of Scotland, and we were hooked. Over a ploughman's lunch, Jane and I hatched a plot.

Why not? A film with the right amount of mood and monster could certainly pass as a worthwhile effort. It would be intended for a family audience and produced solely by our family.

Of course, we could not take cast and crew to Scotland. But, not to worry, I knew just the place. Lake Tahoe is the perfect stand-in for Loch Ness. Its waters are dark and deep. It even has a castle or sorts, Vikingsholm Castle.

Jane would be the producer; I would write the script and direct only. The lead would be our son Barry. A real Scottish lass, Miki McKenzie, would be the love interest. Our daughter Dee would have the part of another village lass, and our two younger sons would work on the technical side. They were already doing crew work for independent producers in Hollywood.

It was an enchanting adventure. This is not to say, however, that we didn't have some close calls with the underwater work and a mechanical Nessie who sometimes balked. We couldn't wait to roll out of the bunkhouse and walk 20 yards to our lakeside "studio."

Playing the Scottish professor was Sandy Kenyon, a friend from as far back as my days in New York. He regaled us all at the long dinners by the fire with his stories from a long career in film and on Broadway. You might remember him as General Stillwell in the film MacArthur with Gregory Peck, or for his costarring role in the series *F Troop*. We had worked together in New York in both film and theatre.

There is a nostalgic whimsy about this film. Working closely with my own and watching them go about their duties (very well, I might add), I realized how much I had been away from them when they were growing up in Dallas and later Los Angeles. I had to remind myself once in a while to mellow out and let them be.

The umbilical cord leading to Nessie could order her to breathe smoke, roll her eyes, surface, submerge, or emit a savage scream. Sometimes the signals got mixed up.

The *Loch Ness Horror* experience was, I think, their gift to me. Now I was on the receiving end of "film as therapy." Watching my three sons and their sister go about their defined duties with zest, totally ignoring me, was an eye-opening journey. In those fleeting weeks they had gone from dependency to adulthood. It was as if they all were saying, "Look, Dad, do your thing. We're ready to do ours — so, not to worry." I am now convinced that this phenomenon must take place in any family for the unit to survive an amiable emptying of the nest.

30. *Down on Us* (a.k.a. *Beyond the Doors*)

I've been called a lot of things. Some ("joke," "minimalist," "plagiarist," "sleazoid," "con-man") were so diminishing that if true, they would drive any rational person to a life in hermitage. Others ("seminal," "genius," "pioneer," "gifted") were embarrassing and overly complimentary.

But the one moniker that baffles me is "conspiratorial theorist." This label was Velcroed to me after my partner Harold Hoffman and I produced *The Trial of Lee Harvey Oswald*. A pivotal sequence in the film is known as the "LBJ ducked" sequence. Carefully researched and documented, it revealed that exactly two seconds *before* the first shot was fired from the Texas School Book Depository, Vice President Lyndon Baines Johnson dropped to the floor of his limousine which followed that of President John Kennedy! The pretense was that he was recovering his Stetson hat which had somehow fallen into the tonneau.

I have recounted earlier that I was at Lake Texoma working with my partner when the terrible chain of events began in the assassination. But Ralph Johnson, one of my cameramen, was working as what was called an IA pickup to help cover the motorcade for one of the networks. Ralph was using a Bell and Howell Eyemo 35mm camera with its 100 ft. load as he focused on the vice president. This was the modus operandi in this kind of coverage. The IATSE (International Alliance of Theatrical and Stage Employees) first-stringers for the networks, such as Jim Davidson, would cover the primary story (Kennedy in this case), and IA pickups, most of whom were non-union itinerants, would cover the "color" or background. These background shots were used for cutaways to enhance the piece and aid with the editorial continuity. (For the record, the very able Jim Davidson would later be the cameraman to shoot *The Trial of Lee Harvey Oswald, Under Age,* and *Sam,* the western with Jody McCrea.)

When Ralph Johnson saw LBJ duck into the tonneau of the limo, his instinctive camera eye knew the cut was over, and he pan-tilted to pick up the president's limo as it made the turn toward the fabled underpass. In the upper right of his frame, scored on the ground glass of the finder, was the ugly brick building housing the school-book inventory for the state of Texas.

After the pandemonium of the next few minutes, Ralph headed for his old yellow Buick convertible two blocks away on Elm St. He expected to find a parking ticket because he had failed to place his press flyer on the dashboard. Because he was running and carrying a strange object, he was stopped by a plain clothes agent, presumably of the FBI or Secret Service. The camera, with its long focal lens, looked much like a gun. The agent wanted to know where he was running so fast, away from the center of the turmoil. Ralph explained that he was hurrying to the laboratory to process film. The lab was my old professional home, Jamieson Film. The interrogator knew of the lab and tested Ralph by asking the address. Ralph quickly responded, "3800 Bryan St." Jamieson Film Lab was then the only facility in Texas which could process 35 mm black and white motion picture film. Ralph was released after giving his ID and address to the agent.

When the negative came out of the soup, Ralph took it to the tiny screening room. No print was made. Rather, an old practice of newsreel cameramen was employed. In the interest of speed in getting stories to the theaters, newsreel operators would risk scratching the original negative by screening it before they made a work print. Then the best takes would be properly timed and printed for the cutters.

Jamieson Labs had an ancient 35mm Simplex projector. Ralph had just threaded the film into the machine when two suited men with pins on their lapels entered the dark room and confiscated the negative film. Ralph told me that they could not possibly have been local feds as their suits were of heavy, dark wool and the Dallas weather that day was almost springlike. Also, Ralph was familiar with most of the federal types who were locally based.

Neither Ralph nor I ever saw the film, and I cannot vouch for what Ralph saw in his finder. But like others in Dallas who knew Ralph, I can vouch for his honesty and ethicality. He joined a long list of pertinent witnesses to that day's drama who were never called by the Warren Commission to testify. Ralph died an untimely death of what was then called in Texas "black cancer."

If *The Trial of Lee Harvey Oswald* first got me branded as a conspiratorial theorist, it was not the last film to do so. For really salacious conspiracy, one need only follow my 1984 endeavor, a triple-threat rock drama variously titled *Down on Us, Beyond the Doors, The Beat Goes On*, and *Who Killed Rock and Roll?* The film actually began in 1970 at a Janis Joplin concert in Lewisville, Texas, a small town north of Dallas on big Lake Dallas. I had never heard "the Pearl" live, and I was floored by my fellow Texan.

Some of my regular crew people had been retained to cover the alfresco event for a possible documentary, so I was able to watch from behind the makeshift stage. After the show I began to follow Joplin's career as well as that of Jimi Hendrix and Jim Morrison.

All three of these artists died at the age of 27 in a period of just one year.

All three were threats to the re-election of Richard M. Nixon to the presidency. They were pied pipers to the young voters, and the voting age had been dropped to 18. This new block of voters alone could make the difference at the polls in trying to stop the devious accident that was Nixon from returning to the Oval Office.

Anyone who knew Janis Joplin would chill at the suggestion that she would overdose at this time in her career. She had just announced an upcoming marriage about which she was girlishly excited. She had just finished a new album which included lyrics and music which really had her turned on.

The same goes for Jim Morrison. Certainly he was always scary and on a razor's edge, but that was just Jim. All he was determined to do was to drop out — certainly not to kill himself with booze and hard drugs.

And Jimi Hendrix? Only now, more than a decade after the revelations of *Down on Us*, is the unvarnished truth of his "overdose" being exposed for the murder it was. Just as Morrison had Paris by the proverbial tail, Jimi Hendrix was the darling of London. Here was the

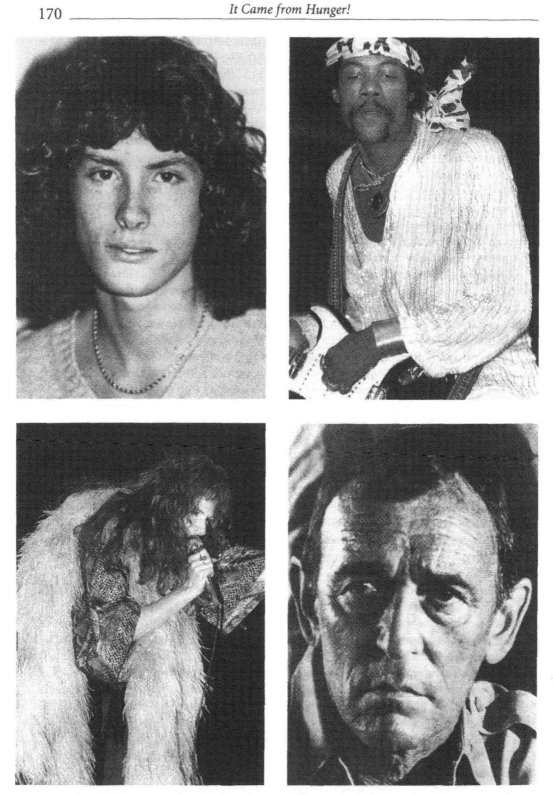

The stars of *Down on Us*: Bryan Wolf as Jim Morrison (*top left*); Gregory Allen Chatman as Jimi Hendrix (*top right*); Riba Meryl as Janis Joplin (*bottom left*); and Sandy Kenyon as the Assassin (*bottom right*).

hippest, most sought-after rock star on the globe dead of what was being called an overdose! I found this scenario impossible to believe.

As George Bernard Shaw said, "Assassination is the sincerest form of flattery." And that, dear reader, is the reason I made the rock drama *Down on Us.*

Permissions to use the hits recorded by the three icons of rock were far more expensive than my budget would allow. So there was the first heavy responsibility: music. Such an obstacle would have been a sobering challenge if there had been only one subject, and we had three. The solution we arrived at was to hire three composers, each with a special affinity for one of the artists, to create new songs in the characteristic styles of Jimi, Janis, and Jim.

Rock guitarist-composer Dave Shorey had the unenviable job of arranging "The Star Spangled Banner" for our actor portraying Hendrix. Imagine being instructed to "make it sound like Jimi, but you can't be too close to Jimi's version as that would be copyright infringement." Of course the national anthem itself had long been in the public domain, but the famous Hendrix version was another matter. The final take on the difficult song was eerie as actor Gregory Chatman, a convincing double for Jimi, mimicked the playback.

We arranged a sneak preview of *Down on Us* in Austin, Texas. The house was the Dobie Twin just off the University of Texas campus. This was to be a genuine sneak preview and I was in town to observe. But the leading Austin paper got wind of the secret playdate. On the day of our test showing, the *Chronicle* carried a "preview" by someone with the initials L.B. (very definitely *not* yours truly) which began, "There is no easy way to deal with filmmaker Larry Buchanan, a cinema talent who, over the years, has turned out some of the most minimalistically weird horror/science fiction films around, including *Mars Needs Women* and *Zontar, the Thing from Venus.*" After characterizing my films as gleefully abandoning "any attempts at linear structure or narrative sense," the piece concluded, "Regardless of its quality, this should be an extraordinary film and an outstanding cultural event. Here at the *Chronicle*, some of us wouldn't miss it for the world."

I had not planned to speak at the screening, so I sat in the rear of the theater where I could make a discreet exit if things didn't go well. I would sign freebies (one sheets) in the lobby. I worried that I had brought too many.

I needn't have worried. The demographics of the patrons arriving would be of interest to any sociologist, or at least to anyone doing a thesis on pop music and rock 'n' roll's impact on the youth culture. The largest group in the audience was University of Texas students, then there were men and women in their late thirties and forties. There was virtually no one in the 25 to 35 age bracket and only a sprinkling of both genders 60 and older. In other words, the attraction was important to the young seeking higher learning and to those who were very young when Joplin, Morrison, and Hendrix ruled the rock 'n' roll airwaves. Those 60 and over couldn't care less about my movie and did not stop to pick up their autographed posters. As I walked into the lobby after the lights came up, I was recognized by a film buff who was part of the university's film studies group. When others saw me signing his little notebook, I was caught up in questions about the "three J's," Morrison, Joplin, and Hendrix. Others, more interested in political science, wanted to talk about Richard M. Nixon and the dirty linen of Washington. Clear-headed, crisp, and aggressive, they did not for a moment doubt what they had just seen on the screen. There were no accusations of "paranoid conspiracy theories" and no demands for documentation. Their loss of innocence about public service was complete. Were they able to recover from Watergate? Do they still call the radio stations and request Joplin's "Down on Me" or Hendrix's "Star Spangled Banner" or Morrison's "Light My Fire"?

Down on Us did a respectable business that week but was not held over. The distributor opined that we should go directly to the new venue of video cassettes. I thought we might have a loser for a while but reminded myself that this was only a sneak preview without any promotion or preopening hype. The modest returns continued, so we temporarily shelved the picture. Recently there has been a stirring of interest in the three rock stars portrayed in *Down on Us*, with filmmaker Oliver Stone and others beginning to mine the rich fields of rock music, and there has been a noticeable change in the video orders. It seems that, along with Elvis, Morrison, Janis, and Jimi are Alive!

31. Goodnight, Sweet Marilyn

Although *Goodbye, Norma Jean* was still in the marketplace via videocassette 13 years after its release, I was haunted by it. Not by what was in the picture, but by what was left out.

In 1975, the final shooting script of *Goodbye, Norma Jean* told the truth of Marilyn Monroe's death. But my backers, both the Australians and the Americans, were running scared. As I have already indicated, they were not known for their savvy or even their artistic responsibility in matters of story content. In the end I could not convince them to film the true story.

I even tried to make it a game for them. I posed the query, "How did Marilyn Monroe die? I'll give you clues. It was not murder. It was not suicide. It was not an accident. It was not natural causes." I offered another clue: "On August 5, 1962, at 10:30 A.M., Thomas Noguchi, deputy coroner for Los Angeles County, conducted the autopsy on the dead Marilyn. It took five hours. Noguchi noted there was [no] trace of barbiturates in Marilyn's stomach or digestive tract." I explained to the backers that the coroner had been wrong and had admitted as much years after the sloppy investigation of Marilyn's death. Small amounts of various barbiturates were found, but not enough to kill her.

I explained the act of mercy that had taken place when Mesquite fulfilled his pledge to Marilyn by administering a suppository loaded with strychnine. I wanted to tell his story, but my timid associates were having

A flyer for *Goodnight, Sweet Marilyn.*

173

none of it. Then, ten years after the release of *Goodbye, Norma Jean*, Coroner Noguchi and others went public and confessed that the only explanation of Marilyn's death was by anal injection of a lethal suppository. So much for backers making esthetic judgments.

Now, in 1988, I could tell the story of Mesquite, his long love for the superstar and his sworn pledge to help her over when the mind was gone. I negotiated the right to use some of the *Goodbye, Norma Jean* scenes to lead into the new story, but I needed an older Marilyn for the crucial night of the death. We found her in Paula Lane, a professional Marilyn impersonator. Paula was a dream to work with, but eerie to watch. She, like some who portray Elvis, had *become* Marilyn. The voice, the breathlessness, and the face all became scary to behold as we worked toward the final whisper from the sex symbol being portrayed.

From the beginning, we believed that our market would be primarily home video. And that was where the film did its business. As of this writing, *Goodnight, Sweet Marilyn* is still on the video shelves.

32. *Works in Progress*

At this writing *Goodnight, Sweet Marilyn* is my most recent completed film, but there are several projects either in the works or on the back burner for possible future production. Here's a rundown:

The Eighth Day. From the novel by Robert Goldstone. An ensemble piece. Seven pilgrims, from different walks of life, come to a mountain monastery in the remote Luberon region of France seeking healing of various kinds. One of them is a homicidal maniac. Before the seven can see the famous monk for healing, he dies and the killer takes his place.

Mars Needs Women 2: Heavenly Bodies. A sequel to my original from 1966. This sci-fi action drama takes place on a colonized and terraformed planet Mars. As has been the custom for any remote frontier colony in history (Australian, America, Alaska, or any other I know of), volunteers are shuttled to the Red Planet as potential mates for the male scientists, pilots, and teamsters who are there in advance. The Love Shuttle, on its run from debarkation at the main colony, is swallowed up in a Marsquake. The multinational colony of young men (Russian, Japanese, Nordics, Americans) join in a race against death to save the valuable cargo.

The Torture Garden. From the novel by Octave Mirbeau, author of *Diary of a Chambermaid*.

An Officer of Color. The story of Lt. Henry Ossian Flipper, first black graduate of West Point. Details his success as the only black officer on the frontier in the 1880s, his serving as a role model for the "buffalo soldiers," and his trumped-up court-martial.

Jimmie the Kid. The life and times of the "Blue Yodler," Jimmie Rodgers. He was the father of country music.

Paso por Aquí. by Eugene Rhodes. Arguably the best western short story ever written.

Wake of the Bounty. In spite of many Hollywood treatments of the *Bounty* mutiny, the best part of the great event has never been told — namely the mystery of what happened on Pitcairn Island.

Norma Jean Wakes Up Screaming. My friend Andre de Dienes, one of the great photographers of the female form, and his love story with the young Marilyn Monroe finally revealed. This would be the last film in my trilogy on Marilyn.

Great Expectations Crushed

The most telling indicator of the dearth of imagination of the major studios and their in-house producers is in their failure to adapt classic older published properties. I speak of novels they sit on which were bought years, even decades, before as well as exciting current novels which they have no knowledge of until some independent soul tries to secure the rights, thus exposing the possibilities. The following are some of the projects I wish I could have undertaken, and the stories of why I couldn't.

McCabe (by Edmund Naughton, Macmillan, 1959).

In the summer of 1964, partner Harold Hoffman and I were still on cloud nine from the success of *Free, White and 21* and *The Trial of Lee Harvey Oswald*. Looking to break out of the confines of studio sets and stuffy sound stages, we began a search for a simple but honest western. We found it in a thin, undersized hardback book called *McCabe*. The publisher gave us the author's agent in New York, who in turn gave us the name and background of the writer.

He was an American who was working in France for the Paris edition of news giant *The Herald Tribune*. After making a flurry of calls and paying a reasonable number of dollars, we had an option to buy the film rights to this minor classic. We were jubilant. From the beginning, we saw one actor who fit the lead like an old glove, Robert Taylor. Bob had fallen somewhat from his lofty reign at MGM but was still in good shape and remembered by many fans. This fall from grace was the very quality that made him a metaphoric match for the once revered *McCabe*. Bob was now long divorced from Barbara Stanwyck and was living with his new wife, gracious and lovely Ursula Thiess, on their ranch well up into Manderville Canyon in Brentwood, California. We pondered and paced. How could we get him?

Enter Lady Luck. My Jane's twin sister Jean and her family lived on Manderville just a mile from the Taylor spread! We commissioned a Dallas artist to do a portrait of Taylor as McCabe. Then we shipped the painting and the only copy of the book we had to Jean, who in turn was to hand deliver the package to Bob. We waited anxiously. Luck was indeed a lady. It turned out that Taylor, along with William Holden, had a financial interest in the classical music radio station in Dallas, KVIL. The principal owner of the station was one of our biggest potential backers, Lee Seigel. We got a phone call from Robert Taylor. "What if Ursula and I came down to Big D as Lee's guest for a couple of days — could we all chew the fat over this book?" Could we!

Bob and Ursula turned out to be two of the most fun-loving, considerate, accessible "movie-people" I have known in 50 years in show business. His laugh bounced off the walls as he called up yarn after yarn from his career in films. Could this be the same lover who held the dying Camille in his arms? In what was surely Garbo's best performance, she met her match in the incredibly handsome Robert Taylor. And that great voice of his, made husky by his chain smoking, filled the room too as he talked of his favorite role.

Bob had brought a leather-bound copy of his shooting script of *Johnny Eager*. He handed it to me for safekeeping while we worked on our screenplay. His tone became serious, his sonorous voice a whisper. "A script needs at least six self-contained scenes that are flawless like a good symphony. The fans will let you off the hook for a lot of filler and puff if you've got the half-dozen moments that really play well. *Johnny Eager*'s got 'em, *Casablanca*'s got 'em, *Double Indemnity* . . . and your book *McCabe* has those scenes in spades. You've got to find them."

We were convinced. I ventured to tap into his vast experience with a question. "Who do you think would be right for the girl?"

He graciously corrected me. "You mean the woman, Larry, the woman — Mrs. Miller?" He then answered with no hesitation. "Anne Francis, no contest."

A recent biographer of Barbara Stanwyck and Robert Taylor bluntly stated that they were both homosexual and that theirs was a marriage of political convenience. For the record, my partner and I saw a great deal of Bob and Ursula, and if ever I saw a loving heterosexual union, it would have to be theirs. My observations are based on 40 years working with crews and casts that invariably treated homosexual conduct in an open and honest fashion.

When we saw Bob and Ursula off in their plane at Love Field, we were supercharged. We would soon learn another in a long line of lessons bought dearly in the film business.

Since we had pulled the obscure, out-of-print novel off the dusty shelves of the Dallas library, we felt ours was the only interest (indeed, until that time, it was), so we had optioned for only six months with no renewal provision in the contract. An entertainment editor on the *Dallas Morning News* picked up the visit by Bob and Ursula and ran a story on "the Dallas whiz kids" and their new project. This information somehow found its way into the Hollywood pipeline, where unoriginal copycats meowed on every stool at the Beverly Hills Polo Lounge looking for a hot property.

Our six months dwindled to a few weeks, and we were still short on investors subscribing to the venture. When we called the author's agent to renew the option, he brusquely dismissed our call with classic Hollywood language, telling us in short, "There's a lot of interest, but we'll entertain your offer too!" Then he stopped taking our calls. Later we learned that Warren Beatty had bought the rights and that Robert Altman would direct *McCabe and Mrs. Miller*.

Beach Red (by Peter Bowman).

In the 1940s, in Manhattan's main public library, I found another little gem that had been abandoned by its publisher. My first partner and friend Lynn Shubert and I optioned a poetic, moving book by a first-time author. *Beach Red* was the *Platoon* of its time, only its theater of war was the Pacific Islands. The novel was really a blank verse poem. Our efforts to translate it into a screenplay were unsuccessful, and we had to abandon the project.

We learned months later that Cornel Wilde, a genuine guerrilla filmmaker, had optioned the book. Sadly, he jettisoned the heart of the story and wrote in a major part for his wife. The result was a somewhat tiresome and formulaic war games story. For all practical purposes he used only the title from a real work of literature.

The Last Picture Show (by Larry McMurtry).

In the early 1960s, with fortune smiling on me with the reception of *Free, White and 21*, I was looking for a serious work to film. My preference was for one indigenous to Texas. Upon opening my copy of *Texas Quarterly*, a learned journal which never failed to please, I found a story titled "The Old Soldier's Joy, an Essay on the Annual Old Fiddler's Reunion held in Athens, Texas." It was by Larry McMurtry, who worked at Cokesbury's book store in downtown Dallas. I became acquainted with Larry and told him I would watch his progress with interest. Shortly thereafter, I was invited to a gathering to celebrate the sale of his first novel to a publisher. Even as the galleys were being sent out, it was apparent we could not possibly bid on this one. It seemed that every responsible producer and director in Hollywood went fishing for the rights to take *The Last Picture Show* to the big screen.

Our loss was tempered with two pleasures. One was seeing the birth of a great literary talent right under my nose. The second was that my favorite character actor in all the world, Billy Thurman, was cast as the coach married to Cloris Leachman in the film. This was Billy's debut into major films. Thereafter, I could not keep up with him. He was a particular favorite of Steve McQueen, who hired him right up to his last western, *Tom Horn*.

33. Epilogue: A Primer for the Maverick Moviemaker

One of the most satisfying projects I've undertaken in recent years is a series of workshops or seminars for aspiring filmmakers. Each seminar is held on a Saturday and lasts all day, and in that time I try to present as much practical information as possible about the reality of making movies on one's own. Film schools cover the artistic and technical aspects; I try to help with the harsh demands of making films in the real world.

The following is a condensed version of the workshop-seminars I have begun, a "mini-seminar" if you will. It addresses some of the most obvious concerns and queries of young filmmakers of disparate interests.

The seminar begins at 9 A.M. I do not mingle with the crowd or even show myself before being introduced, usually by a local filmmaker or cinema department chair from a nearby college. Even that must come after the obligatory announcements have been made: lunch time, location of restrooms and parking, breaks, and the announcement that no taping is permitted. And the handouts must first be in front of the guests. There is no way to open strong if you are caught over your coffee and Danish and pressed to answer a trade question that really should come during the proper Q&A periods, which will be ample.

I check the public address system personally before anyone walks into the hall. Nothing destroys a delivery rhythm more surely than the necessity to tap the mike and count "One, two, three," or whisper, "Is this mike hot?"

I do not ask stragglers to be seated. Promptly at nine o'clock, I work my way to the mike and with a full voice say, "Welcome to the O.K. Corral." I use this as a silencer and will not continue until there is quiet. But I am smiling.

9:15 A.M. State of the Art. Health of the Business.

Your chances at success as an independent filmmaker are rotten! That is of this morning; by Monday, you can be sure they will be better. That, dear friends, is the ornery nature of our business; foul weather and fair, high and low, euphoric and depressed. If you are seeking an excuse for not taking what you will learn here today and hitting the ground running, there will be ample excuses.

If you are one of those "oughta, shoulda, woulda, coulda" people, beware — the industry will devour you.

The state of the art of film now can be best described as quixotic. Never in our one hundred year history have we faced such a quagmire. Producers don't know whether to rent an Arriflex, a Betacam SP or a digital filmless camera. Production managers can't decide between HDTV, Fuji or Kodak stock, fine grain or the new fast Eastman Primetime negative. Because to cover their behinds, they know whatever they do, ultimately, it must look good on the tube. And make no mistake here, we must talk about the tube. TV and cassettes might be your safe harbor. You sure to hell had better explore it in your pitch to your investors.

And sixteen millimeter or thirty-five. Remember when sixteen millimeter was a dirty word? We only used it in the early days in Texas because the difference in price of the two stocks could sometimes be the difference in profit or loss. Today? Today, some of the most creative and successful work coming out of the U.K. and Europe is being captured with Panavision's new sixteen millimeter camera. They call it "Elaine." Look at the Arts and Entertainment specials such as "Sherlock Holmes" and "Inspector Morse": sixteen millimeter Elaines and they are saving thirty cents on the dollar. In Greece and Israel, sixteen is carefully exposed and then optically blown up to thirty-five. Nobody has asked for their money back.

Understand me. I am not here advocating you shoot sixteen. I'm merely showing how we've done an about-face here and sixteen could very well be your first venture. My fellow Texans Tobe Hooper and Robert Rodríguez didn't let the high price of thirty-five millimeter raw stock stop them from making watershed first films. Make the right film and the majors will be happy to pay for the blowup. Later, you will hear me discuss exceptions to this recitative.

Changes. With all the frenetic fury that is going on now, some things remain. There are the majors: Disney, Warners, Paramount, MCA/Universal, Columbia, Tri-Star, and the upstart New Line. The minors are too numerous to mention, but if you are going to try for a precious gem as your first try, remember there are class acts such as Miramax and Samuel Goldwyn Jr.

Finally, there is "Gower Gulch," and even that name is a generic holdover from the seat-of-the-pants era of picture making. But, for better or worse, most of you will start in Gower Gulch. Interestingly, there is no such place anymore. For your edification it was Gower Street in the shadow of Columbia Pictures. The two arenas were light years apart in product. I have told you about the majors, the minors and Gower Gulch because as despicable as they can often be, they are at the top of the food chain. But they are bottom feeders. And what does that mean? You are the prey.

You, in short, are an independent. And that is not all; there is a distinction here. There are the independent independents and there are the dependent independents. Stanley Kubrick, Martin Scorsese, and Woody Allen are independent independents. They begin a project on a whim. No longer do they have to endure the uncomfortable pitches to studio executives or financiers.

And the dependent independent? That would be most of us. We are dependent on a studio, or private capital, or a distributor. They are the power brokers in the industry. They know that all we have is a script, a fragile support system, and a dream. And unless you are careful, they will devour you for breakfast, probably at Nate and Al's Deli in Beverly Hills before they get to the office. There are, thank God, exceptions to this cycle that leaves you vulnerable to these barracudas. Your fortune hinges on the screenplay, the "piece," the property.

9:30 *A.M. Where, Except in Genesis, Do You Find "In the Beginning Was the Word"?*

Hollywood has exhausted its store of gimmicks, special effects, and tired formulas. This means that they have stubbornly, if slowly, begun a migration back to the material. The script. Young writers have gone from ghetto apartments to Brentwood on the strength of an excellent screenplay. Prices are in orbit. Scenarists are being wooed by agents and producers. They have achieved the status of celebrity that only a Robert Bolt (*Lawrence of Arabia*) or a Robert Benton (*Bonnie and Clyde*) enjoyed till now. Even the white-hot Quentin Tarantino (*Pulp Fiction*), in spite of his derivative prowess, knows what a script must be. And, just as important, what it must not be.

Good writers know that good screenwriting is visceral. It is not cerebral, at least for long. A shootable script is like a string of pearls or a link chain. The pearls need not be, in the purest sense, orderly — that is, in the form of a simple narrative. They can be used to violate every rule of classic writing and, in the hands of a scenarist or a director of skill, revolutionize storytelling. And these tools are there for the taking. It is very probable that Tarantino saw Edward Dmytryk's *Mirage* with Gregory Peck (1965) before he edited *Pulp Fiction*.

Novice writers must understand genre before they can break the rules and take their characters in a new direction. The western, horror, sci-fi, period romance, comedy, drama, film noir — all must be understood before embarking on experimentation.

Beware of imitation in the screenplay. One of the saddest displays of ineptness in film usually follows the hit picture. Knock-offs are commissioned and started the minute a winner hits the screen. The players in this game overlook the simple truth that it was the very originality of the hit that made it work. More of same need not apply.

There are two great rules of screenwriting among many that I respectfully submit. The first is, "It's got to be about *something*!" And nobody said it better than the old Irishman himself, George Bernard Shaw: "Scripts are not written, they are rewritten."

[*A question and answer session, then a 10-minute break, now follow.*]

10:25 *A.M. Maverick Financing. Wells Fargo "Jus' Went That-a-Way."*

A brief moment while I dispense with the obligatory disclaimer. I am not a lawyer and cannot offer legal advice without a slap on the wrist from the California Bar Association. Having said that, let me say that some of those barristers who would discipline me would want a fifteen hundred dollar retainer just to answer your simplest concerns on the rules of the game of film finance.

Ergo, my overview will be couched to the side of caution as I take you into the snakepit of finding the backing for your heartfelt project. There *are* options.

THE STUDIO DEVELOPMENT DEAL.

Do you really have three years to lose? And even then, no guarantee of a green light? This avenue has come to be known as "development hell," an apt description. Somebody at Warners has heard of your script and you are called to "take a meeting." What you think is "Hurray, I've made it!" The reality is that the bum's rush is on.

Best case scenario, they option your script for a few thousand dollars. This option of course is just the right to buy the property at a fixed price at a fixed time. For a first-time screenplay from an unknown, the option money and the purchase price will be modest.

The time could be any period from six months to eighteen during which they will hold your precious script hostage. But you are ecstatic.

Suddenly, you find yourself in "development hell." Your contact at the studio wants you to tweak a few elements in the story "to make it more accessible." Translation, he wants you to bring your play into the mainstream to reach a larger audience. He tells you he needs this rewrite before he kicks the script upstairs.

The next several weeks you spend in a fever at the keyboard of your PC word processor (you learned long ago that typewriters are obsolete in the film business). One week you may be asked to change the locale of your masterpiece from Spain to Italy. The next week somebody in Legal insists that the leading lady's name be changed. It seems that he is going through a nasty divorce with his wife of the same name, "Ellen."

After gallons of coffee and months of absurd script changes, you don't even recognize the story anymore. Everybody, and I do mean everybody, has had their say. There have even been some recantings and you've been asked to go back to "that third revision where she doesn't sleep with the guy until page 30."

Finally, it seems that you've done it. There have been no new meetings and no calls to "polish that ending." You feel pretty good and are thankful for the rest. After a few days you would even welcome a call.

It comes. Some stranger from the studio calls asking about this script he is looking at from "the pool." He would like to "take a meeting." It seems that the executive you have been working with for seven months has moved to Paramount and your screenplay has been put into turnaround. That means you are back to square one. The new man wants to talk about some "fine-tuning on the piece."

Your original option money has been exhausted and there are several months to go before you will know if they will pick up the option. Dilemma.

In a burst of anger which you interpret as courage, you ask to have your script back. You are referred to Legal (very probably to the same lawyer who had you change the leading lady's name.) He has happily remarried and doesn't remember your name or your script. However, he will check "development" and get back to you right away. Well, you think, I really showed them I'm no pushover.

Sure enough, the call comes in a matter of minutes. He is blasé but to the point. "The option has seven months to run, so we would only require a rebate of four thousand on that. However, legal and other development to date is thirty-five thousand, secretarial, mailings, telephone, faxes come to seventeen thousand . . . let me see, that would be fifty-six thousand for any other studio to do a pick-up on this one."

You are stunned. You can't bear to look at the PC against the wall. You grab your car keys and head for Mario's for a glass of house red. Welcome to Hollywood.

ALTERNATIVE FINANCING.

It's time we talked about some alternative financing. But for the record, *don't try any of the following without a lawyer's help.* This doesn't necessarily mean an entertainment lawyer, although certainly if you've got the bucks, that's the way to go. Any competent practitioner can prepare your papers with only two or three hours of consultation. Modern legal software with boilerplate language is at their disposal for the preparation of the following instruments.

For the mini-budget film, a private offering is a simple and expedient option. The private offering can be a limited partnership. The simplest such would be you as general partner and thirty-five investors as limited partners depending on your state's law. You would be the responsible party for filings and management of the partnership. The investors would be considered passive and would not and could not be participants in the day-to-day operation of the business. The investors or limited partners are liable only to the extent of their subscription to the entity.

The general partnership is somewhat more complicated. Investors and creators alike are general partners and are mutually liable. They also can and do involve themselves in the day-to-day matters of business.

Caveat: The following vehicles *should not be considered without a competent attorney*. Moving into the area of security offerings, the Securities Exchange Administration on the federal level for some years now has made available to the filmmaker alternative financing vehicles through a policy known as Regulation D. "Reg D" has accompanying rules 504 through 506 which lend themselves well to independent film finance. Rule 504 provides up to one million dollars in subscriptions. It also provides an exemption from the provisions of Section Five of the SEC act for limited offers and allows an issuer to offer and sell its securities (or units) to an unlimited number of persons without regard to their sophistication or experience. Producers in New York employ Rule 504 for the backing of a play or musical. It has become known as the "Broadway Plan." As the rule number goes up, the ante goes up to cover any project within reason.

When I opened this discussion with "Wells Fargo jus' went that-a-way," I meant that in its generic sense. Banks are not a source of film finance without collateral. However, the banking institutions will be a party in the funding device known as presales. It works this way. If you are fortunate enough to have a strong script that has caught the interest of even a modest "name" actor or actress, you can plan on offering the package at one of the film festivals or film markets in the U.S. and abroad.

The choices of these places for no-nonsense negotiation are the Cannes Film Festival in Cannes, France, in May; the Milano Film Festival (MIFED) in Milan, Italy, in October; and the American Film Market (AFM) in Los Angeles in February. You and or your producer's representative will offer the package to distributors and studio reps, usually excluding the domestic United States. The strategy here is to presell countries, large and small. Letters of credit are used to purchase the exclusive distribution rights (or to buy the film outright) within a given country or territory. The monies indicated are due on delivery of the finished film with the promised star or "name" attached.

These negotiable letters of credit are presented to a banking institution which has experience in film production. The bank discounts the notes and makes funds available for production, but only if certain elements, most importantly a completion bond, are in place. This budget figure (rarely used in modestly mounted films) can be as much as six percent of the budget. This is an insurance policy which warrants that the film will be completed. It carries with it a wallop. If the filmmaker, novice or veteran, drops behind in the schedule or demonstrates an ineptness in coping with details confronted, the insurance company has the right to remove the filmmaker and replace him or her.

It gets worse. The bank and the insurance carrier require an Errors and Omissions policy (commonly shortened to "E & O policy") as protection against lawsuits arising out of the script or the underlying novel or story, as in the case of an invasion of privacy or a violation of the right of publicity. This last is a fairly recent wrinkle in protection as far as the untutored filmmaker is concerned, but it is a treacherous area for the modest resources of the neophyte producer, director, and writer.

FRIENDS AND FAMILY FINANCING.

Think about it and then forget it.

CREDIT CARD FINANCING.

Don't even think about it!

"MONKEY POINT" FINANCING.

This device entails giving shares in the profit of a projected picture to the principals (actors, crew, musicians, editor, laboratory, etc.). Payments are thus deferred until the picture makes money. The profits clause is couched in the words "net" and "gross." This manner of putting financing together on a picture was in vogue during the thirties and forties. It has been so unsuccessful and so discredited over the years that it is a wonder it still survives. Probably because it *sounds* so fair and equitable.

A net deal is so vulnerable to theft and waste from so many sources that somehow the dollars never trickle down to the principals who gave their all to make the picture happen. In other words the creative team rarely sees any compensation for its labors. The theaters (not all) hold up the distributor's cut for weeks, even months, then ask for a "settlement." The distributors (not all) load the distribution expense report with phony and outlandish items like junkets to Puerto Vallarta and even call girls.

A most notorious and bitter case in point was the lawsuit filed by comedian Eddie Murphy against a major studio in the 1980s. One of Eddie's blockbuster hits, for which his agent had negotiated net points, had grossed upwards of one hundred million dollars. This was in a time when a hundred million was a nice piece of change, even for a big-budget Eddie Murphy picture. Eddie had received no payment whatsoever from the film's profits.

The lawsuit that followed exposed Hollywood's infamous "rolling breakeven" manner of bookkeeping. Eddie called his promised share of the profits "monkey points" and the phrase entered the Hollywood jargon.

Thereafter, actors and others with clout demanded gross points, which means that if Clint Eastwood has two points in the box-office gross from *Bridges of Madison County*, the amount owed him is documented at the gate when the patron puts his ten bucks down and requests "two for *Bridges*." No deductions!

Another plus for the gross participant. When that ticket you carry into the theater shoots out of the machine, it has a sequential number on it, along with the tax information. Now Uncle Sam is working for Clint, because all across the country, the ticket information is gathered for the proper reporting of income to the theater. Clint may play around with monkeys in *Every Which Way but Loose*, but he won't work for monkey points.

11 A.M. *Producing the Film, Maverick Style.*

Now that you are banked, postpone the start date. I mean this with all sincerity. Fess up. You really need more time for preparation because you fudged when you underestimated your schedule. You owe it to your backers to tell them nothing will be lost by adding a month to the preproduction breakdown. This could make the difference in success or failure on your thinly funded dream. Wasn't it Theodore Roosevelt who said, "An expedition that is well planned usually has luck"? (Incidentally, Teddy would have made a great movie producer. A man with sight problems, he always carried seventeen pair of spare glasses with him on his wild expeditions. History does not record his ever losing or breaking a pair, even charging up San Juan Hill. But he demanded those seventeen pair be there.)

Let's talk about the sixteen millimeter versus thirty-five myth. I explored earlier the rapid advances being made in the use of the narrow-gauge sixteen millimeter image for special circumstances. Those, you should recall, were primarily for special series in the U.K. and Europe, for documentaries and subjects going direct to the television tube or videocassette.

But your introduction to the industry is another matter. Yes, you could save some real dollars in buying and shooting sixteen millimeter. And mobility of movement of camera and crew would be enhanced. I have opted often to do just that.

But you will lose on several counts. Initial savings will be lost in the cost of the optical blowup to thirty-five millimeter for theaters. "Grain" is still a problem, despite new camera stocks that promise very little loss of grain as you move to the interpositive then to the dupe negative process.

Now the most damaging of the several disadvantages of the blowup process. *You must as a matter of principle tell the potential buyer or distributor that this is a blowup from sixteen!* I cannot stress this too much. Ultimately the truth will out and there could be a turndown anyway. That's when things get ugly and the reason for my caution comes into play. The rule goes something like this. You can shop your film all over town, at Sundance, Cannes, the majors and the minors. There is no loss as long as you are not committed to one deal. But once you have signed on with a studio or distributor and you lose the deal for some oversight or something withheld, you will be plagued with the novice filmmaker's worst nightmare. You have a "problem" picture. That is the phrase used in telephone conversations from Burbank to New York City. These talks usually end with one party saying, "We don't buy lawsuits, we buy entertainment."

11:30 A.M. Question and Answer Session.

There is a question from the floor: "To save money, what about using 'short ends' for a camera negative?"

Short ends are unexposed raw stock negative in measures of fifty to four hundred feet which are salvaged from the incredible waste of major studio production. The expression is used also for full, unopened one thousand foot thirty-five millimeter and four hundred foot sixteen millimeter rolls of color and black and white stock. Sometimes this is "outdated" negative, or an end user is overstocked and wants to release material before it is outdated.

I will go on record here that I have used short ends on and off for forty years, depending on the picture. I have never lost a foot of dailies due to a flare, a scratch, or broken perforations. But you must buy from a responsible and experienced dealer.

My personal choice is the veteran house known as Studio Film and Tape. Our relationship goes back to the sixties. Of course, I confess to some prejudice; the company is owned and managed by a lovely Texas lady named Carol Dean.

I never speak to would-be maverick filmmakers but that one of them asks that expected question, "What about the unions — do I have to deal with those people?" This is a very sensitive subject and my response changes radically every five years or so.

The IATSE (International Alliance of Theatrical and Stage Employees) and NABET (National Association of Broadcast Employees and Technicians) have been the bargaining agents for movie and theatrical employees for the better part of a century. The relationship with producers and production companies has been a roller coaster of sweetness and hostility.

Wages are very high for these skilled craftsmen and women, and it is often impossible for the creator of a minimally budgeted film to comply with their union pay scales. Sometimes their meal penalties, golden time, and other fringes seem outrageous to the producer struggling to stay on schedule.

For the record, I prefer not to use union crews although I have done so many times. My reluctance has to do with attitude. So often, the organized worker seems to lack an enthusiasm for the effort. Deportment, too, is a problem. A small dedicated crew fosters a sense of inclusion during a take. The crew members really care about making it play and enjoy their work. A crew of seventy to record a couple in conversation in a diner seems a bit much to me. They spend a large part of the day discussing overtime.

Having said that, my union crews have always delivered in a crisis. And I have to applaud all the craft unions — the Screen Actors Guild, IATSE, NABET, and the Director's Guild for their new low-budget accommodation rates for the production of films with budgets under a predetermined cap.

In summary on actors and crew, don't let them see you sweat. Do trust me when I say wrap day will come sooner than you think.

[*At 12 noon we take an hour for lunch and networking.*]

1:30 P.M. *Making Out.*

Today's marketplace for releasing your film is an exciting menu of venues, many of which did not exist even ten years ago. A release pattern for a film, even a modest one, typically reads in somewhat the following order: theatrical domestic, theatrical foreign, pay-for-view TV, cable nets, free TV, videocassettes, in-flight, and, on the horizon, CD-ROM.

Are you really ready to sell or sign off your picture? Some cautions.

- If they cannot ante up a minimum guarantee, don't expect anything more.
- If you have to pay for the second screening or the first lunch, walk away from the deal.
- Never show a videocassette unless that is the only option, and even then don't roll until the blinds are closed and the buyer's secretary is told to hold all calls.
- Never sign a "memo deal" without a clause providing for a subsequent fully executed contract.
- Never sign a contract that does not provide for arbitration in the event of disputes. Lawsuits can turn your dream flick into a problem picture.

2:40 P.M. *Keeping Yours.*

Let's be optimistic. Your film has a test date and it looks as if it has legs. How do you protect your investors? How do you protect yourself from pirates? Cope with language barriers? How can you find the time to field offers of new opportunities and properly husband the current picture?

Enter the producer's rep. "What?" you might wail. "Another layer of concern? Another hand in the pie!?"

Don't fight it. A producer's rep works on percentages, usually a low three percent. He is usually a lawyer and a whiz with figures and knows how to read a quarterly report from your distributor. He is responsible for the audits and any violation by the distributor. The rep is acquainted with the foreign buyers and agents.

More than ever, now that the venues and markets have grown, the rep can relieve you of a lot of grief. Most important, he or she can free you to do what you started out to do in the first place — make movies.

So, cheer up! So you didn't make Sundance or pay down on that adobe in Santa Fe. You made Cannes and MIFED and you have a rep looking after you and your backers. Agents are returning your calls when you want to talk to talent. And if they are not picking up all the bar tabs, at least you can count on going Dutch. That's progress.

A Guerrilla Filmmaker's Glossary

ADR   Additional dialogue replacement. In films, recorded location soundtracks of the speaking actors are often unusable because of intrusive sounds (e.g., airplanes, motors, room bounce, thunder, rain, air conditioners, or traffic) or an amateurish reading by an actor. The location soundtrack then becomes only a reference track or **click track** which will be replaced later in the controlled environment of a dubbing studio.

AFM   American Film Market. One of the big three annual film markets, usually held in Los Angeles in the early spring. It is actually an international market with thousands of buyers, sellers, and production people gathering from more than 100 countries. Trailers and product reels are shown and deals are made. Buyers and sellers engage in this high-stakes poker game for ten days.

ambient level   In recording motion picture sound, there is always ambience, or surrounding sound. It may be "room tone" or the levels of the dialogue, effects, or music. Sound recordists, working with their Nagra recorders, concern themselves with the signal to noise ratio on the set to achieve an acceptable and natural ambience.

Annie Oakleys   Before the turn of the century, one of the great live road shows was Annie Oakley's Wild West Extravaganza, starring the flamboyant professional cowgirl herself. If the advance man had failed to sell out the opening night in a "dead" town, Annie would make the rounds of the bars and hotels, giving free passes to anyone who could talk up the show (such as the mayor) and handing out "twofers" (two for the price of one) to barflies and traveling salesmen. Later, the Broadway theater adopted this practice to keep shows alive until word of mouth could save them. It was especially effective for comedies as even the funniest play in the world is a bomb if only 12 people are sitting in the house.

answer print   The final print of a film, accepted by the producer and director, which will be the guide for the multiple release printing of a motion picture. Literally the "answer" to the technical requirements of the creators (DP, director, producer) in the lighting, color correction, soundtrack, synchronization, and titles. A responsible laboratory will strike several trial prints to achieve the best from the elements assembled.

Arkoff, Sam   Cofounder, with James Nicholson, of American International Pictures. A legendary Hollywood character and attorney who helped create an amazing library of theatrical films that jump-started the careers of dozens of today's great filmmakers and actors.

artsy-craftsy   (Also artsy fartsy). A favorite expression of Sam Arkoff. No budding filmmaker dared approach Sam with a project that was unfocused or intended as the artist's ticket into the big time. With his unerring eye and ear for commercial viability, Sam was seldom wrong in dismissing the passionate filmmaker and his dream package. There were exceptions witnessed by this writer. One such as a little biker script brought to Sam by Peter Fonda and Dennis Hopper. Sam found it "artsy craftsy" and passed. Another studio thought it had possibilities. It was the watershed film *Easy Rider*.

aspect ratio   The motion picture image reaching the emulsion in the camera is an evolutionary process. In the days of the silent picture, the ratio of height to width was virtually 1:1, producing a nearly square image area. Then, with the introduction of the optically squeezed image in processes such as Panavision, Cinemascope, and VistaVision, the image was skewed more toward the "natural eye" of a long horizontal measurement and shorter vertical. All films produced for television transmission and most of those shot for industrial, documentary, and educational use are photographed in an aspect ratio of 1.33:1. Most films shot for theaters are shot in a system to be projected in an aspect ratio greater than 1.33:1. For example, Panavision is a 2:1 squeeze in the camera. This is unsqueezed for projection at a ratio of 2.36:1. Most films, using spherical lenses and shot for theatrical use with later transmission over television, are shot with a full frame, but the cinematographer frames the compositions so that the principal action is protected within scored lines on the finder which show the TV limits. The most important etchings on the ground glass, however, are the markings showing the limits of 1.85:1, 1.75:1, and so forth, on down to 1.37:1. Prestigious directors who have shot a masterpiece in Panavision or another anamorphic system are having artistic battles with the networks. The conflict arose when the so-called "letterbox" image on the television screen found little favor with audiences either for broadcast viewing or for videocassette sales and rentals. It has the appearance of looking through the wrong end of a telescope. To preserve the full horizontal stretch of the composed images, letterboxing in effect shrinks the image to fit the screen horizontally and inserts blank spaces above and below the image.

   "Panning and scanning" the image and using selective frames to fill the television screen has not proven successful. The carefully composed images are shattered into cropped images that are flat and lifeless.

Automat   An automated cafeteria. Originally indigenous to Manhattan, the Automats were a fast food innovation wherein diners could move their trays along a line, choose foods and drinks by looking at samples in a small window, and pop the posted prices into change slots. The items from the menu were removed as the door to the window opened and closed. Mysterious gremlins, never seen behind the tempting wall of goodies, would then replace the item for the next hungry patron. The Automats were a favorite haunt of the film crowd when I was in New York. As of this writing they have all but disappeared.

baby legs   A small set of tripod legs with accommodation for the friction or fluid head. Used for low angles and hard-to-access vantage points.

bad film   (often one word) A phrase coined by cinema critic Douglas St. Clair Smith which does not necessarily refer to inept filmmaking. To quote another critic on the subject of my film *Zontar, the Thing from Venus*: "It is a measure, perhaps, of the crisis of our 'culture' that we have experienced a swelling wave of interest in 'schlocky' and 'bad' films. In a time when our so-called world is increasingly plagued by wars, crime, suicide, and economic collapse . . . mass audiences turn ever more to seamless escapist fare in movies, TV, and music. Certainly the new-found fashionability of the 'bad' can be viewed as at least a partial antidote to the smotheringly slick product of today."

   An article in *Zontar, the Magazine from Venus* offered the following thought: "As for Larry Buchanan, perhaps no other 'Bad Filmmaker' has produced such a consistent *narco-mystical* body of work with its obsessive themes of alienation, loneliness, entrapment, and the love-hate relationship between an isolated, misunderstood man and his own personal *rubber monster . . .* the living antidote to the effects-crazed *gore-schlock* and *Spielbergian space-slush* of the 1980s."

bankability   When producers offer a film package for pre-sales either to foreign interests or to a major studio, the script or source material will be accompanied with star names attached or considered as attached to the property. These stars must be of a certain stature so that the lending institution feels secure in its financial exposure. At any given time, certain players are hot and others are not, regardless of their box office pull in the past. Bankable names can ensure the funding of marginal subject matter.

blaxploitation   A genre of film that emerged in the sixties. The term tends to connote films that depict blacks in unrealistic or stereotypical ways, but can also apply generally to films with black characters and themes. *Free, White and 21* is an early example of the latter type of film. Until the late fifties, most black-oriented films were carefully constructed, socially conscious and politically correct efforts such as *Home of the Brave*, *The Defiant Ones*, *To Sir with Love*, or *Pinky*. These worthy films were popular but sometimes token offerings which perpetuated the very offenses they decried. The blacks were "near-blacks" or sometimes called "white-blacks" in studio story conferences. Light-skinned blacks and, early on, sometimes whites in black makeup were preferred in casting these films. With the release of *Free, White and 21*, the floodgates opened for hits such as the *Shaft* series, *Penitentiary*, *I Spit on Your Grave*, and *Sweet Sweetback's Baadasssss Song*. These were made by, of, and with African Americans. Their energy, audacity, and cinematic hipness allowed them to cross over to broad success.

Brando   An actor who, aping his idol Marlon, mumbles and slurs his dialogue. The sound man finally has to tell his director, "We got a Brando." Directors who don't know much about sound will ask the recordist to bring up the sound level, whereas an experienced director will patiently explain to the player that if the level is boosted to accommodate him, the audience will be able to hear the mice in the rafters and the Coke machine in the hall. The guerrilla director will not waste the time. He will use the actor's voice only as a click track and loop him with some deserving beginner.

breakdown   Part of the planning process for a film. Long before a screenplay goes to camera, all locations, props, wardrobe, cast, and special effects must be planned precisely. A breakdown and a "crosshatch" of the 120-odd pages of screenplay are scientific processes that bring the undertaking of the film into the realm of reality. All the elements are a slave to the scene numbers. All the scenes in a tavern, for instance, are shot together even if they appear in the script separated by days or even years. This necessity can introduce major complications when you consider that the actors will have changes of wardrobe from Scene A to Scene E, the props will change over the story years, the lighting will be at different levels to represent day and night, and the decor will reflect the passage of time and circumstance. Then there is the need for different makeup if the characters have changed over the intervening hours, days or years. The crosshatches, call sheets, and other concerns committed to paper will exceed the 120-page script manifold.

Cannes Film Festival   Each spring, in May, the world's most famous, flashy, expensive and sexy gathering of movie people convenes on the Croisette of Cannes, France. It is a nightmare of deal-making, partying, boozing, gourmet dining, gaming, and uninhibited showing off of the human animal and its excesses. Thousands of the mighty and the obscure of filmdom debark from the jets at the Nice airport, eyes shining and pitches practiced. For two weeks, much of it without sleep, the players dance out the ritual of buying and selling. Early in the festivities, a secret list of "who's in and who's out" circulates to the initiated. A few choice "art" films are celebrated. The astonished filmmaker is on cloud nine for a short while. Typically, his film will flare like a votive candle, flicker and be lost. These sacrificial works are a cover for the hot commercial titles that are the main course of the Cannes feeding frenzy. Those bidding for rights often have not seen the film. The food chain here is short, and nobody takes prisoners. Slowly, as the week ends, the migration to the airport begins as wallets flatten and hopes dissolve into booze and blues. Cannes has devoured another season's Young Turks and old warriors.

"Carmen Miranda"   Many actresses, especially dancers, wear no underwear in movie scenes. The camera favors this practice because there are no unsightly seams or stitching to disrupt the body's curves in a form-fitting evening dress. When the player waltzes across the dining room to her table or the high-stepping dancer twirls in her partner's arms, the illusion is film fantasy.

But sometimes things go wrong, as in *Down Argentine Way* (Fox, 1940) when vivacious and high-spirited Carmen Miranda was lifted by her partner in the big finish dance number. All four cameras recorded more of Carmen than they expected, settling once and for all the question of whether or not she was a brunette. At the time 20th Century–Fox was delivering these musicals like sausages, so the Technicolor laboratory "check printed" them at high speed — 64 frames a second. Somebody blinked, and the peep-shot was not discovered until deep into the editing, by which time Miranda was back home in South America. To reshoot would have been prohibitive even for 20th Century–Fox, given producer Darryl Zanuck's boast of an ability to "fix" any cutting problem and his refusal to cut to co-star Don Ameche at the crucial moment.

The advance prints shipped into the Fox exchanges across the United States became collector's items. Projectionists would cut the scene out and offer it to the highest bidder.

Thereafter, crews and editors alike became more aware of the crotch shot, which was nicknamed a "Carmen Miranda." If anyone saw such a shot in a production number, he would call out, "We've got a Carmen Miranda!" A retake was in order. Times have changed. It is said that Sharon Stone's crossing of her great legs elevated *Basic Instinct* to a mega-hit.

check print   A print of a film from a newly conformed negative, used to verify proper lip synchronization and the success of optical effects that have been cut into the originals. This is especially vital when the originals have been cut with A and B rolls. A and B roll conforming facilitates the inclusion of multiple dissolves and faces without losing a generation of quality in the negative. Once the above concerns have been satisfied, the color timer can proceed with full color timing and correction for that most important answer print.

click track   Many scenes are recorded on location under adverse audio conditions. When the scene cannot wait and must be shot, the sound man may record the scene "under protest" or else all agree that the tape in question will function as a reference track only and be used in the postproduction phase to aid the actor involved in re-recording or ADR (additional dialogue replacement).

closed set   A circumstance in which only essential personnel may be present during filming. Almost always applies to a scene wherein there is serious nudity and the actress or actor requests that only the director and key crew be present. Another reason to close the set is if an actor has a difficult histrionic passage and is seeking total concentration. Sometimes political subject matter or a need for secrecy can close a set.

cocktail shot   The last set-up of the day and the last "print" take of that set-up. Just about everybody but the poor director heads for the favorite bar.

completion bond   No banking house or lender will stand behind a shoot just because there have been presales. Until those presales have been collected and discounted, and throughout principal photography, the bank demands that a completion bond (a guarantee of the completion of the film) be in place. The bonding company takes a fee of up to 6 percent, and, depending on the prestige and clout of the director and producer, may reserve the right to step in and take over the production if too many problems arise. They avoid doing so if humanly possible because such action tends to get a film tagged as a "problem picture."

continuity   A typescript or computer printout of an abstract of the dialogue and general action of the final cut of a film. This is not a screenplay as such but instead represents what is actually said and done in the fine cut, even down to the smallest grunt or sigh made by the actors. The reason for all this precision is that the continuity (in translation) is used by the foreign buyers for dialogue dubbing into languages other than the original.

contract player   During the 1940s and 1950s, major studios searched for talent in amateur theatrical productions, beauty contests, county fairs, college campuses and anywhere else where young people gathered. Talent scouts, when finding a promising prospect, would arrange for a screen test at the studio. The tests are simple, sometimes nothing more than the player taking directions from off camera: "Walk this way . . . right profile, please . . . smile right into the camera." If the subject showed real promise, a second test was made using the help of one of the stars on the lot in a real scene which the neophyte would memorize.

With a pretty face, sexy body, vivacious personality, or any combination of these factors, a stock contract would follow. The studio then would schedule classes for the contract players in diction, deportment, wardrobe, and even fencing. One of the functions of the young men and women would be as escorts around town. If a studio had a rising star on its hands, it would arrange dates with the contract players to see that she or he was properly entertained. This meant dinner and dancing at the Trocadero, Ciros, or the Mocambo on the Sunset Strip. When I had this pleasant chore, I would choose the Palm Room at the Beverly Hills Hotel. That meant a prime rib dinner, Pupi Campo's rhumba band, and the company of an actress "about to happen"—all on Darryl F. Zanuck and the 20th Century–Fox treasury.

Corman, Roger   Arguably the most successful independent filmmaker on the globe. He is the only producer-director that I tip my hat to as my superior in being able to deliver the most with the least. This immodest statement stands after nearly 40 years. Most producers and directors in Hollywood are really traffic cops. They are given an obscene amount of money to hire the most gifted cinematographers, actors, cutters, and writers in the business. Then they boast when the film comes in "under budget." In most cases the $30 million "miracle" really should have been a budget of $5 million.

My valued friendship with Roger goes back to the years when we both scratched and wheeled our way into the business of making films. We've had a casual acquaintance since his *Bucket of Blood* and *The Little Shop of Horrors.* But I believe our first really good talk came on a Saturday morning at the Sunset Boulevard offices of American International Pictures. Roger was on a roll with his Edgar Allan Poe series. My partner Harold Hoffman and I were basking in the theater returns from *Free, White and 21.* We had flown to Hollywood for meetings with AIP honcho Sam Arkoff to discuss new projects. While most of the heavy players in Hollywood were on tennis courts all over town sipping gin and tonic and networking, in bounced Roger in jeans and sneakers. He was as high as we were with his box office reports from his *Masque of the Red Death.* Harold and Sam drifted off to smoke some of Sam's Havanas, and Roger and I traded horror stories about the making of horror films.

I believe Roger's book *How I Made a Hundred Movies in Hollywood and Never Lost a Dime* (Random House) should be required reading for young cinéastes before they make a first pitch for their masterpieces. The same goes for *Fast and Furious: The Story of American International Pictures* (McFarland) or its expanded 1995 edition, *Faster and Furiouser.* Roger, like me, has been called a lot of things. I call him the Master.

Cukor, George   An incredibly cultured, gifted director who was hopelessly flawed in his relations with anyone not "above the line." I first was floored by his *Romeo and Juliet* with John Barrymore, Norma Shearer, and Leslie Howard. He excelled at "women's pictures" set in effete, high key-light. But he could be a tyrant with minor female players, saving his graciousness for young males on the set. Working for him on *The Marrying Kind* in New York, I was appalled that producers would give this man so much money to do so little with his pictures.

cut-aways   In breaking down a day's work, a director will allow a number of isolated cuts (usually close-ups) of the principals and objects. These reactions and inanimate set-pieces can be a life-saver for the editor for pacing and as simple escape cuts to smooth out a mismatch in action.

dailies   The first work print struck from the negative as it comes into the lab. Some cinematographers ask for dailies fully corrected for color and density, which makes the craftsman look good but can be treacherous. I prefer one-light dailies, which, although harsh, can tell us if we are on target with F-stops and determine if retakes are necessary.

day-for-night   Imagine trying to shoot a nighttime cattle stampede in a western. There is no logical source of illumination. Even arc lights with blue gels representing the moonlight can only cover the first 40 head of beef. Day-for-night is called for. Some cinematographers will build a filter pack that will do the job. Others prefer the simpler method: remove the Wratten 85 filter and underexpose two or more stops. If the elements are just right, a polarizing filter can do the job. Veterans of this technique will avoid the horizon and will always find an excuse for an incandescent light source as an accent — a lantern in a western, a porch light for the front of a house, the lighting of a cigarette, a flare by the roadside, a campfire, or a flashlight.

dead track   In film editing, a period of silence when sound effects and even music do not completely fill the shot time. These quiet interludes are not acceptable. The editor either fills them with "room tone" or secures a loop from the ambient level of the particular set-up or location.

DGA   Directors Guild of America.

director's cut   A final cut made by the director him- or herself, a privilege sometimes demanded if the director has enough clout. After a rough cut is completed, the director is called in and can make changes or deletions, or even decide to make retakes. This last is of course an expensive undertaking, as it may involve collecting actors already dismissed or reconstructing sets which have been struck.

Director's Fortnight   A special category of competition at the Cannes Film Festival.

director's line   The very first rule of cinema grammar. In theory it is elementary, but in practice it can be a quagmire. It is an imaginary line drawn between the noses of the two actors closest to the camera. In planning shots, the director crosses that line at his peril. Consider the following example: A novice combat cameraman is covering a military parade on Main Street. As the tanks approach, he is shooting from the right side of the frame. Suddenly, he thinks he needs better light and he crosses the street to shoot from the left. The clouds pass and he returns to his original position. In the cutting room, the editor is puzzled by the shot slated as #2. "Who is that, the enemy?" It simply won't cut.

Had the novice been in the field longer he would have made a critical shot, one of several ways: (1) As a head-on cut as the tanks approach; (2) as a subjective shot from the point of view of the turret gunner; or (3) as a tail-away shot showing the trailing tanks. Now he has a cutting sequence not only to accommodate the director's line but also to give rhythm and pace to the sequence.

In time, a director learns to violate this rule on occasion as second nature. Some directors, such as David Lean, John Ford, and Howard Hawks delighted in doing so. They had earned the right to experiment and could "feel" the cut, many times over the objection of their director of photography.

"direct to"   A phrase which entered the lexicon of the industry when cable and television movies began to go "direct to" television without a theatrical release. I peg this time about 1985. Features that were without stars of real box office power or without a compelling and original story simply could not support the horrendous cost of delivery to theaters.

The only remaining theatrical outlets for such films, thank God, are the specialized or "art" houses. A personal, heartfelt story, however modest, can go into these selected venues and make a lot of noise and respectable grosses. This is done with limited print and advertising orders, allowing the picture to grow with word of mouth. Viva the specialized house!

dirty dupe   A black and white mylar or one-light color print used for editorial work, looping (ADR), and final dubbing or "mix" of the picture. Dirty dupes are made with reversal stock and are contact printed from the fine cut color print which has been pronounced as final. Sometimes several of these edge-coded dupes are made to permit simultaneous progress in music scoring, sound effects, and optical effects. These operations can be at different locations. The edge-coding is the control factor. Breaks and losses can be "slugged" with plain or color leader. This is a luxurious technique not often available to the guerrilla filmmaker.

"doing a Von Stroheim"   Many actors and some directors (including, famously, Erich Von Stroheim) are not mindful that the only thing that really matters is what is transmitted through the optical glass that makes up the lens on a camera. If an actress is told to drive a car toward the camera but she insists she has on the wrong shoes, she is "doing a Von Stroheim." She could have on sneakers and be wearing jeans as far as the lens is concerned. This example is banal, but it is surprising how often this particular nuisance crops up on the set and how many players will argue the point.

The phrase originated when Erich Von Stroheim, directing his fiasco *Greed*, ordered army officer's underclothes to be made in silk and monogrammed with the regimental colors. When told the audience would not be aware of the horrendously expensive wardrobe, he answered, "Ah, but the officers will!"

Dove, Billie   A stunning, if somewhat controversial, star of the thirties. Her daughter was married to Paul Bertoya, one of the stars of my film *Strawberries Need Rain*.

"drugstore Kodachrome"   A recent phrase for bright, vivid color. Directors of photography have gone far toward desaturating color in their scenes. Many films today are so filtered that they might as well be shot on a monochrome stock or vat-dyed as in the days of Griffith's *Intolerance*. Some films need full brilliance and saturated colors to have story integrity. Musicals, westerns and pictures with tropical settings are obvious examples of films that should have the whole palette to work from. Imagine *Singing in the Rain* in only sepia color. Or a story of Gaugin in Tahiti with his voluptuous nudes and sarongs in the impotent salmon colors so prevalent on today's screens. This has given rise in the last few years to the expression, as in "This is a rich and bold adventure; I want drugstore Kodachrome."

dry run   A rehearsal without film being exposed in the gate.

E&O Policy   Errors and omission policy. Insurance protection against putting in something you shouldn't or leaving out something that should be included.

This is one of the most abused tools of the Hollywood legal fraternity. Certainly, care should be taken in the construction of any script to avoid invasion of privacy, use of actual telephone numbers, defamation, libel, slander and an endless list of other improprieties. But today's barristry has found a "bird's nest on the ground" in the E&O's, and the cost is obscene. To take an extreme example, Shakespeare's *Hamlet* has been in the public domain for centuries, but many lawyers (whose knowledge of classic drama is suspect anyway) will not proceed with studio or venture capital funding until the shoot is covered by an errors and omission binder.

edge code   Edge numbering, in sequential digits which are inked onto one side of work prints, magnetic soundtracks, and optical tracks to maintain synchronization during the editing and dubbing stages. Differentiated from "edge numbers," which are built into negative stock and transfer to the work print for conforming the negative cut.

Forte, Fabian   A teenage idol during the 1960s, and the star of my feature *A Bullet for Pretty Boy*. I had a script on the 1930s gangster Charles Arthur ("Pretty Boy") Floyd, and AIP had a "play or pay" contract with Fabian. That meant that earlier they had signed him to a multiple picture deal which guaranteed him the action. If they failed to find something suitable, he would be paid his $30,000 for doing nothing. This is not the way I like to make pictures, but it came from hunger. We got off to a bad start. We were shooting in Texas in the summer, and the cast was wearing double-breasted wool suits. Fabian, although a conditioned athlete, was exhausted from the intense sun. His costar Adam Rourke, a buddy of mine, came to my rescue, and the three of us had a good heart-to-heart. I put Fabian on salt pills and he recovered his energy. Thereafter, it was "Fabe" and "Tex." Fabian Forte is an underrated actor who has taken punishment for his good looks and Aquarian nature.

fanzines   Magazines published by and for fans. There are various fanzines devoted to the horror and science fiction genres and to "bad film" in general. Colorful and well-read by film lovers, they have functioned to preserve the obscure for generations to come. Ed Wood Jr., Val Lewton, Ted Mikels, Monte Hellman, Joe Dante, Roger Corman and yours truly are indebted to their tenacity and kindness in lionizing our bad films. Favorites of mine include *Schockxpress* and of course, *Zontar, the Magazine from Venus*.

"faux 4-F"   A falsified 4-F document used to avoid military service on the grounds of an imagined disability. When the draft for World War II began, many young and able men looked for ploys that would keep them from suiting up for Uncle Sam. Those with flat feet, impaired hearing, or any of a whole menu of disabilities were spared serving their country and could sit out the war. Actors, some of them household names, panicked. Enter the "second handers." Agents, friends in high places, and studio bosses devised a variety of afflictions to protect their investments and calm the fears of the reluctant draftees.

first refusal   A contract clause by which a buyer (e.g., of a screenplay) is granted the first opportunity to accept or reject the seller's next product. This can apply to screenwriters, actors, and technicians. I find the expression odious because it presumes a turndown of one's heartfelt work.

front slate   see **tail slate**

"Fuzz at two o'clock!"   A warning that a policeman or other official has been spotted. One of the guerrilla filmmaker's tactical tricks is to shoot on location without permits. In such a situation, or in the midst of a dangerous stunt, a shouted "Fuzz at two o'clock" warns all that the company may be the guests of the city that night unless they can come up with a convincing reason for their transgressions on the spot.

good-bad film   A kind of film, defined by a secret, cloistered body of critics, which achieves artistic effect through or despite consciously poor production values or technique. For us true guerrilla filmmakers, this can be a coveted honor, sharply distinguished from simply "bad film." For example, *It's Alive!* is a "bad film," whereas *Zontar, the Thing from Venus* has passed inspection after 30 years as a good-bad film.

Great White Way   In Manhattan, Broadway from 42nd St. to 49th St. No longer a viable expression, it said everything in the 1920s when there were 90 legitimate playhouses lighting up the sky.

gross deal   Payment based on the gross receipts, rather than net profits, of a film. It is no longer a secret that this is the only way talent with points in a film can expect real money. A net deal is worthless. The so-called "rolling break-even" means that every time a hit picture threatens to make so much that checks should go out, the studio financial wizards go into their creative mode and find some way to charge off the big dollars so that the movie is always just breaking even on the books.

A gross position, on the other hand, can't be tinkered with. The grosses are out there, protected by Uncle Sam's interest. A dollar comes into the box office, a nickel goes to Jack Nicholson or whomever. No discussion, no sweat. No "rolling break-even."

guerrilla filmmaker   Sometimes the only way to get your picture in the can is to head for the hills. With no money for permits or to pay off corrupt cops and firemen, or even really to pay the lab, you go undercover. You work weekends or whenever your mostly volunteer crew and cast can gather at some risky location to grab a shot that would be impossible otherwise. The only ingredients in abundance are a love of filmmaking and a hunger to be in the game.

You are a guerrilla filmmaker. You work by the seat of the pants, rolling with the punches, without fiscal backup, on the run, exhausted, stealing shots, feinting, pulling back for reloading, facing an endless succession of perils.

ham   An overacting performer who chews the scenery.

"Heat 'em up"   A gaffer's order to turn on the sound stage lights for the first set-up of the day.

hi hat   A bracket, shaped like a top hat, which can be clamped or nailed for a locked-off shot in difficult camera positions. Used where a tripod or baby legs cannot function.

hot set   When a break for lunch is called on a sound stage or on location, the set is marked as "hot." Lunch or visiting is prohibited on the set. Roped off, the set must be undisturbed so that all props, lights, and furniture will match the last set-up before the caterer's truck arrived.

Huntsville Prison   An ancient and brooding state prison near Huntsville, Texas, that has the distinction of having held felons as disparate as Clyde Barrow, Bonnie Parker, and Huddie Leadbetter (Leadbelly). Barrow cut off one of his toes with an ax so that he would be sent to the prison hospital where he could make an escape and join his sweetheart, Bonnie. Leadbelly composed a blues song about the prison and sang it to the warden, who promptly pardoned him. This is not apocryphy.

IA   see IATSE

IATSE pickup   A union substitute for a film crew member. When a crew is short for illness or other reasons, the production manager can call the union and pick up a craftsman or craftswoman. Organized labor pools in other fields, such as dock-working longshoremen, call it "shape up."

IATSE   International Alliance of Theatrical and Stage Employees (often abbreviated to IA). The once powerful parent union of theater and film workers. The IA has a rocky history, including labor-relation crimes committed by some of its top executives in the labor wars of the early forties. Scholars researching the subject should investigate the Bioff and Brown extortion and bribery scandals of that time. With some shabby exceptions, my own experience has been good with the IA. They came to know, in Texas at least, that when the budget allowed, I called upon their undisputed excellence at their skills.

interlock   A selsyn motor–driven "locked" screening of the fine cut work print of a film and its accompanying voice track or multiple tracks.

key art   A basic illustration or photo which carries the campaign theme of a released film. This key art is couched in a variety of sizes and catchlines to hook the filmgoer.

looping   The forerunning technique to post synching dialogue. Until the perfection of ADR (additional dialogue replacement), actual loops of the line to be dubbed ran in the projectors and the actors mouthed their lines until there was a good match. With the refining of ADR, the loops were jettisoned for the high tech of "push-pull" and "pick-up."

made for   Literally, "made for" television. When a subject and chosen players are marginal and do not warrant the "A" film treatment, which may involve large print orders and millions of dollars in promotion, the wise choice is going directly to television and thence to the relatively safe harbor of home video.

M&E tracks   Music and effects soundtracks. Sometimes called "foreign backgrounds," these separate elements, independent of the English dialogue, are necessary for sales to foreign countries.

magic hour   A very critical few moments in a day's shoot, immediately after the sun has disappeared from the sky but while there is still a radiance that can produce a good exposure and a safe F-stop. Crew members have been known to whistle "When the Deep Purple Falls" to alert others to the approaching moment. The "fill" that lingers is like magic when coupled with some practical lamps or other incandescent illumination. Taking advantage of this brief moment can save tortuous night lighting that will be required just minutes after the magic hour.

matching   In shooting a scene which is covered from several angles, the steps taken to ensure that everything caught by the cameras remains identical throughout the scene. Care must be taken to avoid any mismatch of lit cigarettes, hats on heads, body movements, lighting, etc. Editors go bonkers when there is a mismatch of any kind, forcing them to use an unwanted cut-away and lose the editorial pacing. To try to place the responsibility of catching a mismatch is an exercise in futility. Everybody on the set, from script supervisor to craftsperson, should be attuned to this potential nightmare.

meal penalty   Under union rules, a heavy charge that is to be levied against a production if a meal is not called after a certain period of work time. I absolutely refuse to honor or sign on to this stipulation. I may have worked painfully for hours to get a scene just right only to confront the penalty clock just when everything is perfect. I reserve the right to put that shot in the can if it takes only a few more seconds to finish a print take. In 40 years, I have never paid a meal penalty. I have the same intolerance of this practice as I do of that scam the "after-dinner drink."

Method Ass   A Method Asshole; i.e., a devotee to the Method, a conscious acting technique taught by the late Lee Strasberg, the artistic director of the Actors Studio in New York. Although Strasberg was perhaps the most revered acting coach of our time, many film and theater directors wince when told they will be working with a practitioner of the Method. Strasberg's classes were celebrity-studded, and many greats and would-be greats worked out their angst and histrionic insecurities employing the Method. Marlon Brando and Marilyn Monroe were star pupils. Strasberg, who died in 1982, left a curious legacy.

M.G.   Minimum guarantee; an advance a filmmaker is offered for the ultimate distribution or sale of his project (usually 10 percent of the agreed price in cash with the remainder to follow). This is a popular device for distributors at Cannes or other festivals and markets to steal a film. All too often, the advance is all the filmmaker will ever see. Those who do not learn guerrilla tactics are doomed to get lost in the jungle.

Mikels, Ted   The director of such exploitation classics as *The Doll Squad* and *The Worm Eaters*, and one of very few filmmakers I have encountered who qualifies for the overused title of auteur. The students who have worked with him know him to be kind, caring, generous, tireless and spontaneous. A prince among thieves.

Minimalism   A studied style in films for some, an inevitable necessity for others. It all comes from hunger for some of us. The minimalist introduces only razor-sharp elements to make his scene: limited cast, props, effects, even theme, with the action usually played out against bare walls or over formica tables. I have been called by respectable fanzines the supreme minimalist.

The truth of the matter is best illustrated in a sketch by the greatest comedian of his time, the late Benny Hill. Benny is portraying a film director on a talk show. The host, a fawning pseudo-intellectual, rhapsodizes, "I loved the way you abruptly went from color to black and white in the love scene. What was your motivation?" Benny answers, "There was no motivation; we ran out of color film."

mix   The British term for the final integration assembly of the many sound reels of a feature. Dubbing, à la Hollywood, is really a misnomer. Dubbing is copying one track, any gauge, whereas "mix" encompasses all of the operations that take place. I have always preferred it for that reason, and it is pleasant to see Hollywood coming around.

"Moola at nine o'clock!"   A warning that the backer or backers are crossing the stage or location ninety degrees to the left. Look sharp! No off-color jokes.

Movie Master   The best screenplay software I have found to date. If I woke up tomorrow and found there was no Scriptor, Movie Master or other software for me and I had to return to my ancient Remington manual typewriter, I would quit writing scripts and use a tape recorder.

MPAA   Motion Picture Association of America.

multiple   The happy circumstance in which two or more theaters in the same community play a picture on the same date. Sometimes called "day and date." This is a filmmaker's dream. The outrageous newspaper ads are suddenly affordable, even at sizes larger than a postage stamp. You don't have to give the lab a "Godfather" print order. You can "bicycle" your prints (i.e., shuttle them between theaters) for maximum returns. You might even be asked to fly in for a morning talk show in Tucson because of the generous TV buy you can now afford. Hey, take your leading lady. You'd be surprised how decent these regional stations can be, and lunch is on them. Multiples are still available to the guerrilla filmmaker with the right feature. On *Goodbye, Norma Jean*, we had only 50 prints and played out the whole country before the scratches got some attention.

NABET   National Association of Broadcast Employees and Technicians. Its members are a special breed of cat. They love film and are sympathetic to the guerrilla filmmaker. Even so, sometimes we have to pass because of budget restraints. Just be straight with them. Don't push them for concessions then boast of your "sweetheart" deal. Always return their calls and use them when you can.

negative pickup   A distributor of films likes your picture. He offers at first only a percentage deal. You balk. If he loves your picture, he then offers a negative pickup, meaning he advances the costs to date at completion. Your backers or the bank are smiling again.

net deal   A deal in which payment is based on a percentage of net profits, an arrangement very unattractive to the filmmaker (see **gross deal**). Eddie Murphy calls them "monkey points."

But sometimes when your picture has been on the shelf too long, and it's the only game in town, close your eyes and sign. First, though, build in some escape clauses: (1) Get a guaranteed number of playdates; (2) in a package deal with other titles sold to television or cable, demand a pari passu share with the other losers in the package; (3) try to qualify the distributor as a producer's representative rather than a full-service distributor. Be wary of words like "exclusive" and "expenses."

We are moving faster and faster on the entertainment highway and witnessing new methods of delivery. Theatrical release is more and more an expensive delivery system for only the monstrous titles featuring megastars, with rare exceptions for specialized product. (There, I've said it, *product*. I hate it, but I love "specialized.") This may portend the era of the producer's rep (the filmmaker's employee). If the film doesn't perform as hoped, the producer can reclaim it from a producer's rep, whereas a "distributor" might sit on the picture for his full seven-year, all-territories, all-markets deal. He's forgotten that eager young guerrilla and his "showcase" picture. After all, that was Cannes two years ago!

Nicholson, James H.   Partner in American International Pictures with Samuel Arkoff, and a gifted and sensitive filmmaker. When we screened our picture *A Question of Consent*, he quietly whispered "The title has to go." In less time than the length of the showing, he came up with *Free, White and 21*, a money title. Salvation. Guerrilla filmmakers lost a booster in Jim.

one eighty five (1.85:1)   The most common aspect ratio used by projectionists in theatrical screenings. This is accomplished with a hard matte in the gate of the projector. (See also **aspect ratio**.)

one sheet   A trade name for the posters that herald a coming show. Usually about 30 × 40 inches, these lithographs can make or break a guerrilla flick. One sheets of certain films are becoming collector's items.

overcrank   To set the camera motor at speeds higher than the sound speed of 24 frames per second. The effect is slow motion when played back at 24. This device is being used to excess in violent scenes in today's features. In the hands of a sensitive director, it can be an effective storytelling tool.

ozoner   A drive-in theater.

Papa Bear shot   A cut-away shot grabbed for no immediate function. Usually shot when there is only a short end in the camera and not enough footage to do a complete scene. Before reloading, throw your principal against the wall and run out the short end on a variety of "looks" right and left. Laugh if you will, but this guerrilla move has saved many a sequence. Sergei Eisenstein would love you.

Pasadena money   Sweet little old ladies who are ready to finance a film about their grandfather who came west before the freeways. If the story is not there, it's best to avoid the project. Otherwise, when things go sour, that watery look in her blue eyes will haunt you forever.

Pickup   see **negative pickup.**

platform   Sometimes the producers of a film, mega-budget or no-budget, are not too sure what they have in the first showings of their project. It could be one of those "fish or fowl" dilemmas. Platforming is an alternative to going for a multiple or the "now at theaters everywhere" assault.

The first platform could be a specialty art house in New York City, an ethnic house in a Chicago suburb, or a middle-class "grind" four-plex in Dallas, the goal being to find a venue where the film's subject matter and style will be welcome. If the picture has legs, that means no tweaking has to be done and the distributor can carefully play off this positive basis and allow the picture to grow. Many prints are struck and the picture goes wide to the next platform.

An example of a work needing this treatment could be a new art film or a new director's iffy first film that could die or go through the roof. Such films are kindly referred to as "specialized."

points   Percentages of a film's income offered as payment. There are gross points, which come only to the heaviest of players. There are net points, which are an exercise in futility. There are genuine points if you can tie your points in a pari passu deal with the CEO of the distributor or studio. Points also seem more likely to return dollars when you have a picture or two in the pipeline or the cutting room and there is noise out there as to your whereabouts.

presales   The selling off of territories or rights to various media to finance the nut of the film. Money does not change hands. You are given instead letters of credit, which must be irrevocable and bankable. They are discounted by the lending institution after you have a completion bond in place. There are a lot of wrinkles and perils in this approach.

problem picture   A film whose progress is interrupted or blocked by any of an infinite number of possible problems. The picture itself may be viable, but a distributor reneges on the advance, an actor calls in some phantom promise he says you made, the writer bad-mouths you around town, or a deal goes sour. These conflicts must be addressed or they can guarantee a problem picture with a reputation for trouble.

producer's representative   Someone hired to work on the producer's behalf in promoting a film and negotiating deals. Reps are becoming increasingly popular. If you have one, he or she can do all the dirty work and you can play Mr. Nice Guy.

When the first returns were in on *Free, White and 21*, Harold Hoffman and I were told to get a producer's rep pronto. We got the best, Robert Shaefer. After working our way past two or three lovelies with the British accents that were chic at the time, we were ushered into the beige domain of a well-dressed and articulate pro. We told him we knew we were going to be had in the Hollywood jungle. He studied us for a moment. Then, warming to his subject, he rose. The room was filled with polysyllabic phrases and genteel metaphors as he walked the deep-pile rug. Then, finally, he turned and softened his tone. "What I am trying to say here, Larry and Harold, is that we must first determine who is the fucker and who is the fuckee!" We laughed until tears blinded us, but we never forgot that caution.

product reel   A sample reel of a film. Very handy when you are still in the cutting room and the Cannes Film Festival is only three weeks away. Since nobody in Cannes looks at the whole film anyway, you make up some good scenes and top off at no longer than 20 minutes of this better stuff. Product reels are also shown by the major studios at the annual Show West in Las Vegas, but these are for exhibitors and many times the contracts are already in and the studio is just showing off.

public domain   The realm of property rights that are publicly owned and unprotected by copyright or patent. There is a wealth of material out there for the asking, but the filmmaker interested in adapting an existing work must understand the basics of the international laws of copyright. The old U.S. rule of a term of 28 years' protection plus a renewal right of another 28 years went out of effect when the copyright laws were changed in 1978. Essentially, the rules for works created on or after January 1, 1978, now follow those in practice for decades in France and the U.K.: life of author plus 50 years.

But there is a caution before you start adapting into screenplay form that great novel whose creator joined the heavenly choir more than 50 years ago. The period of copyright protection for works published before 1978 has been increased to a maximum of 75 years. The initial copyright still lasts 28 years, but if renewed, it gains another 47 years. So a novel published in 1930 will enter the public domain in 2005, assuming its copyright was renewed in 1958. And a 1978 work by an author who died in 1980 will go to the public domain in 2030.

The new laws are tricky at best, and the guerrilla filmmaker, bold and daring as he is, cannot afford to stumble into legal quicksand. There are always oddball cases to watch out for, too; for example, the beloved *Peter Pan* by James M. Barrie was penned before the Earth cooled, yet when you are ready to do your play or musical adaptation, you'd best deal with the British Crown. It seems that an unusual exception was made upon the demise of Barrie because he willed the worldwide royalties to charity. The creaky old work is therefore not readily available.

I have two pieces of advice for aspiring filmmakers. First, beware of Texans praising lawyers. But having said that, I strongly urge you to seek counsel from a copyright attorney on any uncertainty in this legal area. Copyright lawyers are a special breed of legal beagles. They love their work and take pride in searching your property. The Library of Congress is courteous, kind and cheap, but they take an eternity to respond. I have always frosted when some "expert" automatically suggests calling a lawyer on some simple matter. This usually entails a retainer of $2,500 or more. But when it comes to copyright status or underlying ownership of literary property, I do urge you to call a copyright lawyer.

Rear Window decision   Imagine the bewilderment of Jimmy Stewart and the heirs of Alfred Hitchcock when they learned that, although they had properly purchased the rights to *It Had to Be Murder*, which later became *Rear Window*, continued distribution of the movie infringed the copyright of the underlying story! The United States Supreme Court rendered this decision on April 24, 1990, in *Stewart v. Abend*. The lawsuit was settled. Although only certain types of works are affected, a producer of derivative works should be aware of this decision. Essentially, the high court decision in *Rear Window* means that continued distribution of a derivative work during the renewal term of the work upon which it is based constitutes copyright infringement if the following three conditions are met: (1) the underlying work was created or first published before 1977; (2) the author of the underlying work died before the renewal term began; and (3) the author's heirs did not grant the derivative work's producer the rights to use the underlying work.

right of publicity   The most confused and murky legal tenet in American jurisprudence and entertainment law. Essentially, it holds that if a public figure capitalized commercially on his notoriety while alive, his image, persona, or voice cannot be used for trade or endorsements without the permission of heirs or assignees. Whereas the First Amendment protects the scenarist in a screenplay featuring a deceased celebrity, the use of that celebrity's photo or film clips to sell products must be negotiated with the heirs or their representative — assuming that celebrity "exploited" his right of publicity while alive. Because of the big bucks that are changing hands in this area, the guerrilla filmmaker should know that this is a rapidly evolving area of law. Professional legal advice is essential here.

roadshow men   A special breed of showman who made a lasting imprint on America's filmgoers in the Thirties, Forties, and even into the Sixties. He was a loner with no ties to studios or independent producers. He was the original "exploitation man." He would acquire the distribution rights to some old, out-of-release film and hit the road with a few prints in his used Cadillac. But first he would change the title and, more important, the "campaign." The roadshow men had an unerring instinct about their audiences. They saw, in the film abandoned by Hollywood, some special "hook" or controversial element that was never exploited by the original owners. A local illustrator would create key art under the roadshow man's knowing eye. Usually it was daring and provocative, and the ads were often rejected by small town newspapers.

They crisscrossed the heartland but found their biggest grosses in the South, especially in the drive-in theaters. Many times they would show short subjects on the birth of babies ("SEE IT FOR THE FIRST TIME . . . THE BIRTH OF TRIPLETS!") or the exotic ("TRIBAL SEX ORGIES FROM DEEPEST AFRICA!"). Secondhand Plymouths and Fords and pickup trucks would be backed up for miles waiting to enter the drive-ins.

Often a roadshow man would pretend to be a medical doctor and appear in a white coat for authenticity. These were genuine characters, the likes of which cannot be found in the Spielbergian slush that passes for showmanship today.

I had the great pleasure to know and learn from the best of them. The big daddy of the roadshow was Kroger Babb, a rotund, jolly giant who traveled with his most famous title, *The Prince of Peace*, which was nothing more than a 16mm blowup of a filming of a passion play performed annually in the American South.

The most colorful however, was my friend Claude Alexander. His golden inspiration was *Mom and Dad*, an early black and white, minimalist drama of out-of-wedlock pregnancy. At the end of the show, "Dr." Alexander, in white coat, would sell sex books and menstrual rhythm calculators, "all approved by the Catholic Church." These were sold from the trunk of the Caddy. Claude had to sew extra pockets onto his white coat to hold enough money to make change as the yokels pressed their dollars into his hands. I loved him like a brother and learned from him like a father.

"A rock's a rock"   As the motion picture medium matured, ambitious directors sought approval to shoot in exotic locales. Since the silents era, they had mostly been locked into filming within Los Angeles. The producers, removing their stogies for a moment, would silence them with their cost-saving solution: "A rock's a rock, a tree's a tree . . . shoot it in Griffith Park!"

room tone   The ambient sound in a room. After a scene is played out in a setting, stage or location, the recordist takes a quiet run on tape of the ambience in the room. This is used to smooth out the final mix of that scene, correcting dead track and refining balance.

rough cut   The first assembly of all elements from the Moviola editing machine, flat bed, or digital software composite. This is usually a deliberately long cut for discussion and refinements.

Sabu reading   Sabu was a young East Indian actor who starred in a number of successful Oriental exotics in the 1940s. His histrionic prowess was quite limited. Sometimes, when an actor or actress keeps flubbing and trashing script lines, I will have to print a bad take and move on. I may mumble my disappointment. "Sabu could have read it better." This has been heard from other directors and has gone into the filmmaking lexicon.

"Sadie Thompson"   Put bluntly, a prostitute hired to service a film crew on location (named after Somerset Maugham's character in his Micronesian play *Rain*). She can be recruited locally or brought in on the day player roster. This is a fast-fading practice in cinema folklore. Marriage and the increasing presence of wives and children on location have diminished the Sadie Thompsons.

Santa Fe Chief   In the 1930s and 1940s, before the ease of air travel, there were only two towns in America as far as the film business would acknowledge — Hollywood and New York. The umbilical cord that united these two was a fast train, the Santa Fe Chief. Deals were made, marriages shattered, romances begun, careers dissolved, and great scripts written (and badly rewritten) on board. Sex was rampant and booze flowed copiously as the Chief rolled through the night of rural America. Warm inside, with eyes glazed by booze and praise, the players acted out their little vignettes, protected from the masses by the Chief's steel hull and its great speed.

"Save 'em!"   Turn off the lights. Or we need a rehearsal. Or it's lunchtime.

Schwab's Drug Store   A networking haven for working and "between engagements" actors on Sunset Blvd. in Hollywood. The classic story of Lana Turner being discovered there is true. But then, hundreds were discovered there over the decades. You pulled yourself out of bed, made for Schwab's, picked up the trades (daily trade papers), ordered a cup of coffee and Danish, flirted with the waitress (usually herself a would-be actress), and picked up tips on current casting around town. Then it was off for the rounds. Today, Schwab's is a remodeled, slick, sterile, cold formica bunker.

Scriptor   A popular screenwriting software.

second handers   The leeches who prey on the creative works of writers, directors, and others. They can be agents, lawyers, critics who have failed as filmmakers, or anyone who soils works from the heart under the guise of "fine-tuning." This species was first identified by Ayn Rand in her novel *The Fountainhead*.

set-up   A camera position from which a number of takes may be shot until the scene is printed.

sexploitation film   A film shot with the promise of lurid sex or sleaze as its hook.

short ends   The last 20 to as much as 300 unused feet of picture negative on a roll. These film scraps are created when the DP decides that the scene being retaken cannot be completed on the remaining footage. These short ends are broken off and repackaged for sale to brokers. In turn, the low-budget filmmaker buys the rolls at a tremendous discount. They are the guerrilla's friend. The most famous and, for me, the most dependable short end supplier is Carol Dean's Studio Film and Tape, in Hollywood and New York.

slate   see **tail slate**

spec script   A screenplay written without money and with no guarantee. The commissioner of the effort will pay for what is written.

stalker   A fan who becomes obsessed with an actress (or, less commonly, an actor) and follows her around. Very few films finish principal photography without at least one incident of sexual obsession by a stranger not attached to the company. A stalker begins his quest with small talk, flattery and cheap gifts, making the target uneasy with his unblinking stare. I watch for certain signs. The stalker will sit in the actress's chair "holding" it for her. He takes a protective interest in her wardrobe. He tries to impress her with his nonexistent "wealth." A real danger signal is his bringing photos of himself, usually nudes, to the set for her perusal. At first he is shy, but then he becomes aggressive and possessive. When we identify a possible danger, the code is whispered: "Stalker at three o'clock." We proceed to eighty-six him and try to determine how he gained access to the shoot.

state's righters   Deals common in the fifties and sixties wherein independents would actually sell exhibition rights to a theater chain, limiting the territory to a defined area.

"Stix Nix Hix Pix"   A long-ago headline from trade magazine *Variety*, in its characteristic style. Hollywood tried to capture bucolic audiences with simple homespun stories. The pictures died. Translation: "Middle America says no to pictures about their lives of quiet desperation."

Strock, Herb   Director of such films as *I Was a Teenage Frankenstein* and *Blood of Dracula*; a bona fide guerrilla filmmaker. When frustrated by minuscule budgets and players who could not act their way out of a paper bag, he would groan, "Oh, for the time for another take!" As I moved into the coveted position of being able to shoot multiple takes, I would sometimes say out loud, "This one's for Herb Strock."

subtitles   Dialogue and other information ("Years later," etc.) translated from the language being spoken on the screen and converted to actual printing at the bottom of the screen. This was done by matte printing for years, but now it's a breeze with the character-generating capabilities of computers.

supplemental rights   The rights on a film that go beyond theater distribution into an ever-increasing number of venues, spinoffs and technologies. Theatrical release begat television, television begat cable, cable begat made-for, made-for begat home video, home video begat pay-per-view, pay-per-view begat CD-ROM, CD-ROM begat virtual reality, and so forth. The mind boggles, the franchising continues. Our timid, hitchhiking thumb waves as we stand on the information highway with no idea of where it will lead.

Taft-Hartley   A labor law, narrowly defined for actors working on films, which stipulates that a non-member of a guild can be used on one casting call with only a written representation (known as the Taft-Hartley letter) that the performer was hired on short notice. A second such call for work requires that the performer join the craft union. The law is named after the senators who introduced the bill.

tail slate   In filming, scenes are marked with the snapping of the familiar clapperboard, one function of which is to provide a point for perfect synchronization between soundtrack and film (since the snapping of the slate is caught by both the audio recorder and the camera). Usually this is done before the scene is filmed, for what is known as a front slate. But there are instances when a director will call instead for a tail slate — that is, the marking of a scene at the end of its filming. This decision may be based on his instinct that a performer is ready and in character for a difficult passage and might be unnerved by the long process of front slating and its mood-shattering bellows of "Quiet on the set," "Roll sound," "Speed," "Roll camera," "Rolling," etc. plus the shattering sound of the slate itself. If a tail slate is called for, the scene will be played out and then, while the camera and recorder are still rolling in sync, the slate will be turned upside down and snapped. This latter twist is a warning flag for the editor that the scene must be synchronized from the end of the scene. As a badfilm auteur, I have had to work with many location people whose histrionic prowess is nil. I will coax the actor quietly until I see he is in character. A slight wave of my hand and the cameras turn. The scene is good. I call for the slate person to run into the scene with his upturned "sticks" and secure sync and the moment forever.

temp track   A temporary music track, usually consisting of library music, which is used for previews and fine-tuning of a picture before the composer's score is laid in for the trial printing. This is an obnoxious practice that is unfair to the other crafts and their efforts, but it is sometimes necessary in extreme circumstances.

territory   A particular geographical area within which the rights to distribute a film are sold. Foreign sales are broken up into a puzzle of territories by independent producers and sold at film markets. A single country may constitute a territory, as does Greece, or several countries may be grouped together as in the case of Australasia (consisting of Australia, New Zealand, and many neighboring islands). The most recent such territory is Benelux, an amalgam of several Nordic states.

turn-around   A dreaded condition under which a script optioned by a studio is moved backward in the development process. Consider the following scenario: You've sold a script to a major studio. You let it go cheap, intoxicated by thoughts of the classy treatment it would receive. The legal papers fly and a polish is ordered, but you don't get the job. Somebody's buddy or nephew is given more than you got for the script to fine-tune the work and beef up the male role to sound like Tom Cruise. Months pass. There are flurries of interest. More months pass. The material suddenly shows up in other new films. Your baby seems dated. It goes into turn-around. Eventually there are no longer even promises of "It's a go—for sure."

You are now in turn-around hell. Oh, yes, you can reclaim your work, but you must ante up the charges to date, and they look something like this: two rewrites ($116,000); legal fees ($48,000); overhead ($35,000); meals, travel and entertainment ($15,000); misc. title and copyright searches; clerical time; and that bastard bane of all, an errors and omissions policy ($55,000).

Van Dyke, Willard S.   A director with real ability. Cinema history has not treated him kindly, but he was one of the giants. The original *Thin Man* pictures with William Powell were only some of his solid credits. In the early forties, he was the only film school in town for the novice. He was first and foremost a great editor, and had a small group of us youngsters to the kitchen of his house on occasion to allow us to actually cut and hold 35mm film in our hands. He would "borrow" equipment from his studio, MGM. I remember his putting his hand on a noisy old black Moviola and growling, "Don't laugh—this miserable wreck saw the first screening of *Gone with the Wind*!"

"Walk away from it!"   A command to abandon an effort that has proven futile or is producing tension. When they hear this, electricians split pronto. Example: a particular light has held up production because of its high frequency hum. It is lunchtime, and tempers are short. A half dozen crew members try their magic, but the singing, 10,000-watt monster won't hush. Then, quiet. The production manager bellows, "Walk away from it!" They do. The scene is canned. The expression is used whenever the PM sees wasted effort on any level.

Westwood Village Theatre   Not a movie house but a small live playhouse at Westwood Blvd. and Santa Monica that was a haven for contract players with studio ties in the 1940s. After standing around all day at Fox, working unpaid at this Shangri-la until midnight soothed our souls somewhat. Lots of growth took place here. The place is now a Pontiac dealership.

wrap   The end of filming, as in "It's a wrap. The party's over. Now it's up to God and Eastman Kodak." A big moment for any filmmaker; for the guerrilla, it's the moment at which a small band of Gypsies who love film and want a part of the fragile joy of making one have triumphed over a myriad of hostile elements that would have us fail in our storytelling. We have suffered the production stage of our storytelling for the euphoria that will follow the shoot as we put the pictures together to tell a story. The director's emotion at this moment is encapsulated in a story about France's great director Jean Cocteau. Exhausted and ill after finishing the wrap shot on his *Beauty and the Beast*, he turned to his crew and cast and hoarsely whispered, "Ah, maintenant . . . le montage!" ("Ah, now . . . the editing!").

The Larry Buchanan Filmography

The Cowboy. First Departure Films, 1951. Producer/Director/Screenplay: Larry Buchanan. Directors of Photography: Hal Hunt, Larry Buchanan. Editor: Larry Buchanan.

Apache Gold (a.k.a. *Grubstake*). Tejano Productions, 1952. Producers: Larry Buchanan, Lynn Shubert. Director: Larry Buchanan. Screenplay: Lynn Shubert, Larry Buchanan. Cast: Steve Wyman, Jack Klugman, Neile Adams, Lynn Shubert, Kort Falkenberg. Director of Photography: Karl Sturges. Assistant Cameraman: Gil Margolis. Sound Recordists: Sol Fol, Kort Falkenberg. Wardrobe Mistress: Toby Wyman.

Venus in Furs. Unreleased, 1956. Producer/Director/Screenplay: Larry Buchanan (From a novel by the Marquis de Sade) Director of Photography: Ralph K. Johnson

The Naked Witch. Alexander Enterprises, 1957. Producer: Claude Alexander. Director/Screenplay/Editor: Larry Buchanan. Cast: Libby Booth, Robert Short, Jo Merryman, Howard Ware, Dennis Adams. Director of Photography: Ralph K. Johnson.

A Stripper Is Born (a.k.a. *Naughty Dallas*) Various Distributors, 1958. Producer/Director/Editor: Larry Buchanan. Cast: Dallas showgirls. Director of Photography: Ralph K. Johnson.

Common Law Wife (a.k.a. *Swamp Rose*) Mike Ripps Company, 1960. Producer/Director/Screenplay/Editor: Larry Buchanan. Cast: Lacy Kelly, George Edgely. Director of Photography: Ralph K. Johnson. Sound Recordist: Sherrill Alcott.

Free, White and 21. American International Pictures, 1963. Producer: Falcon International Pictures. Director: Larry Buchanan. Screenplay: Harold Dwain (Hoffman), Larry Buchanan. Cast: Frederick O'Neal, Annalena Lund, William McGee, Shirley McLine, George Russell, Joreta Cherry, Johnny Hicks, Jonathan Ledford, Bill Thurman, Anne MacAdams, Tommie Russell. Director of Photography: Ralph K. Johnson. Sound Recordist: Robert Redd. Production Design: Dennis Adams. Special Legal Consultant: Charles Tessemer.

Under Age. American International Pictures, 1964. Producer: Falcon International Pictures. Director: Larry Buchanan. Screenplay: Harold Hoffman, Larry Buchanan. Editor: Larry Buchanan. Cast: Anne MacAdams, Judy Adler, Roland Royter, Tommy Russell, Johnny Hicks, Regina Hicks, George Russell, George Edgely. Director of Photography: James R. Davidson.

The Trial of Lee Harvey Oswald. Falcon International Pictures, 1964. Producer: Harold Hoffman. Director: Larry Buchanan. Screenplay: Harold Hoffman, Larry Buchanan. Editor: Larry Buchanan. Cast: George Russell, George Edgely, Arthur Nations, Charles Mazyrack, Bill Carter, Joreta Cherry, Howard

Ware, Wallace Edwards, Don Gillispie, Dave Terrell, Bill Peck, Max Anderson, Theodore Mitchell, Jan Altgers, Charles McLine, Bob Dracup, Jonathan Ledford, Shirley McLine, Anne MacAdams, Armand James, William McGee, Barnett Shaw, Bob French. Director of Photography: James R. Davidson. Camera Operator: Henry Kokojan. Assistant Cameraman: Jack Specht. Sound Recordist: R. Shields Mitchell. Sound Mixer: Bruce Howard. Set Decorator: Bill Mitchell. Script Supervisor: Betty Sooter.

The Eye Creatures. American International Pictures, 1965. Producer/Director: Larry Buchanan. Screenplay: R. Taylor, Larry Buchanan. Editor: Jim Ferguson. Cast: John Ashley, Cynthia Hull, Ethan Allen, Shirley McLine, Bill Peck Jr., Warren Hammack, Anthony Houston.

High Yellow. Dinero-Thunder Distributors, 1966. Producer/Director/Screenplay/Editor: Larry Buchanan. Cast: Cynthia Hull, Warren Hammack, Kay Taylor, Bill McGee, Anne MacAdams, Robert Brown, Bill Thurman, Jonathan Ledford, Max Anderson.

Zontar, the Thing from Venus. American International Pictures, 1966. Producer/Director/Screenplay/Editor: Larry Buchanan. Cast: John Agar, Pat Delany, Anthony Houston, Susan Bjurman, Anne MacAdams, Bill Thurman, Neil Fletcher. Director of Photography: Robert Jessup.

Curse of the Swamp Creature. American International Pictures, 1966. Producer/Director/Editor: Larry Buchanan. Screenplay: Anthony Houston. Cast: John Agar, Francine York, Jeff Alexander, Cal Duggan, Charles McLine, Bill McGee, Ted Mitchell, Roger Ready, Bill Thurman, Gail Johnson, Michael Tolden, Annabella Weenick, Pat Cranshaw, J. V. Lee, Naomi Bruton. Director of Photography: Ralph K. Johnson. Unit Manager: Jim Sullivan. Sound Supervision: Bruce Shearin. Recordist: Ted Lyles. Special Effects: Jack Bennett. Art Direction: Robert Dracup. Key Grip: Jack Carney. Script Supervisor: Joreta Cherry.

Mars Needs Women. American International Pictures, 1966. Producer/Director/Editor: Larry Buchanan. Screenplay: Larry Buchanan/Anthony Houston. Cast: Tommy Kirk, Yvonne Craig, Byron Lord, Roger Ready, Barnett Shaw, Neil Fletcher, Chet Davis, Ron Scott, George Edgely, Dick Simpson, Don Campbell, Bob Hazlett, Anne Palmer, Gordon Bulow, Bill Thurman, Pat Cranshaw, Claude Farls, Bob Lorenz, Sylvia Rundell, David England, Terry Davis, Sally Casey. *The Martians*: Tommy Kirk, Warren Hammack, Anthony Houston, Larry Tanner, Cal Duggan. *The Women*: Yvonne Craig, Pat Delany, Sherry Roberts, Donna Lindberg, "Bubbles" Cash. Production Coordinator: Joreta Cherry. Director of Photography: Robert Jessup. Assistant Cameraman: Robert L. Buchanan. Gaffer: Robert Dracup. Sound Supervisor: Rex Cromwell. Boom Man: Don Ross. Key Grip: Jim Finley. Makeup: Annabelle Weenick.

The Hottest Fourth of July in the History of Brewster County (a.k.a. *Sam*). Larry Buchanan Presents, 1966. Producer/Director/Screenplay/Editor: Larry Buchanan. Cast: Jody McCrea, Pat Delany, Anthony Houston, Caruth Byrd, Bill Thurman, Jack Carney, Ethan Allen, Neil Fletcher. Director of Photography: James R. Davidson. Camera Operator: Henry Kokojan. Production coordinator: Joreta Cherry.

In the Year 2889. American International Pictures, 1967. Producer/Director/Editor: Larry Buchanan. Screenplay: Harold Hoffman. Cast: Paul Petersen, Quinn O'Hara, Charla Doherty, Neil Fletcher, Hugh Fagin, Max Anderson, Billy Thurman, Byron Lord. Director of Photography: Robert C. Jessup. Assistant Cameraman: R. L. Buchanan. Sound Supervision: Rex Cromwell. Gaffer: Robert Dracup. Key Grip: James Finley. Special Effects: Jack Bennett. Dialogue Direction: Annabelle Weenick. Production Coordinator: Joreta Cherry.

Creature of Destruction. American International Pictures, 1967. Producer/Director/Screenplay/Editor: Larry Buchanan. Cast: Pat Delany, Les Tremayne, Aron Kincaid, Anne MacAdams, Neil Fletcher, Byron Lord. Director of Photography: Robert C. Jessup.

Comanche Crossing. Caruth Byrd Productions, 1967. Producer/Director/Editor: Larry Buchanan. Screenplay: Anthony Houston. Cast: Cynthia Hull, Anthony Houston, Caruth Byrd. Director of Photography: Ralph K. Johnson. Production Coordinator: Joreta Cherry.

Hell Raiders. American International Pictures, 1968. Producer/Director/Screenplay/Editor: Larry Buchanan. Cast: John Agar, Richard Webb, Joan Huntington, Bill Thurman, Anne MacAdams, Jeff Alexander. Director of Photography: Robert Jessup. Special Effects: Jack Bennett. Production Coordinator: Joreta Cherry.

The Other Side of Bonnie and Clyde. Dal Art Distributors, 1968. Producer/Director/Screenplay/Editor: Larry Buchanan. Cast: Joe Entrentree, Lucky Mosley, Bill Thurman, George Edgely. Narrated by Burl Ives.

It's Alive. American International Pictures, 1968. Producer/Director/Screenplay/Editor: Larry Buchanan. Cast: Tommy Kirk, Shirley Bonne, Billy Thurman, Anne MacAdams, Corveth Ousterhouse. Director of Photography: Robert Allcott. Sound Supervision: Conrad Lee Redd. Special Effects: Jack Bennett. Paleontology: Skip Frazee. Production Coordinator: Joreta Cherry.

A Bullet for Pretty Boy. American International Pictures, 1969. Producer/Director: Larry Buchanan. Screenplay: Larry Buchanan, Anthony Houston, Henry Rosenbaum. Cast: Fabian Forte, Jocelyn Lane, Adam Rourke, Astrid Warner, Michael Haynes, Morgan Fairchild, Billy Thurman, Jeff Alexander, Charlie Dell, Anne MacAdams, Hugh Fagin, Neil Fletcher. Director of Photography: James R. Davidson. Special Effects: Jack Bennett.

Strawberries Need Rain. Dinero Distributors, 1970. Executive Producer: Leslie Lagoni. Producer/Director: Larry Buchanan. Screenplay: Anthony Houston, Larry Buchanan (Based on the novella *In a Certain Village* by Victor Bruns). Editors: Larry Buchanan, Jeff D. Buchanan. Cast: Les Tremayne, Paul Bertoya, Terry Mace, Gene Otis Shane, Monica Gayle. Director of Photography: Robert Jessup. Camera Operator: Lynn Lockwood. Sound Supervision: Bob Reagan. Art Direction: Byron Lord. Key Grip: Bill Thurman. Production Coordinator: Joreta Cherry. Music: Ray Martin.

The Rebel Jesus (a.k.a. *Live from the Dead Sea*). (A work in progress.) 1972. Producers: Larry Buchanan, Anthony Houston. Directors: Larry Buchanan, Anthony Houston. Screenplay: Anthony Houston, Larry Buchanan. Cast: Gene Otis Shane, Garth Pillsbury, Leigh Cavanaugh, Howard Rubin, Warren Hammack, George Costello. Director of Photography: Robert Jessup. Camera Operator: Don Reddy. Assistant Cameraman: Phil Pfeiffer. Production Coordinator: Joreta Cherry. Music composed and conducted by Alex North.

Goodbye, Norma Jean. Austamerica Distributors, 1975. Executive Producers: Mark Josem, Robert Ward. Producer/Director: Larry Buchanan. Screenplay: Larry Buchanan. Editors: Larry Buchanan, John S. Curran. Cast: Misty Rowe, Terrence Locke, Patch McKenzie, Preston Hanson, Marty Zagon, Andre Philippe, Garth Pillsbury, George Costello, Sal Ponti, Adele Claire, Paula Mitchell, Charles Aidikoff, Jean Sarah Frost, Lilyan McBride, Burr Middleton, Stuart Lancaster, Ivy Bethune, Robert Gribbon, Steve Brown, Anthony Giger, Darla Leroy, J. R. Clarke, Frank Curcio, Duncan McCloud, Charles Edwards, Laurel Barnett, Steve Sikes, Don Brodie, Bill J. Stevens, Debbie Daniels, Sheri K. Campbell, Harry Woolman, Shiela Sisco, Edward Ansara. Director of Photography: Robert B. Sherry. Assistant Cameraman: Kalman Masaros, Nicholas von Sternberg. Production Manager: George Costello. Assistant Director: John Curran. Sound Recordist: Henri Price. Wardrobe: Alexis Seepo. Script Supervisor: Debra Hill. Grips: Barry Buchanan, Bob Brill. Still Photography: Garth Pillsbury. Comptroller: Kay Campbell. Property Assistant: Debbie Daniels. Miss Rowe's Makeup: L. Marie Carter. Makeup: Zoltan Elek. Art Direction: John Carter. Gaffer: Tommy Estridge. Best Boy: Stuart Lancaster. Executive Assistants: Frank Curcio, Bernice Napolitano.

Hughes and Harlow: Angels in Hell. Pro International Distributors, 1977. Producer/Director: Larry Buchanan. Screenplay: Lynn Shubert, Larry Buchanan. Editor: Robert A. Fitzgerald. Cast: Victor Holchak, Lindsay Bloom, David McLean, Adam Rourke, Royal Dano, Eric Holland, Nelson Olmstead, Barry Buchanan, James E. Brodhead, Charles Aidikoff, James Appleby, Adele Claire, Rita Convi, Tony Cortez, John Curran, Rick Davis, Charlie Dell, Clement St. George, Stuart Lancaster, Marius Masmanian, Garth Pillsbury, Duncan McCloud, Walt Robin, Toni Sawyer, Tommy Silberkleit, Marty Zagon.

Director of Photography: Nicholas Josef von Sternberg. First Assistant Cameraman: Lowell Petersen. Second Assistant Cameraman: Davie Schmier. Assistant Director: John Curran. Production Manager: Joe Price. Sound Mixer: Al Ramirez. Boom Operator: Mark Brickalew. Makeup: Ray Sebastian. Script Supervision: Jackie Saunders. Costume Design: Lennie Baron. Key Grip: Robert C. George. Gaffer: Ron Batsdorff. Gaffer's Best Boy: Ernie Roebuck. Art Direction: George Costello. Music composed and conducted by Jimmie Haskell. Opticals: Metro-Goldwyn-Mayer.

Mistress of the Apes. Cineworld International, 1981. Executive Producer: John F. Rickert. Producer/ Director/Screenplay/Editor: Larry Buchanan. Cast: Jennie Neuman, Garth Pillsbury, Walt Robin, Stuart Lancaster, Barbara Leigh, Marius Masmanian, Barry Buchanan, Blaine Dennis, Burr Middleton, S. Mandell, Mark Rudy. Director of Photography: Nicholas Josef von Sternberg. Camera Operator: Lowell Petersen. First Assistant Cameraman: David Schmier. Second Assistant Cameraman: David Boyd. Associate Producers: John Curran, Joe Price. Unit Production Manager: John Curran. First Assistant Director: Thomas Keir. Script Supervisor: Kathie Zatarga. Sound Supervision: Norman Haughey. Makeup Assistant: Rob Bottin. Special Lighting Consultant: Ron Batsdorff. Special Primate Makeup: Greg Cannom.

The Loch Ness Horror. Cineworld International, 1982. Executive Producers: Clan Buchanan Production, Jane Buchanan. Producer/Director: Larry Buchanan. Screenplay: Larry Buchanan, Lynn Shubert. Editors: Larry Buchanan, Jeff D. Buchanan, Randy Buchanan. Cast: Sandy Kenyon, Barry Buchanan, Miki McKenzie, Eric Scott, Darcy-Louis Scott, Doc Livingston, Stuart Lancaster, Preston Hanson, Garth Pillsbury, David Clover, Pat Musick, Kort Falkenberg, Don Myshrall, Dee Myshrall. Director of Photography: Robert Ebinger, Jr. Assistant Cameraman: Steve Mann. Sound Supervision: Wayne Berwick, Randy Buchanan. Gaffer: Ernie Roebuck. Best Boy: Jeff D. Buchanan. Key Grip: Adam Jones. Script Supervisor: Dee Buchanan. Production Manager/First Assistant Director: John Curran. Second Assistant Director: Hans Beimler. Associate Producer: Irv Berwick. Music composed and conducted by Richard Theiss. Special Effects: Image Engineering. "Nessie" created by Tom Valentine & Peter Chesney.

Down on Us (a.k.a. **Beyond the Doors, The Beat Goes On** and **Who Killed Rock and Roll?**). Unicorn, 1984. Executive Production Company: Omni-Leisure International. Executive Producer: Murray M. Kaplan. Producer/Director/Screenplay: Larry Buchanan. Production Manager/First Assistant Director: John Curran. Director of Photography: Nicholas von Sternberg. Cast: Sandy Kenyon, Gregory Allen Chatman, Riba Meryl, Brian Wolf, Steven Tice, Toni Sawyer, Jennifer Wilde, Susan Barnes, Stuart Lancaster, Randy Buchanan, Jeff Buchanan. Musical Supervision: Jeffrey Dan Buchanan, David Shorey, Richard Bowen.

Goodnight, Sweet Marilyn. Arkoff International Pictures, 1988. Producer/Director: Larry Buchanan. Screenplay: Larry Buchanan, Lynn Shubert. Editors: Jeffrey D. Buchanan, Randy Buchanan, Larry Buchanan. Director of Photography: Miles Anderson. First Assistant Camera: Dave Drysdale. Sound Supervision: Peter Wolf. Boom Operator: Skip Clarke. Makeup: Constance Gamieire. Script Supervision: Kathe Hoogner. Gaffer: Jack Wiley. Art Direction: C. Cracko. Music Supervision: Richard Bowen. Cast: Paula Lane, Joyce Lower, Phyllis Coates, Kenneth Hicks, Jerry Hopkins, George Niles Berry & Jeremy Slate as "Mesquite". Associate Producer: Marlene O'Connell. Production Supervisor: Jeffrey D. Buchanan.

Index

19673716R00131

Made in the USA
San Bernardino, CA
23 December 2018